Mussolini in the First World War

Mussolini in the First World War

The Journalist, the Soldier, the Fascist

Paul O'Brien

BERG

Oxford • New York

First published in 2005 by
Berg
Editorial offices:
1st Floor, Angel Court, 81 St Clements Street, Oxford, OX4 1AW, UK
175 Fifth Avenue, New York, NY 10010, USA

Berg is the imprint of Oxford International Publishers Ltd.

Library of Congress Cataloguing-in-Publication Data
O'Brien, Paul, 1962-
Mussolini in the First World War : the journalist, the soldier, the fascist / Paul
O'Brien.— 1st. ed.
p. cm.
Includes Mussolini's writings, translated into English.
Originally presented as the author's thesis (doctoral)—Trinity College, Dublin.
Includes bibliographical references and index.
ISBN 1-84520-051-9 (cloth) — ISBN 1-84520-052-7 (pbk.)
1. Mussolini, Benito, 1883-1945—Political and social views. 2. Press and politics—
Italy—History—20th century—Sources. 3. World War, 1914-1918—Sources. 4.
Fascism—Italy. 5. Italy—Politics and government—1914-1922. I. Title.
DG575.M8O26 2005
945.091'092—dc22   2004020618

British Library Cataloguing-in-Publication Data
A catalogue record for this book is available from the British Library.

ISBN 1 84520 051 9 (Cloth)
1 84520 052 7 (Paper)

Typeset by Avocet Typeset, Chilton, Aylesbury, Bucks
Printed in the United Kingdom by Biddles Ltd, King's Lynn

www.bergpublishers.com

Contents

List of Figures

Abbreviations

ACS	Archivio Centrale dello Stato (Rome)
ANC	Associazione Nazionale Combattenti
ANMIG	Associazione Nazionale fra Mutilati e Invalidi di Guerra
AUSSME	Archivio dell'Ufficio Storico dello Stato Maggiore dell'Esercito (Rome)
A5G	An ACS reference to distinguish documents related to the First World War from those related to the Second World War
b.	*Busta* (archive folder), bb. is *buste* (plural)
fasc.	*Fascicolo* (file inside archive folder)
ins.	*Inserto* (subcategory of fasc. and s.fasc.)
Min. Int. Dir. Gen. Ps, Div. AA. GG. RR.	Ministero degli Interni. Direzione Generale di Pubblica Sicurezza. Divisione Affari Generali e Riservati
MRF	Mostra della Rivoluzione Fascista
OO	Opera Omnia of Benito Mussolini
PCM	Presidenza del Consiglio dei Ministri
prot.	*Protocollo*
PSI	Partito Socialista Italiano
s.fasc.	*Sottofascicolo* (subcategory of fasc.)
SPDCR	Segreteria Particolare del Duce, Carteggio Riservato (1922–43)
UIL	Unione Italiana del Lavoro

Acknowledgements

Many are the people to whom I shall be eternally grateful for their assistance in seeing this book through to completion both during its previous incarnation as a Ph.D. thesis and in the transition from the Ph.D. to the book. In particular these include my parents, Nora and Paul, my late and beloved uncle Jack, my by now numerous brothers and sisters, my friend Jim Larragy and my 'old mate' Andy 'I have taken the liberty' Pickering. I am also indebted to Paul Corner of the University of Siena and Alan Kramer of Trinity College Dublin for their detailed advice on how to prepare the manuscript for publication. Special thanks to Tom Gray and to Michael Rosen for their guidance and encouragement during the book-proposal/publisher-seeking process, and to Berg Publishers for their decision to take the project on. The maps contained herein were designed by Professor Giorgio Rochat of the University of Turin, to whom many thanks are due for the kind permission to adapt and use them from his and Mario Isenghi's recent volume on the Great War (Isenghi and Rochat, 2000). Unless otherwise stated, all translations from Mussolini's writings are mine. Finally, there are two people who tower over this book and who lend most weight to the theory according to which there is no such thing as an individual author. The first is Professor John Horne of Trinity College Dublin, who remained a firm, imperturbable, humane and professional term of reference during the many years of uncertainty and despair which have accompanied this work through its various phases. The second is my wife, Giusi Dossena. This endeavour began at the same time as our life together and is virtually synonymous with it. Why, despite everything, she has chosen to believe in both me and this project is the main unresolved mystery of the project itself, and it is to her, therefore, that I dedicate this book.

Introduction

Fascism is a religious conception in which man is seen in his immanent relationship with a superior law and with an objective Will that transcends the particular individual and raises him to conscious membership in a spiritual society. Whoever has seen in the religious politics of the Fascist regime nothing but mere opportunism has not understood that Fascism, besides being a system of government, is also, and above all, a system of thought ... Therefore, for the Fascist, everything is in the State, and nothing human or spiritual exists, much less has value, outside the State. In this sense Fascism is totalitarian, and the Fascist State, the synthesis and unity of all values, interprets, develops and gives strength to the whole life of the people ... Outside the State there can be neither individuals nor groups (political parties, associations, syndicates, classes) ... For Fascism, the growth of empire, that is to say the expansion of the nation, is an essential manifestation of vitality, and its opposite a sign of decadence ... But empire demands discipline, the coordination of all forces and a deeply felt sense of duty and sacrifice: this fact explains many aspects of the practical working of the regime, the character of many forces in the State, and the necessarily severe measures which must be taken against those who would oppose the spontaneous and inevitable movement of Italy in the twentieth century.

Mussolini, *Dottrina del fascismo*, 1932

In 1925 Giovanni Gentile, philosopher, former Minister for Education, and fascist ideologue, argued that fascism had emerged as the expression of a search for a renewal of Italian political and spiritual life. He contrasted this project with the failure of the liberal State to realize the nation-building project of the small group of idealists who had led the struggle to unite Italy. Recalling the religious-style language of 'sacrifice' and national 'mission' of Giuseppe Mazzini's Young Italy movement, Gentile went on to aver that this was directly comparable to the youthful ideals, romanticism and heroism of the fascist squads. These in turn were wearing black shirts reminiscent of the élitist *arditi* founded as special shock troop units during the Great War. The actions of these men were thus informed by reference to the memory of the experience of that conflict, now mythologized as the great founding event of fascism but nonetheless rooted, via Mazzini, in the very origins of Italian unity (G. Gentile, 1975).

How justified were these fascist claims to Italy's past? In his analysis of the means by which the regime sought consensus and consolidation through a cosmos

1

of cultural representations, Pier Giorgio Zunino argues that the themes of the Great War and Mazzini were components of a discourse to which fascism itself was essentially extraneous. But Zunino also concedes that while fascism sometimes stretched the heritage of Mazzini to suit itself, many aspects of that tradition, such as the nation seen as an organic whole, were 'anything but outlandish' in their applicability to the regime (Zunino, 1985: 90, 99–107). Might it not also be true, therefore, that fascism's claim to the cultural legacy of the Great War – codified in the subcategories of Intervention, Victory and the Cult of the Fallen Soldier (E. Gentile, 1993) – was not altogether unfounded? It is with this and related issues – in particular the historical question concerning the role played by the Great War in the transition from the liberal to the fascist State (Procacci, Giu., 1966; Rochat, 1976: 82–6; Vivarelli, 1981; 1995; Fava, 1982; Procacci, Gv., 1989), and the crucial problem of 'continuity' and 'fracture' between the liberal and fascist periods in general (E. Gentile, 1986: 195ff) – that the present study will engage.

The approach adopted follows those which seek to reassess the significance of the First World War from the point of view of political and cultural mobilization. By this is meant both a commitment to political action and the means for translating this commitment into action. Symbols and cultural representations are called upon in order to communicate the values and goals of the mobilization to those who are to be mobilized into achieving them. Since this involves specific groups, classes or even entire societies, political and cultural mobilization entails a social interaction in which roles may be crystallized, and structures and collectivities altered. While, therefore, mobilization, as thus defined, is generally articulated through ruling *structures*, it is also a social, political and cultural *process* in which the authority of political organizations, and perhaps even the State, is reconfirmed and reinforced, or contested and undermined (Nettl, 1967: 32–3 and Ch. 5, esp. p. 143). However, political and cultural mobilization is not necessarily effected through State organizations and structures. In countries such as Britain, France and Germany, the outbreak of war in 1914 saw significant levels of what has been termed political and cultural 'self-mobilization' on the part of broad sectors of the population, including intellectuals, artists, school teachers, workers' organizations and ethnic minority groups (Horne, 1997: esp. Introduction and Parts. 1 and 2). The degree to which this 'self-mobilization' was effective in any given country depended, naturally, on the character of political and cultural development in the period preceding the outbreak of the war. The decades prior to the conflict had seen the ruling classes of the above-mentioned countries involved in the veritable invention of traditions which sought to bind the population to the nation and national institutions. This enterprise formed part of a practical response to the failures of empiricism and rationalism to provide theories of social cohesion in the wake of industrialization and mass involvement in political activity (Hobsbawm, 1983).

As is now well known, Italian intervention into the Great War in May 1915 was marked by sharp divisions between the minority of Italians who wanted the war and the vast majority of the population, especially (but not only) the working population, which did not. For its part, the State, controlled as it was by anti-popular conservative élites, deemed mass political mobilization to be both unnecessary and dangerous (Corner and Procacci, 1997). 'Self-mobilization' in Italy was, therefore, always going to be something of a subversive phenomenon. In his analysis of the Italian primary school system between 1915 and 1918, Andrea Fava deals with the implications arising from the fact that the mobilization of national values through the schools to a large extent fell on the teachers themselves. He reaches the conclusion that while, during the war, the teachers were to a considerable extent victims of what he calls a 'false consciousness' concerning the level of autonomy they believed they exercised with respect to the State, their crucial role in the process of cultural mobilization nonetheless laid the basis for a delegitimation of the ruling élites. This was accompanied by a rejection of the pre-war optimistic positivism of the governing class associated with the name of the moderate liberal Giovanni Giolitti. Fascist education was one possible alternative to this cleavage, as it provided a nationalistic response both to the unwillingness of liberal conservative élitism to mobilize popular sentiment, and to the socio-political evolutionism and universalist humanitarianism of Giolitti who, it was believed, had failed to forge a national consciousness and had left Italy unprepared to conduct a national war (Fava, 1997).

This approach provides methodological keys for the present book. Fava does not begin from war's end in order to investigate the manner in which the conflict was retrospectively reflected upon, but examines the ways in which meaning was produced during the conflagration. It is also noteworthy that while Fava is concerned with the social production of beliefs and values through symbol and signification, he takes the issue beyond sociological observation and description and stresses an epistemological approach. This seeks to establish how conflicts in the realm of signification, including the role of 'false consciousness', come to bear on the legitimation or delegitimation of the political authority of the State. The present book can therefore be defined as a study in political legitimacy as expressed in and through the process of political and cultural mobilization within the war. It will attempt to identify the social and political character of a 'self-mobilization' which sought to bridge the cultural and political cleft between State and society, and will assess the extent to which that response helped generate fascism.

Before coming to a discussion of the main subject of the book, it is necessary to define four key terms: fascism, State, imperialism and ideology. Only the meanings used in this book are explained here, since a justification of the terms would take us into enormous and contentious debates on political theory. The general definition of 'fascism' informing this study will be the one outlined by Mussolini in his *Dottrina del fascismo* in 1932, some key quotations from which have been presented at the beginning of this Introduction (Oakeshott, 1972; Kreis, 2003). We can add to this the further theorization of fascism elucidated by Leon Trotsky in the 1930s. Fascism, in this view, is a seizure of political power in order to alter the conditions of capitalist production in favour of the ruling classes in a period of systemic crisis. This type of power is, however, unachievable by a normal military or police dictatorship. Fascism emerges as a movement which adopts methods of physical confrontation to terrorize and crush workers' organizations. It is in terms of the social character of this movement that fascism is best understood, since it is not readily identifiable with the capitalist interests that it represents. Fascism derives its numbers primarily from the lower middle classes who have been hit by the profound economic crisis and who are psychologically mobilized through resentment, nationalism, crusades against real or perceived internal enemies, and quite often anti-capitalist phraseology. Once power has been consolidated and opposition crushed, fascism's historical mission is to reorganize society militarily, industrially and psychologically in preparation for imperialist war (Trotsky, 1971).

For the purposes of the present study the term 'State' will be used to distinguish the political formation and the repressive and legal apparatuses (army, police, bureaucracy, courts etc.) from society both before and during the war. As thus defined, State will appear throughout the book with a capital *S*, whereas 'state' defined as the totality of social, economic and political relations within a given territory will appear with a small *s* and will apply to such phenomena as the endeavours of the southern Slavs to form a state. We can add to this one further analytical specification, given that along with the above-mentioned restructuring of power the fascist State would develop new forms of authority and political mobilization. While, to be sure, fascism's historical function was one of violence, terror, repression and war, it also sought consent through language, gesture and symbol. Fascism attempted to dissolve society into the State, or, in short, to edify a totalitarian State. Following the overthrow of the pre-existing political regime and the installation of a system of terror to safeguard the new State against the 'enemy within', the politics of the totalitarian party and State are, to use Emilio Gentile's definition, based on the idea that 'the meanings and purpose of human life are expressed in myths and values that constitute a secular religion whose aim is to make the individual and the masses one'. The totalitarian State 'aims to bring about an anthropological revolution that will create a new type of human being, totally dedicated to achieving the political aims of the totalitarian party' (E. Gentile, 2002: 143). Gentile perhaps overstresses the symbolic dimension to the issue. Indeed, his study on the fascist system of political religion tends to divorce the analysis of the relative symbols from their social significance, thus allowing the realm of cultural representation to become too free-floating and self-referential (E. Gentile, 1993). The same can arguably be said, to give one further example, of

George Mosse's trailblazing study on the Myth of the Fallen Soldier in modern European history (Mosse, 1990). At any rate, while for the present study we have defined State as distinct from society, we also need to assess the degree to which the process of political and cultural mobilization in the Great War revealed elements of their envisaged conflation, and to analyze the social and political character of the symbols called upon in this process.

The term 'imperialism' will be used to define the essence of the era under examination. It expresses the nature of the world economy as dominated not by laissez faire liberalism but by giant monopolies and multinational corporations based in a small number of economically powerful countries. The process of concentration, which began around the 1870s, witnessed a transformation in the role of the banks and their increasing intermeshing with major industrial firms. By imperialism, then, is meant the growing fusion of banks with industry and the dominating effects of this on the life of nations and continents. However, since different economic powers had different spheres of influence and interest, imperialism did not stop at the phase of 'competition' between finance capitals but went on to create the conditions for military conflict between states, and this defines the character of the 1914–18 war (Lenin, 1974; Etherington, 1984). The way imperialism, thus defined, developed in Italy in the decade leading up to the First World War has been documented by Robert Webster (1975).

Finally, since we are dealing with the role of cultural representations in the transition from one form of political rule to another, it becomes crucial to isolate the conjuncture between power and representations or, in a word, ideology. From here on ideology will mean the point at which issues related to the production and reproduction of dominant social and political relations have imposed themselves upon language and cultural representations, and where the latter 'spontaneously' readjust their meaning to conform to the power-reproduction process (Eagleton, 1991).

The aim of this book is not so much to offer a new interpretation of fascism as to contribute to a better understanding of the circumstances of its origins. To this end it will attempt to answer its broader questions through an analysis of the writings and speeches of Benito Mussolini between July 1914 and June 1919. Much ink has been spilt over Mussolini's political career and personality, but there has been no in-depth and critical study of his activities in the First World War. The early biographical endeavours of Emilio Settimelli (1922), Antonio Beltramelli (1923) and Giuseppe Prezzolini (1925) are not historical biographies at all, but hagiographies which focus mainly on Mussolini's physical features, on the influences of family and childhood environment, and on explaining away his changes of mind, with particular reference to his break with socialism in October to November 1914. Also in this category is Margherita Sarfatti's *Dux*, which dedicates over thirty pages to the war, replete with Mussolini quotations which, however, unfold in an unexplained and in any case clearly uncritical framework (Sarfatti, 1926: 162–92). Guido Dorso's *Benito Mussolini alla conquista del potere* is a more interesting and fast-moving account which nevertheless remains substantially descriptive and far from exhaustive in the material it examines (Dorso, 1949: 127–72). In 1950 Paolo Monelli gave a brief analysis of Mussolini in the war, though not with a view to understanding the possible origins of fascism. Rather, he was concerned to ridicule 'Mussolini the petty bourgeois' as a shirker and contradictory hypocrite (Monelli, 1950: 83–5). Much more detailed and documented on Mussolini in the First World War is the first of Giorgio Pini and Duilio Susmel's four biographical volumes. Unfortunately, this work's formally scholarly bent does not conceal the fact that it is a descriptive narrative as uncritical as it is hero-worshipping (Pini and Susmel, 1953, I: Chs 10–11). Christopher Hibbert's 1962 biography refers to Mussolini's position in relation to Italian intervention in terms of 'the seed of Fascism [being] sown'. But this tantalizing statement is dissipated by the end of the first paragraph of the following page when Mussolini is already out of the war (Hibbert, 1962: 39–40).

More informative, because based also on documentary material from the Italian State archives opened in the 1960s, is the first volume of Renzo De Felice's biography. This gives an account of Mussolini's 'conversion' to the cause of the war and touches on his activity in the rest of the period of Italian neutrality between August 1914 and May 1915 (De Felice, 1965: Chs 9–10). However, it is not altogether clear who De Felice's Mussolini is, since no sooner does the author make a statement than he goes on to affirm its contrary. De Felice's interpretation of Mussolini and fascism in 1919 as left-wing and revolutionary (Ch. 12) – a characterization which he would go on to apply to Italian fascism as a historical phenomenon (De Felice, 1975) – appears to be more a point of departure than arrival, and as such must *perforce* colour De Felice's assessment of Mussolini in the period 1914–15 and thereafter up to 1919. De Felice argues that Mussolini's right-wing nationalist involution began after Italy's military defeat at Caporetto in October–November 1917 (1965: Ch. 11), a position which is difficult to reconcile with his left-wing and revolutionary interpretation of Mussolini and fascism in 1919. More puzzling still is the fact that De Felice skips over Mussolini's experience at the front between September 1915 and February 1917. He notes that a war diary existed without giving one quotation from it or discussing what it might mean in terms of Mussolini's political evolution in historical context (De Felice, 1965: 322–3). For this period, De Felice refers readers to Pini and Susmel's biography: an invitation to accept as good coin what is effectively a fascist hagiography. This scholarly abdication deprives us of De Felice's insights into Mussolini's political evolution before late 1917. His theory concerning Mussolini's repositioning in 1917–18 thus loses force, since it remains unsubstantiated with reference to what went before, including Mussolini's stance on the February Revolution in Russia. Granted, during the war Mussolini wrote virtually nothing about the October Revolution, but, as we shall see in Chapter 6, he was prolific on Russia between March and November 1917. That the entire De Felicean proposal rests on tenuous presuppositions was shown by Roberto Vivarelli, who while ultimately accepting De Felice's thesis concerning Mussolini's post-Caporetto political redefinition nonetheless argued in 1967 that Mussolini was drawing upon nationalistic terminology long before 1917 (Vivarelli, 1991, I: Ch. 3).

Emilio Gentile's painstaking 1975 investigation into the origins of fascist ideology is not dedicated wholly to Mussolini; though to be sure the political formation and ideas of the duce are central to it. While Gentile has tended to reproduce De Felice's notions according to which scholars who disagree with his (De Felice's) findings and method are dogmatists who allow politics to interfere with their analyses, whereas those who accept them are blessed with the 'intellectual courage' and 'cultural open-mindedness' of the 'new historiography' (E. Gentile, 1986: 182; 2003a; O'Brien, 2004), in his 1975 book and in later efforts (E. Gentile, 2002; 2003b), Gentile would go on to reassess significant elements of the De Felicean interpretation of fascism. In particular, this involves the latter's reluctance to define the regime as totalitarian (De Felice, 1968: 9; 1975: 108) or to at most concede that it was a 'left-wing totalitarianism' (De Felice, 1975: 105). Gentile's 1975 book nevertheless borrows heavily from the De Felicean methodological framework, particularly at the point where it argues in favour of Mussolini's post-Caporetto shift away from socialism and where it theorizes fascism in early 1919 as an ideologically undefined urban phenomenon. It therefore sees Mussolini's right-wing turn as having begun after Caporetto and having reached full fruition only after the war, more specifically in the early 1920s when the arrival of huge quantities of new (overtly reactionary) members meant that fascism was forced to redefine its programme (E. Gentile, 1975: 40–41, Ch. 4). Hence Gentile's book does not go into any significant detail about Mussolini's war experience, and in fact is dated from 1918 onwards. His more recent studies on fascism as political religion (1993) and on the pre- and post-war radical vision of the authoritarian myth of the new State (1999) likewise leave out any systematic treatment of the war.

A. James Gregor's 1979 study on the intellectual life of the young Mussolini was hatched in order to throw further light on what in a 1974 book Gregor had argued to be the 'progressive revolutionary' nature of fascism due to its focus on industrialization. But the American scholar's dependence on abstract sociological typologies is taken to extremes. Not only does he not apply his heuristic model to concrete social relations, but he rather disparagingly dismisses attempts to understand fascism in social, class-struggle and politico-strategic terms (Gregor, 1974: esp. Ch. 5). Yet Gregor's approach leaves him quoting uncritically from Mussolini's writings. The latter's political and military activities during the First

World War, touched upon only briefly (Gregor 1979: 205–7), are set within the 'historically progressive', i.e. 'bourgeois industrial' (in the abstract) categories which Gregor applies to his quotations from Mussolini and, from there, to his interpretation of fascism in general.

Mario Isnenghi's all too brief 1985 analysis of Mussolini's 1915–17 war diary approaches the entries as a composite text rather than as a document which responded to the unfolding war. His conclusions, such as that already at that stage Mussolini was behaving like 'the duce among his people' or that he 'brings the world of the officers to the men', are insightful but remain disconnected from the subject's broader wartime activity, and we are therefore not told what they imply (Isnenghi, 1985). Luisa Passerini's treatment of the construction of the Mussolini myth opens with a series of quotes from Mussolini's war diary and examines the ancient-mythological manner in which his injury of February 1917 was treated by his supporters (descent into the underworld to then re-emerge). But she effectively leaves the diary quotes without comment in relation to the unfolding war, and therefore does not fully enter into the otherwise enticing title to this section, namely 'Death and resurrection' (Passerini, 1991: 15–32). Aurelio Lepre's reconstruction of Mussolini between myth and reality furnishes quotes from the war diary, but not as part of a detailed examination of that text or of Mussolini's war experience in general. Lepre does, however, concisely observe that from an early point in the war Mussolini had adopted a Manichean perspective – a universe divided into black and white, good and bad, ins and outs, those with us and those against us (Lepre, 1995: 67–73). Finally, the most up-to-date biography, by Richard Bosworth, makes no critical reassessment of the war texts of Mussolini that it cites, and interprets the material as being of no meaningful ideological significance (Bosworth 2002: 114–21).

Drawing upon sociological, anthropological, cultural and literary theory, the present book conducts a contextualized exegesis of Mussolini's writings and speeches between July 1914 and June 1919. The two main sources of the book are Mussolini's newspaper, *Il Popolo d'Italia*, and his war diary, all of which is published material. Central State Archive documents are also referred to, as is the official diary of Mussolini's regiment. These unpublished documents nevertheless remain secondary to the far greater quantity of published articles and diary entries whose importance is underscored by their contemporary diffusion and socio-political influence. An exception is represented by Mussolini's military and health records for 1917, which, however, formed the basis of a previous publication by the author (O'Brien, 2002a; 2003) discussed briefly at the end of Chapter 5. The underlying proposition of this book is that Mussolini textually reinvented himself through the experience of the war in a way that reveals the nidus of fascism, fascist ideology and the system of cultural representations – including Mazzini, Intervention, Victory and the Fallen Soldier – later adopted in the consolidation of the regime. Rejecting dismissals of Mussolini as an empty rhetorician incapable of anything metaphysical or logical (Eco, 1994: xii), the book explores what marked Mussolini out from even the most similar of political militants and how this distinction formed the basis of fascist power.

–1–

Stating the programme
November 1918–June 1919

Then they said . . . that we were an ephemeral movement; they said we had no doctrine.

Mussolini, Speech in Milan, 28 October 1923

I conclude my speech with a question; but before you reply, bear in mind that the great King, the Father of the Fatherland is watching you, and the Unknown Soldier is listening: now, if it is necessary, will you do tomorrow what you did, what we did, yesterday?

Mussolini, Speech in Rome, 4 November 1928

The Programme of San Sepolcro, March 1919

In December 1918 nationalist imperialist Alfredo Rocco argued that while the recently concluded conflict was commonly seen as one between a democratic Entente on the one hand, and German imperialism and militarism on the other, each of the Great Powers had in fact conducted a war for the preservation and expansion of its own empire. The principle of nationalities was only a democratic smokescreen that allowed the Yugoslavs 'to perpetuate foreign control' in the Balkans, and at Italy's territorial expense. Italy therefore needed to abolish the democratic basis of her national life and to reorganize her social formation in preparation for ongoing war. The State had to impose 'the discipline of inequalities' and, from there, 'hierarchy and organization' (Rocco, 1918).

From the very beginning of his post-war journalistic campaign in *Il Popolo d'Italia*, a newspaper which he had owned and run since November 1914, Mussolini supported a different interpretation of Italy's war. On 4 November 1918, the day on which the armistice between Italy and the now defunct Austro-Hungarian Empire came into force, he defined Italian victory with reference to Giuseppe Mazzini, the democratic prophet of national independence during Italy's Risorgimento. He wrote that Mazzini was among the Italian dead 'who are still living' and who had 'led the armies' (OO, XI: 458–9). In his *Questione morale* of 1866, Mazzini had argued that Italy's international and humanitarian mission was identifiable with a victorious war against Austria-Hungary that would liberate both Italy and the Balkan peoples (Mazzini, 1961: 52–3). On 5 November Mussolini reproduced this idea as a dominant feature of Italy's war: '[The Austrian] corpse', he wrote, 'will no longer stifle the atmosphere . . . Italy, the nation of the future . . . has liberated the peoples' (OO, XI: 460).

Yet in February 1923, just four months after the fascist March on Rome, the Associazione Nazionale Italiana, of which Rocco was a member, dissolved into the Partito Nazionale Fascista led by Mussolini. The two organizations had found what, in a joint statement, they termed a 'unity of ideals' (De Felice, 1966, Appendix: 773–4). What had come to pass that such a fusion was now possible? According to De Felice, an examination of the kind of people present at fascist meetings in 1919 and the early 1920s is crucial for understanding the political transformation that fascism underwent in its ascension to power. In early 1919 there were the 'old guard' socialist, syndicalist and anarchist revolutionary inter-ventionists of 1914–15. These attest to the 'markedly left-wing' character of the original fascist movement. When, however, it comes to the congresses of Rome (November 1921) and Naples (October 1922), a radical transformation can be noted: now predominant among fascist ranks were agrarians and industrialists reacting against land and factory occupations. For De Felice, 'in the two sets of names is already synthesized the [progressive] evolution [and then reactionary] involution of fascism' (1965: 504–6). Even with this involution, however, the orig-inal fascist movement would continue to exist throughout the fascist period and, according to De Felice, 'is the "guiding thread" which links March 1919 to April 1945' (1975: 28). Elements of this argument were later taken up by Emilio Gentile, according to whom the fascism of 1920 was revealing a 'progressive moving away from the fascism of the original programme' (1975: 192). More recently, Richard Bosworth has spoken of the fascist programmes of 1919 as having contained 'radical plans to push society towards equality' (2002: 21).

To what extent do these assessments conform to the documentary evidence? On 18 March 1919 Mussolini announced the aims of the founding meeting of the *fasci di combattimento* which was to be held five days later. He continued to differ rad-ically from Rocco in his characterization of the war's legacy: fascism, he stated, was out to achieve 'political and economic democracy'. But he also specified that fascism would be setting out 'from the terrain of the nation, of the war, of the victory'. In short, it would be starting 'from interventionism'. For Mussolini, Italian intervention in May 1915 had represented a revolution, or rather 'the first phase of a revolution' that was '*not finished*' and in fact '*continues*' (Mussolini's emphases). To bring this 'revolution' to completion was the purpose of nascent fascism (OO, XII: 309–11). Hence even at this early stage Mussolini, like Rocco, placed emphasis on the nation and shared with the nationalist imperialist the view that the war was an ongoing process. In Piazza San Sepolcro in Milan five days later Mussolini presented the fascist programme, which is reproduced in full here:

I.

The meeting of 23 March dedicates its first salute, its memory and its reverent thought to the sons of Italy who fell for the greatness of the Fatherland and for the liberty of the World; to the mutilated and the invalid; to all the combatants and to the ex-prisoners who carried out their duty. It declares itself ready to energetically support the claims of a material and moral nature put forward by the combatants' associations.

II.

The meeting of 23 March declares itself opposed to the imperialism of other peoples to Italy's detriment and to any possible Italian imperialism to the detriment of other peoples. It accepts the supreme postulate of the League of Nations which presupposes the integration of each nation, an integration which in Italy's case must be realized on the Alps and on the Adriatic with the claim to Fiume and Dalmatia and their annexation.

III.

The meeting of 23 March commits all fascists to sabotaging the candidacies of the neutralists of all parties by any means necessary. (OO, XII: 321–3)

A number of issues are at work here. In section I reference is made to Italy's fallen soldiers and these are linked to 'the greatness of the Fatherland'. But any notion that this somehow implies egotistic expansionism is offset when those same soldiers are said to have fallen for 'the liberty of the World'. In any case, in section II Italian imperialism is rejected and fascism's adherence to the American proposal for a League of Nations is stressed. By the same token, however, Italian imperialism may be acceptable once it is not carried out 'to the detriment of other peoples'. In his spoken comment on the programme, Mussolini qualified this by saying that 'what distinguishes one imperialism from another are the means adopted' and that Italy would never adopt 'barbaric means of penetration'. He also noted that Italy had a population of 40 million which, he claimed, would be 60 million 'in 10 or 20 years time'. This contrasted with the fact that 'we have barely 1.5 million square kilometres of colonies, for the most part sandy, towards which we will never be able to direct the majority of our population' (OO, XII: 323). There is also some sabre-rattling in section II where it declares that fascism is opposed to whoever may be considering the practice of imperialism 'to Italy's detriment'. The same section's territorial claims to Fiume and Dalmatia therefore represent something of a bull in a shop whose anti-imperialist and pro-nationalities china has already been precariously placed.

Similar contradictions abound. Mussolini's already-quoted 5 November 1918 article de-emphasized the State, seeing the war as 'a people's war' and victory as 'the victory of the people'. Also, in his above-mentioned spoken comments on the San Sepolcro programme he argued that 'in none of the victorious nations can the triumph of reaction be seen. In all of them there is a march towards the greatest political and economic democracy.' This differed from Rocco, who, as we have seen, envisaged an authoritarian role for the State in reorganizing Italian society in a decidedly reactionary direction. Yet neither was Mussolini without his ambiguities on this issue, some of which reveal a concern to reaffirm and bolster State authority. In reference to section I's salute to the former prisoners of war who had 'carried out their duty', for example, Mussolini specified in his spoken comment that 'evidently there were those men who surrendered, but these are known as deserters' (OO, XII: 322). The need for this distinction originated in the fact that during the conflict the military authorities had treated Italian prisoners of war as little more than deserters. The government blocked public aid, thereby contributing to the deaths of about 100,000 Italian captives through starvation and exposure (Procacci, Gv., 1993: 167–75). In December 1918 Mussolini had visited the detention centre at Gossolengo near Piacenza, where newly released Italian POWs were being interrogated about the circumstances of their capture. He remarked that among the 40,000 men there was 'no "political" ferment' and concluded by calling for an end to what he saw as the 'ridiculous speculation of certain people' who were trying to 'deviate towards Italy that deeply felt hatred which our brothers have towards that contemptible Austria'. He praised the camp's officers for everything they were doing to treat the men with 'a sense of comradeship and humanity' (OO, XII: 56–9). In short, Mussolini's main objective was to redirect any political implications deriving from the prisoners' grievances about their (mis)treatment during the war. If there was any anti-State sentiment in this stopover camp, it was anti-Austrian.

Furthermore, there is an all-important question of State about which the programme of San Sepolcro says nothing – the Monarchy. In his ultimately failed attempt in November 1918 to convene a Constituent Assembly of Interventionism, Mussolini specified that the Assembly was not to have a republican character. 'We will make the republic when a change in the institutions seems necessary to ensure national development', he wrote on 14 November (OO, XII: 3–5). Arguably this position reflected a desire not to preclude the participation of non-republicans in the Constituent Assembly. This, indeed, was De Felice's view (1965: 470). But in February 1919 Mussolini affirmed that, along with everything else, 'we are also *conservative*' (OO, XII: 230–3. Mussolini's emphasis). Was his non-committal stance on the Monarchy the expression of the tactical shrewdness of a left-wing militant, *pace* De Felice? Or might it have reflected a concern to underpin the central symbol of State authority and social hierarchy? We can begin to examine these various possibilities by further exploring the San Sepolcro programme's territorial claims (section II) and its internal social policy (sections I and III). Particular attention will be paid to the role ascribed to Italy's fallen soldiers, whose centrality is evidenced by the fact that they initiate the programmatic declaration.

Blood and Soil, Old Friends for New

It should be noted that the San Sepolcro programme appeared at the time that the Paris peace conference was entering a crucial phase as regards Italy. Italy was represented in Paris by Prime Minister Vittorio Emanuele Orlando and Foreign Minister Sidney Sonnino. Sonnino was a key architect of the Pact of London, a secret agreement signed with Britain, France and Russia on 26 April 1915 as the basis for Italian intervention into the war. In the event of an allied victory the Pact promised Italy the Trentino and Upper Adige as far as the Brenner pass; Trieste; Istria as far as the Quarnaro to include Volosca and the Adriatic islands of Lussin and Cherso; Dalmatia as far down as Cape Planka; the port of Valona and a protectorate over Albania. The Pact also recognized Italy's control of the Dodecanese Islands, and granted her compensation in North Africa if England and France increased their influence in that region. Fiume, however, was to remain in the Austro-Hungarian Empire as part of Sonnino's strategy of containing 'pan-Slav' influence in the Balkans and using a territorially reduced Austro-Hungarian Empire as a guarantee against the union between Croatia and Serbia (Albrecht-Carrié, 1938: 334–9; Vivarelli, 1991, I: 172–3).

Despite the fact that the two main pillars of the Pact no longer existed at the end of the war (Austria-Hungary was no more, and Russia had withdrawn from the conflict following the October Revolution), Sonnino continued to defend the accord. Indeed, Orlando and Sonnino used the dissolution of Austria-Hungary to increase Italy's territorial claims. Orlando was prepared to sacrifice elements of the Pact in exchange for a line along the Alps and the annexation of Fiume and Zara, while Sonnino continued to downplay the annexation of Fiume in favour of full recognition of the Pact of London. The compromise position was a claim for the Pact of London territories *plus* Fiume, and even a hint at the annexation of Splate. All this amounted to only slightly less than the demands of the nationalist imperialists, whose congress of 15 December 1918 had demanded Italy's annexation of the whole of Dalmatia plus Fiume (Albrecht-Carrié, 1938: 370–87; Vivarelli, 1991, I: Ch. 2).

For reasons which are unclear, but which are probably linked to his status as a political journalist and owner of a Milan-based newspaper, Mussolini was a guest at the gala dinner given in honour of American President Woodrow Wilson on 5 January 1919 in the Scala Opera House in Milan. Wilson received a tremendous popular reception during his visits to Rome and Milan on 3, 4 and 5 January and during his brief stopovers in Genoa and Turin on his journey back to Paris (Mayer, 1968: Ch. 7). On 3 January Mussolini wrote: 'It is not being adulatory towards the President of the great Republic of the stars if we say that today he is our guest and that Italy, by spirit, tradition and temperament is the most Wilsonian nation of all.' Mussolini linked this pro-Wilson discourse to Italy's fallen soldiers: 'The people of the dead, which has tied a terrifying inheritance to the living, and the living, who propose to be deserving of the people of the dead, all today gather in body and spirit in the streets of the Eternal City to greet Wilson and recognize themselves in him' (OO, XII: 106–9). Wilson's visit to Italy came at an important moment in Italian political life following the resignation from government of reformist socialist Leonida Bissolati on 28 December 1918. This was occasioned by a disagreement with Sonnino over the Foreign Minister's insistence on pursuing the Pact of London. Bissolati argued for a policy of friendship with Yugoslavia and Italy's full insertion into Wilson's New Diplomacy. He discussed these views personally with the American President in a meeting of 4 January 1919. At that encounter, and later during a speech at the Scala on 11 January, Bissolati outlined what he considered the necessary Italian territorial concessions to achieve alignment with Wilson. He argued that Italy should forgo its claims to the Upper Adige beyond Bolzano, leave Dalmatia to the Dalmatians, and renounce control of the Dodecanese Islands (Bissolati, 1923: 392, 394–414; Colapietra, 1958: 272–9; Mayer, 1968: 213). Correspondence between Mussolini and Bissolati in late November and early December 1918 had been extremely cordial (OO, XII: 37–8, 50). One would assume, therefore, that Mussolini's support for Wilson's mission in Italy also meant that he sided with Bissolati in his disagreement with Sonnino, and that the territorial claims of the programme of San Sepolcro emerged later and for reasons which need to be explained.

Yet nothing could be further from the truth. On 29 December Mussolini affirmed that, like Bissolati, he accepted Wilson's proposals for the League of Nations and disarmament, but added that this was also Sonnino's position. His point was that Sonnino was no more or less Wilsonian than France (which would never consider a plebiscite in Alsace-Lorraine), or Britain (which would never give back Gibralta, Malta or Cyprus, or consider reducing its fleet), or even America itself (which while calling for arms reduction was going ahead with its own naval programme; OO, XII: 88–90). On 1 January Mussolini accused Bissolati of causing 'extreme humiliation' for Italy in the run-up to the Paris conference (OO, XII: 100–103). Mussolini was present at the Scala on 11 January and was among those who shouted the speaker down when he began to discuss territorial issues (De Felice, 1965: 487–8). On 12 January Mussolini explained that he had not mentioned Mazzini recently because Mazzinians like Bissolati had been dishonouring his name (OO, XII: 134–6). Two days later he affirmed that Bissolati had become 'the "leader" of the Germans, their man, their banner, their evangelist' (OO, XII: 141–3).

How, then, did Mussolini's pro-Wilson stance, given symbolic expression in a pro-nationalities unification of the living and the dead, fit with this public attack on a key Italian representative of Wilson's position? Italy's territorial ambitions stood in sharp contrast to the claims brought to the Paris conference by the

Yugoslav delegation headed by Nicola Pasić and Ante Trumbić, a Serb and a Croat respectively. The Yugoslav state had been proclaimed on 29 October 1918, and on 1 December King Alexander had announced the existence of the Kingdom of Serbs, Croats and Slovenes. While Yugoslavs were confused as to which territorial claims they should make as a unified state, they had no doubts about their desired borders in relation to both Italy and Austria. They traced a line ranging from Pontebba in the north right down to the Adriatic. This stretched fifteen kilometres beyond the west side of the river Isonzo and went down as far as Monfalcone, which, however, was to remain in Italy. Into Yugoslav territory were to go the counties of Gorizia and Gradisca, Trieste, the whole of the Istria peninsula, Fiume, the islands of the Quarnaro and all of Dalmatia with its Archipelago (Lederer, 1966: 57–9, 101, 119, 129). Working in the Yugoslavs' favour was the fact that one aim of Wilson's fourteen-point speech to congress on 8 January 1918 (Wilson, 1969: 88–93) had been to reduce the import of Italy's war. Following the October Revolution in Russia, the ideological struggle had intensified, rendering more urgent a reaffirmation of the democratic and anti-imperialist ideals for which, it was claimed, the Entente and America were fighting. Italian imperialism clashed with this strategy (Rossini, 1991: 488). In short, Italy was heading for a collision with the United States.

Immediately after the cessation of hostilities the Italian Army occupied the whole of the Pact of London territory and on 17 November 1918 moved into Fiume. Admiral Enrico Millo declared himself Governor of Dalmatia, and American observers in Fiume got the distinct impression that the Italians were there to stay (Lederer, 1966: 79–82, 91–2). On 22 November Mussolini dealt with Yugoslav animadversion to the Italian military occupations. In particular he rejected Croat disapprobation, the most vociferous in as much as Fiume had been occupied. He claimed that the Croats were 'heroes of the last hour' who had defected to the anti-Austrian side in 1918 'only when the die was cast'. He specified that 'nobody contests the right of the Yugoslav people to unite and live in freedom', once it did so in those territories left over after Italy had occupied Fiume and the territories promised by the Pact of London. At this point Italy's fallen soldiers were again invoked:

> Would Italy have made 42 months of war, would it have sacrificed the flower of ten generations (all Italian blood, since we didn't put coloured or colonial troops in the line!), would it have subjected itself to the hardest of Calvaries, would it have slashed its veins, only to then hand over Trieste and Gorizia, which are Italian, to the Slovenes; Fiume and Zara, which are Italian, to the Croats? This is the most absurd of absurdities. It cannot and will not be. (OO, XII: 22–4)

In early to mid-December 1918 Mussolini initiated a collection campaign for the mother of Nazario Sauro (OO, XII: 61). Sauro, from Capodistria, had been an officer in the Austrian Merchant Navy, but had fought with the Italian Navy during the war. He was captured by the Austrians while attempting to enter Fiume with the submarine *Pullino* in late July 1916 and hanged for treason in August. Mussolini aimed for contributions of 25,000 lire, but claimed to have received more than three times that amount. He asked whether there was anything behind the generous donations and answered:

> Yes. There is. Nazario Sauro is the martyr of our sea [the Adriatic]. The consecrator and claimant of its two shores. On the sea that is Sauro's there is no place for other flags which are not those of peaceful commerce. Where there is the *martyr*, there is uncontested and incontestable right. Where there is heroism there is no place for bargaining. The sea of Sauro is the sea of Italy. (OO, XII: 67–8; Mussolini's emphases)

The dead revivified were not only those from the Great War. In Trieste on 20 December Mussolini called up the ghost of the local patriot Gugliemo Oberdan, hanged by the Austrians in 1882 for possession of a bomb with which he intended to assassinate Emperor Franz Josef. Mussolini remarked that 'death cannot end with death itself'. Italy had to arrive in Trieste 'not only because 200,000 suffering living men are waiting, but because that Dead Man is waiting' (OO, XII: 71–3). Nine days later Mussolini was in Leghorn for the unveiling of a memorial plaque to Sauro, Oberdan and Cesare Battisti. Battisti, a Trentino socialist and member of the Austrian parliament, had campaigned for the annexation of the Trentino to Italy. He returned to Italy in 1915 and subsequently enlisted. He was captured by the Austrians on 10 July 1916 and hanged two days later for treason. On unveiling the monument to the three national heroes Mussolini said: 'We must have the religion of memory, not to remain locked in the past, but to set out on the triumphal march and to prepare for the difficult tasks that await us' (OO, XII: 91–5).

Hence with reference to Italy's fallen, Mussolini presented the victorious powers with an incontestable past, present and future Italian right to expansion to the north and east of its actual frontiers. As regards the League of Nations, he concurred that this was necessary for dealing with problems of national rights, but defined Italian expansionist claims as precisely that, namely 'clear and legitimate [national] rights', which again were non-negotiable since '460,000 dead men don't permit [negotiation]' (OO, XII: 110–12). It was not, however, until April 1919 that Mussolini felt he had enough evidence with which to assail Wilson. Prior to this he had limited himself to dealing with British and French demurral over the Italian military occupations and what he defined as their 'complicity' with the 'Yugoslav imperialist thesis' (OO, XII: 25–6, 42–4, 47–9, 62–3). Even on 9 March his invective was still aimed primarily against these two allied powers (OO, XII: 278–81). The shift occurred because on 14 April Wilson accepted the Pact of London in the north and a division of Istria between east and west, the so-called 'Wilson line'. He also conceded to Italy the island of Lussin, control of Valona, the demilitarization of the other Adriatic islands, and the transformation of Fiume into a free city under the Yugoslav customs system (Lederer, 1966: 225–6). This, however, was insufficient for the Italian delegation in Paris, which merely reiterated its demand for the Pact of London plus Fiume. Mussolini agreed, and on 15 April invoked the dead 'from the trenches beyond the Isonzo and the Piave'. Fiume was Italian 'through a plebiscite of the living and the dead'. For Mussolini, Wilsonism was revealing itself to be 'the idealism of business dealings' (OO, XIII: 57–9).

Despite the placatory tone of Wilson's 23 April appeal to the Italian people (over the heads of its rulers) for a reasonable position on territory, the Italian delegation took it as an affront. Orlando's response, published in the Italian press alongside Wilson's message, was a diplomatically worded but nevertheless sharp rebuttal (Albrecht-Carrié, 1938: 498–504). By 24 April the Italian delegation was on its way home. This withdrawal from the Paris conference received Mussolini's support. He urged the parliamentary sitting of 29 April to proceed towards decreeing the annexation of Fiume and Dalmatia (OO, XIII: 85–7, 90, 101–3). However, the government merely sought (and received) parliamentary approval for its conduct at the negotiations. Ten days later it was back in Paris, cap in hand. On 9 May Mussolini declared that Italy, 'the "Great Proletariat"', was 'ready to take up the class struggle once more' against 'an exquisitely plutocratic and bourgeois alliance' of France, Britain and America (OO, XIII: 107–9). On 20 May he wrote that 'if we are "betrayed" – and the word isn't a big one – by the Anglo-American coalition, we will fall, fatally, in spite of all the moral and physiological repugnance that the Germans inspire in us, into the block of anti-English forces'. In order to arrive more quickly at the Italo-German realignment, he urged Germany to sign the peace terms imposed by the allies (OO, XIII: 140–41). On 29 May, when the German Foreign Minister, Count Brockdorff-Rantzau, presented further objections to the conditions, Mussolini implored him to 'not get lost in note upon note', to accept that Alsace-Lorraine had to be returned to France and to get on with the signing (OO, XIII: 157–9). On 19 June Mussolini assured Germany that 'the roads of the future are still open' (OO, XIII: 195–7). As had been promised in the lead up to San Sepolcro, the 'revolution' was continuing, and new battle lines were being drawn.

The Early Fascists: Social Composition and Ideology

Who were the fascists of San Sepolcro? And what does their social and ideological composition tell us about the origins and nature of the fascist programme of 23 March 1919? On 24 March *Il Popolo d'Italia* claimed that 'many friends, officers, soldiers and workers' had attended the previous day's assembly. It went on to provide a list of names, of which we have counted ninety-seven (OO, XII, Appendix: 337–40). This does not mean that there were only ninety-seven people at the meeting, and a contemporary police report gave the number as around 300, though to be sure this included journalists and curious passers-by (De Felice, 1965: 504). The list in *Il Popolo d'Italia* can, however, provide a useful analytical source. Taking workers first, a look down the roster shows the presence only of representatives of the Milanese section of the Unione Italiana del Lavoro (UIL). This was a national syndicalist organization founded in September 1914 by Filippo Corridoni and Alceste De Ambris after they had failed to convince the majority of the Unione sindacalista italiana (formed in November 1912 following a split by 'revolutionary syndicalists' from the Confederazione Generale del Lavoro) of the need for workers to support intervention in the 'revolutionary war' (De Felice, 1965: 163ff, 237ff). These representatives did not speak at the meeting. Out of the ninety-seven identifiable people we find perhaps three 'soldiers', none of whom bore military rank. Then there are the names of sixty or so people without any professional title or military rank (the Unione Sindacale Milanese representatives included). There are seven lieutenants and five captains, plus a lieutenant colonel and two majors. Also present were two members of parliament and one senator. The rest of the list is composed of the middle-class professions: six are 'prof.' (university lecturers or schoolteachers), and of these one was both a lieutenant colonel and doctor, while another also bore the title 'avv.' (lawyer); another six were in fact lawyers, one of whom was also a captain, another of whom was one of the above-mentioned soldiers without rank, and yet another of whom was the already-mentioned 'prof. avv.'; there was also one 'ing.' (an engineer), and four people bearing the title 'dott.' or 'dottor' (either university graduates in letters or medical doctors). Thus despite the presence of UIL representatives, when officers are taken together with the professions the list becomes very much a middle-class one. Since many of the names without professional titles or military rank were delegates from the cities and towns of Italy, it is likely that they, too, were from the middle classes.

In the Mostra della Rivoluzione Fascista (MRF) in the Archivio Centrale dello Stato (ACS) in Rome are contained 222 documents of various nature (long and short letters, postcards, telegrams, notes) which declare allegiance to fascism in the spring of 1919. These tend to confirm the above sociological analysis and moreover reveal the understanding of nascent fascism nurtured by those who recognized themselves in it. A certain Torgelio Seniade, for example, told Mussolini on 25 March that 'whoever understands and follows you is Italian, whoever understands you and doesn't follow you is a false Greek who croaks the song of the socialists and the renunciators: i.e. the song of the enemy . . . Whoever sabotaged, whoever betrayed, whoever thanked the enemy, will have their hands full in today's supreme hour' (ACS, MRF, b. 17, s.fasc. 18). On 11 April Lieutenant Pietro Gorgolini assured Mussolini that he could count on 100 or so officers and university students to form a local *fascio di combattimento*. Gorgolini boasted of having 'slapped a Bolshevik without pity' and of having 'labelled as infamous' four socialists (ACS, MRF, b. 17, s.fasc. 30). From other letters to Mussolini dated 5 April and 13 May we discover that Gorgolini was part of a pro-Fiume and Dalmatia society whose governing body was made up of a university dean, a lieutenant colonel and a number of officer students. He himself was just finishing his law degree (ACS, MRF, b. 17, s.fasc. 16 and b. 20, s.fasc. 206). Amedeo Rebora wrote to Mussolini on 3 April of the local anti-German action league among whose 'best and most combative friends' were nationalists and monarchists who, while being unable to adhere loyally to the *fascio,* 'nevertheless share our general postulates' (ACS, MRF, b. 19, s.fasc. 117). An undated list of members of the Rome section of the *fascio di combattimento* reveals men with titles such as cap. avv. (a captain and lawyer), ten. rag (a lieutenant and accountant) and cap. rag (a captain and accountant), all of whom were keen to guarantee Italy's 'territorial and economic compensation' against the 'internal and external enemies' (ACS, MRF, b. 19, s.fasc. 122).

In short, while many of these documents simply ask for assistance in the formation of a local *fascio,* those which reveal a political content are overtly anti-socialist and in open opposition to what is deemed an external and internal plot to rob Italy of the fruits of its 'victory'. There is no organized support from members of the working class or the peasantry. Only one document, dated 14 June, asked for 'pamphlets and books for socialist propaganda' (ACS, MRF, b. 20, s.fasc. 179). These are the letters, postcards and telegrams of reactionary elements of the middle and lower middle classes, many of whom were former officers, and junior officers in particular.

One of the few speeches made at the meeting of 23 March (published in *Il Popolo d'Italia* the following day) was by Michele Bianchi, who in obvious reference to Mussolini (since only Mussolini spoke at length) demanded that the meeting not make demagogic promises to workers that it was unable to keep. De Felice defines this as 'more realistic' than Mussolini's contributions (1965: 508). Another way of looking at it, however, is that Bianchi wanted to make no commitments whatever to the labouring classes, whom he defined as 'incapable'. But the real reason is undoubtedly to be found in Bianchi's political past. A one-time 'revolutionary syndicalist', between 1910 and 1912 he led the Camera del lavoro in Ferrara. He was later involved in an immense political and ideological shift which culminated in the issue of intervention in the war in 1915. This concerned the forging of an alliance between local landowners, the Catholic Church, urban-based lawyers, teachers and the commercial classes of Ferrara. The genesis of this coalition went back to a reaction against the farm workers' strike of 1897 and it solidified even further after 1901 when those same workers began to organize into socialist leagues. When the interventionist crisis arose between 1914 and 1915, the shift by many middle class 'friends of labour' to the side of anti-socialist nationalism completed the realignment of forces into this aggressively conservative and now pro-war bloc. Bianchi was among those who made the transition (Corner, 1975: Ch. 1).

The foregoing sociological and ideological analysis of the San Sepolcro meeting needs to be taken further, for the meeting was chaired by Feruccio Vecchi, a member of the *arditi*, who were further represented by Captain Mario Carli, founder of the Associazione Arditi, president of the Fascio futurista politico romano, and editor of *Roma futurista*. Other futurists present were Achille Funi, Mario Dessy, Gino Chierini (all lieutenants), and the writer and poet Filippo Marinetti, their leader. What exactly did the presence of these two currents represent at the founding meeting of fascism?

The futurists argued for the absolute freedom of the individual from what they perceived to be the obstacles of law and tradition. As in art, so too in politics were all previous forms to be violently swept away. In the *Manifesto del Futurismo* (1909) Marinetti argued: 'There is no more beauty, if not in struggle. Any work which does not have an aggressive character cannot be a masterpiece.' Art itself 'cannot be but violence, cruelty and injustice'. Futurism's mission was to reconcile aesthetic individualism with the collectivity by placing the artist at the head of a new social and political formation. The most potent expression of this relationship between the individual, the nation and art was war: 'We want to glorify war – the only cleanser for the world.' As part of the break with the stultifying past, Marinetti insisted on the need 'to destroy museums, libraries, academies of every type' (1996: 7–14). In a December 1913 speech in defence and celebration of Italy's invasion and occupation of Libya (1911–12), he demanded 'a ferociously anti-clerical and anti-socialist Nation' and warned that the socialists 'should convince themselves that we representatives of the young Italian artistic youth will fight with all means and without truce their cowardly manoeuvres against the politico-military and colonial prestige of Italy' (Marinetti, 1996: 499–502).

In short, through his writings and speeches Marinetti made an artistic virtue out of nationalism, imperialism, militarism, anti-socialism, unabashed philistinism and unthinking violence. From the front in December 1915 he, together with a number of other futurist soldiers, issued the document *Orgoglio italiano* (Italian pride) in which they lauded 'the superiority of Italian genius' and promised 'slaps, punches and shootings in the back' for anyone who did not express this pride or who worked against its being brought to full fruition (Marinetti, 1996: 502–6). In February 1918 the futurists announced the formation of a political party whose programme repeated previously expressed imperialist, anti-clerical and anti-socialist themes (Marinetti, 1996: 345–52). In September the journal *Roma futurista* was founded to promote the party and the latest version of the programme, also dated September 1918, a medley of demands for electoral reform, sexual parity, anti-clericalism, militarism and vague notions of land reform (De Felice, 1965, Appendix: 738–41). At the beginning of 1919 the Fasci politici futuristi sprang up in various Italian cities, and were mainly composed of petty bourgeois intellectuals and NCOs (E. Gentile, 1975: 109–28; 1999: Ch. 4; Marinetti, 1996: 508–509). These formed the basis of what in March would become the *fasci di combattimento*.

The *arditi* were special assault troops founded in 1916 but given greater importance from late 1917 onwards following Italy's strategic defeat at Caporetto. Their adoption of black standards, skulls with daggers in their teeth, flames and black shirts all symbolized the desire to face danger and overcome death. Seeing themselves as the elect few over against the dormant mass, the *arditi* were convinced that Italian victory had been very much due to their own heroic acts of individual daring. This was not true, but it did nothing to alter their sense of election, expressed most lucidly in their continuous use of the term 'religious'. In November 1918 General Francesco Saverio Grazioli called for their demobilization and disbandment, and by March 1919 the only ones remaining were sent to Tripolitana. The *arditi*, however, had different ideas, forming into a combatants' association on 1 January 1919. They intended to regroup those who had fought 'for the greatness of Italy' and to continue in peacetime 'the ascension of the great Italian nation'. For the *arditi*, the war had been a revolution which could not finish in the blink of an eye but which had to continue without, and, if necessary, *against* the masses. As they saw it, the war had done away with distinctions between bourgeois and proletarian parties and had exalted the nation above both. In particular, they nurtured an enormous bias against the Italian Socialist Party (PSI), which as a mass organization and anti-war party contrasted with their élitism, nationalism and militarism (E. Gentile, 1975: 98–109; Rochat, 1981: 23–7, 118, 123–4, 140–41, Chs 4 and 7). In the week following the end of the war, Mussolini was to be found in the company of a number of *arditi* at the Caffè della Borsa in Milan. He said, 'I feel something of you in me and perhaps you recognize yourselves in me' (OO, XI: 477). On a visit to *Il Popolo d'Italia*'s offices the following day a group of *arditi* declared to Mussolini that they wanted to be at his side 'to fight the civil battles for the greatness of the Fatherland' (quoted in Rochat, 1981: 115). By mid-January 1919 *Il Popolo d'Italia* was arranging finance for the Milanese *arditi* from local industrialists, and this probably explains why the *arditi* only had any real success in Milan (Rochat, 1981: 115–16).

Social Conservation, Anti-Socialism and a 'Mystique' of Violence

The San Sepolcro meeting seems, therefore, to have represented a merger between Mussolini and certain middle-class interests, upon which the presence of UIL representatives has no significant bearing. It is noteworthy in this regard that the programme of March 1919 makes no reference to the labouring classes or to agrarian reform. No certain data exists for the social composition of the Italian Army

during the Great War, though rough estimates see the peasants as having represented about 46 per cent of Italy's fighting army and they thus account for the vast
majority of casualties (Serpieri, 1930: 41–2; 48ff). Mussolini knew that the peasants had provided the majority of Italy's combatants: 'The immense masses of
infantry', he remarked on 16 November 1918, 'were recruited from the agricultural proletariat of the Po Valley and southern Italy where three quarters are agricultural labourers or day workers'. Yet this article did not call for a radical,
pro-peasant transformation of relations on the land, in particular the expropriation
of southern *latifondisti* and the breaking up of their large, technologically back-
ward and historically anchronistic estates. It limited itself, rather, to demanding a
reduction of the working day which, it stated, 'would represent the first step
towards a less bestial life' for Italy's peasants (OO, XII: 9–10). A week before the
appearance of this piece, Mussolini claimed that 'the project of "land to the peasants" has been supported in these columns', though we are not given to know when
and where, and it is not listed among the same article's socio-economic demands,
such as the eight-hour day by 1920, an improvement in working conditions and a
minimum wage (OO, XI: 469–72). In any case, in April Mussolini informed
readers that 'we don't have land to offer to the peasants' (OO, XIII: 35–6). In a pio-
neering article in 1963 Giorgio Rumi seriously questioned the historiographical
orthodoxy being uncritically reproduced in that period concerning the existence of
a presumed 'fascist' programme which included a call for land to the peasants.
Rumi discovered that a similar programme appeared only in the newspaper
Battaglie, the organ of the UIL, and further observed that in his spoken comments
on the San Sepolcro programme Mussolini only generically alluded to the UIL's
demands when stating that 'we have already made this programme ours'. For
Rumi, this deliberately avoided dealing concretely with the issue in the here and
now. Rumi also noted that a resolution proposed by Mussolini in favour of
accepting the UIL's claims was said to have been voted upon and passed unanimously, but that the text of this motion cannot be found in *Il Popolo d'Italia*. In
short, the UIL programme was *not* the programme of San Sepolcro (Rumi, 1963:
21–4, esp. n. 77).

While, as we have seen, nothing concrete was mentioned in the programme of
San Sepolcro about the industrial proletariat, Mussolini's speeches at the meeting
supported the eight-hour day, old-age and invalidity pensions, and even workers'
control over industries. He also came out in favour of an expropriation of war
profits (OO, XII: 320–27). However, such proposals were few and far between
after mid-November, when his proposed Constituent Assembly of Interventionism
had come to nought (OO, XI: 469–72; XII: 3–5, 9–10, 172–4, 193–6, 222–4,
242–5, 249–52, 256–8). Moreover, other types of discourse were contained alongside and within Mussolini's 'pro-worker' utterances. In his 9 November 1918
article, for example, he defined the war as revolutionary 'in terms of what it

demolished and created in the international political field'. The question, however, was 'how to impede – now – the "social" repercussions of this revolution initiated and completed by the victorious war' (OO, XI: 469–72). Not social revolution but calls for a pre-emptive re-channelling of imminent social grievance *before* it got out of control and veered towards anti-State militancy characterized Mussolini's 'pro-worker' writings. His 14 November article noted that the purpose of calling for the minimum wage and a reduction of the working week was 'to keep the proletariat on the [national terrain]' (OO, XII: 3–5). Three days later he wrote that this 'economic democracy' was aimed at 'renovation, not revolution' (OO, XII: 11–14). In his article of 18 March 1919 he wrote that by 'political democracy' he meant 'conducting the masses towards the State' (OO, XII: 308–11). On 1 April he admonished Orlando for what he saw as the lethargy with which social issues were being tackled by the State: 'If you don't [accept social reforms], then without having to be prophets we believe that you will compromise the fate of the institutions and it will be all your fault because we told you how you could direct the movement towards a peaceful outcome' (OO, XIII: 52–4).

In February 1919 Mussolini wrote that economic concessions were necessary so that 'the function of the workers is not tyrannical or destructive' (OO, XII: 242–5). What this 'tyrannical' and 'destructive' tendency amounted to had already been clarified in an article of 17 November when he described 'political socialism' as 'destructive'. In his view, the working class had to 'reject the confused and ridiculous "anticipation" of socialist politics' and it was his and his supporters' job to 'fight without truce the [PSI] that continues its sordid speculation to the detriment of the working class' (OO, XII: 11–14). Conversely, when the working class rejected political interference it could be 'creative'. What all this meant practically was evidenced during the occupation of the Franchi-Gregorini steelworks in Dalmine, Bergamo, between 14 and 17 March 1919. Workers' demands included the eight-hour day, Saturdays off, a minimum wage, union recognition and the right to be consulted on the implementation of new technology. Influenced as they were by the national syndicalism and interventionism of the UIL, strikers continued production, even raising the national flag over the occupied plant (Pozzi, 1921: 33–96). In an unsigned article of 19 March (which is attributed to him in the list contained in OO, XII: 335, but which can be consulted only in *Il Popolo d'Italia*) Mussolini defined the strike as a 'likeable gesture' because it had not interfered with production and because it had demonstrated the ability of the workers to run a factory without the supervision of the owners. But Mussolini said nothing about the Dalmine workers or the workers in general being ready to take over production. And rather than call for an extension of the agitation to other factories and industries, he passively settled for the fact that the strike had come to an end due to 'the inexorable exigencies of the class law which today dominates social life'. He argued that the decision to raise the national flag was 'more than a likeable gesture' because it had been done in a period when 'a pile of bastards, of vipers and chimpanzees blaspheme and deride more obscenely than ever the triumphs, the fortunes and the future of their own country'.

Mussolini was obviously concerned to see the Dalmine strike end as quickly as possible to then use it for propagandistic purposes of a nationalistic, pro-war, anti-strike and anti-socialist nature. This was evidenced by his reference to Italy's fallen soldiers during his visit to Dalmine on 20 March (hence after the strike was over). He stated that the Dalmine workers were right not to deny the nation 'after 500,000 of our men have died for it'. These dead men he then linked symbolically to the national flag which the workers had raised over the factory: 'The national flag is not a rag even if by chance it was dragged through the mud by the bourgeoisie and its political representatives: it is the symbol of the sacrifice of thousands and thousands of men.' Most important of all, he praised the workers for the fact that they had 'kept away from the games of political influences'. The PSI, he added, 'despoils the dead' and was 'an instrument of the Kaiser' during the war. For this reason, 'I won't cease the war against it.' Mussolini's visit was thus transformed into a pro-war and anti-German ceremony. Indeed, there was something of a military atmosphere about the event: on his arrival at Dalmine Mussolini was met by a number of students and officers and was greeted by strike leader Secondo Nosengo who was wearing military uniform (OO, XII: 314–16).

Why did Mussolini base himself on the *arditi* and the futurists and not on the Associazione Nazionale Combattenti (ANC) which was being formed in the same period? While the ANC was a new organization, it was a direct emanation of the Associazione Nazionale fra Mutilati e Invalidi di Guerra (ANMIG), the central committee of which was behind the 12 November 1918 declaration of the imminent birth of the ANC. The ANMIG had been founded in June 1917 under the surveillance and with the consent of the government and the High Command, and on the understanding that it would adopt a strictly non-aligned approach to the political parties. This it did, and its declared aim was to organize all future returnees irrespective of their interventionist or neutralist background. The ANMIG saw all combatants as the basis of a new society, and believed that this noble, altruistic and self-sacrificing fraternity had already been realized in the trenches as a living and functioning reality. But the organizers themselves were urban petty bourgeois junior grade officers, and the ideology of the organization reflected *their* worldview: the programme issuing from the ANMIG as it announced its dissolution into the ANC was in fact vacuous, ingenuous and profoundly cautious at both the political and social levels. Despite the fact that the ANC grew most rapidly in those areas where the land question was most acutely felt (such as Apulia), programmatic vagueness is once again what defines the document emerging from its first congress in June 1919 (Sabbatucci, 1974: 54, 64–78, 390–93).

Section I of Mussolini's programme of San Sepolcro was of similar bent, since it stated that the meeting of 23 March 'declares itself ready to energetically support the claims of a material and moral nature put forward by the combatants' associations', without Mussolini then specifying in his spoken comments what the 'material and moral' demands might or should be. In other words, by not entering onto the terrain of concrete issues related to the mass peasant base he was taking a similar approach to the ANC leadership itself. It is legitimate to conclude that the reasons for the organizational differentiation between the *fasci di combattimento* and the ANC lie in the fact that nascent fascism had no intention of allowing its politics to be even remotely informed by, or answerable to, the masses of peasants who were joining the ANC. Where politics was to be pursued this was to be by the self-proclaimed élites of the *arditi* and the fascists. Not for nothing did the *arditi* decide to go it alone in forming their own association rather than join the ANC (which nobody prevented them from doing). This act confirmed precisely the extremism of their anti-democratic and élitist patriotism (Rochat, 1981: 118). But there was more to it than just this. When calling on 9 April 1919 for the numerous combatants' associations to form into one movement, Mussolini claimed that this was necessary 'if the combatants want to confront the internal danger which amounts to the taking of power by a party to the detriment of the whole nation' (OO, XIII: 37–9). Yet while the ANC hailed the war and the victory, and while it was at times prepared to inveigh against the PSI for its opposition to the war, with its evolutionist notions of society it did not foresee civil war against 'Bolshevism' (Sabbatucci, 1974: 48, 68–9, 72–3, 98–119). It was here, then, that the most profound difference between nascent fascism and the ANC lay. Mussolini's originally positive judgement of the ANC's nationalism, its support for the claims to Fiume and Dalmatia and its decision to practise 'politics' (which he put in inverted commas) were quickly transformed, in an anonymous article of 24 June, into insult (this article is attributed to Mussolini by Sabbatucci, 1974: 107, correctly in our view, but not by E. and D. Susmel in OO, XIII, where it does not appear). He had in fact come to realize that the ANC was not going to be influenced in a subversive direction (OO, XIII: 201–3, 207–9) and that it did not share the thirst for anti-socialist violence of the *arditi*, the futurists and the *fasci di combattimento*.

It is worth noting in this regard that Mussolini's invocation of the fallen soldiers in his Dalmine speech means that we can fine-tune our previous understanding of the role of the dead in the San Sepolcro programme. Not only were they symbolically representative of territorial expansion, but they cut across social divisions, subsuming all classes into their nationalist and anti-socialist religious mystique. On 18 February Mussolini wrote that 'you cannot give or take away the party card of the dead. They don't belong to a party but to the Nation.' Against the socialist 'hyenas' who wanted to 'rummage through the bones of the dead', he called on war imagery which neatly tied in with his understanding of the conflict as a *continuing* process not only in the Balkans but also in Italy: he promised to defend 'all the dead, even if it means digging trenches in the squares and streets of our cities' (OO, XII: 231–3). One form this 'defence' of the dead was to take was the haranguing of Bissolati by Mussolini, futurists and *arditi* at the Scala Opera House in Milan on 11 January 1919. This, indeed, can be defined as the first act of organized fascist violence (Franzinelli, 2003: 16, 278). What the physical dimension to this strategy of silencing opposition meant on the streets became clear when on 13 April the Milanese socialists took advantage of the government removal of the wartime ban on public meetings and organized a rally which was attacked by the police. By way of protest against the killing of a demonstrator, a one-day strike was called for 15 April to be topped off with a rally in the Arena in Milan. As demonstrators were making their way towards the rally, they were attacked by *arditi* and futurists, including Marinetti and Carli. These went on to ransack and burn the offices of *Avanti!* in Milan. Four people died (three workers and one soldier) and thirty-nine were injured (De Felice, 1965: 519–21; Rochat, 1981: 116; Marinetti, 1996: 516–17; Franzinelli, 2003: 22ff). Already on 15 November 1918, the anniversary of the founding of *Il Popolo d'Italia*, Mussolini's article bore the title 'Audacia' (Daring), which he had used for his first front-page piece four years previously. In it he argued that 'violence is immoral when it is cold and calculated, not when it is instinctive and impulsive' (OO, XII: 6–8). Here, as with the futurist manifestos or the *arditi*'s mysticism, acts of gratuitous and illegal violence were justified by their arbitrary, irrational and passionate character. However, it is crucial to note that the attack on the *Avanti!* offices occurred precisely in the period during which Italy's war aims were being brought up for discussion at the Paris peace conference. On 15 April Mussolini in fact tied the incident into Italy's territorial dispute with nascent Yugoslavia. He noted that the Milan strike 'has given Mr [Wickham] Steed [journalist for *The Times* in London and supporter of the Yugoslav cause] the motive for writing a number of articles aiming to describe Italy as being on the verge of a Bolshevik revolution' (OO, XIII: 57–9). Mussolini declared that 'the Leninist horde, which believed and still believes that it can sabotage and mutilate our victory has, from the outset, found itself up against those Italians who are ready to save that victory's fruits' (OO, XIII: 60). He remarked that the role of the fascists in the *Avanti!* incident was to guarantee that the strike did not assume 'anti-interventionist and anti-national directives' (OO, XIII: 61–3). The attack was not, therefore, 'instinctive and impulsive'; rather, Mussolini's statements show it to have been planned and rational, an example of the sabotage of anti-war and anti-expansionist activism portended by the programme of San Sepolcro.

The foregoing discussion of the ideas and actions of early fascism suggests that De Felice's characterization of it as 'markedly left-wing', plus his view that the original movement represents 'a guiding thread' throughout the history of fascism, and that this movement was based on 'emerging', that is socially mobile and revolutionary-progressive elements of the middle classes (De Felice, 1975: Ch. 3), are mistaken assumptions. It is noteworthy, indeed, that when asked (twice) by Michael Ledeen, in the well-known and controversial 1975 interview, to explain what type of world these 'emerging' middle classes actually envisaged, De Felice went round the question and effectively did not answer it (De Felice, 1975: 31–2). Equally untenable is the biographer's conviction that the few announcements of Mussolini on 23 March were 'certainly not sufficient to define [the San Sepolcro programme] as a programme', and that the real programme was developed in the weeks and months after 23 March, culminating in a document published in *Il Popolo d'Italia* on 6 June. For De Felice, the latter declaration 'can be effectively considered the programme of fascism "of the origins" or of San Sepolcro as it has been improperly called' (1965: 513).

According to Enzo Collotti, however, it is precisely our knowledge of the existence of the San Sepolcro programme which allows us to characterize the early fascist government's bombastic militarist rhetoric as representing something other than a merely formal transfer of the foreign policy baton from the liberals to the fascists (Collotti 2000: 10). Moreover, in the period between the meeting of San Sepolcro and 6 June, Mussolini published sixty-six pieces of which twenty-three, that is 34.8 per cent, were given over to attacks on the PSI or included such attacks as a significant part of the speech or writing (OO, XIII: 5–9, 12–13, 14–16, 21–4, 28–30, 31–4, 35–6, 37–9, 40–42, 43–4, 45–6, 52–4, 60, 61–3, 64–6, 67–9, 73–4, 77–9, 91–2, 94–7, 120–23, 128–30, 168–70). A further thirty-one, or 47 per cent, were dedicated to the Paris peace conference and/or to issues of a territorial nature (OO, XIII: 10–11, 57–9, 70–72, 75–6, 80–81, 82–4, 88–9, 93–4, 98–9, 101–3, 104, 107–9, 110–12, 115–16, 124–7, 131–3, 134–6, 137–9, 140–41, 142–6, 147–9, 150–53, 154–6, 157–9, 160–61, 162–3, 164–5, 166–7, 171–3). Moving further back, between the end of the war and the meeting of San Sepolcro Mussolini's campaign for social reforms was, as we have seen, sporadic and unorganized, while his attacks on socialism were substantial and systematic, accounting for nineteen of the 110 pieces, or 17.3 per cent (OO, XII: 29–32, 96–9, 124, 151–2, 180–82, 183–6, 200–202, 203–207, 231–3, 253–5, 259–61, 272–4, 275–8, 285–7, 291–4, 301–5, 314–16, 317, 318–20). During this same period, the Paris peace conference accounted for fifty-nine of the 110 pieces, which amounts to 53.6 per cent (OO, XII: 17–19, 22–3, 25–6, 33–4, 42–4, 45–6, 47–9, 60, 61, 62–3, 64, 67, 68, 71–3, 74–77, 78–9, 82–4, 85–7, 88–90, 91–5, 100–103, 104–6, 107–9, 110–14, 113–15, 116–17, 118–20, 121–3, 125–30, 131–33, 134–6, 137–40, 141–3, 144–5, 153–5, 156–8, 161–3, 164–6, 170–71, 175, 176–9, 187–92, 208–10, 214–16, 217–18, 219–21, 215–27, 228–30, 234–7, 238–41, 262–4, 265–8, 269–71, 279–81, 282–4, 288–90, 295–8, 306–8, 312–13). These two central themes of anti-socialism and territorial expansion combined with the street violence which *arditi* and futurist participants at the San Sepolcro meeting had long been advocating, and the fascist programme was thus defined in March 1919.

The key issue, therefore, is not whether nascent fascism was right- or left-wing. It was clearly the former. Rather, we need to ask where it sprang from. Did it emerge solely in the late winter and early spring of 1918–1919? Or did it not in fact come from the Great War which had so dominated Italian life since 1915? If it did, to what extent was it an expression of the war's social, political, military and cultural character? One way of answering these questions is to relate our interpretation of the San Sepolcro programme to the wartime experience and writings of the man who defined it – Benito Mussolini. The initial focus will be on his stance during the tense months between the diplomatic crisis of July 1914 and Italy's intervention in the war on 24 May 1915.

–2–

Man of Straw
July 1914–May 1915

We cannot accept humanitarian morality, Tolstoyan morality, the morality of slaves. We, in time of war, adopt the Socratic formula: be better than one's friends, be worse than one's enemies.

> Mussolini, Speech in Milan, 4 October 1922

One can say of Enrico Corradini that he appears at the beginning of the present century as the prophet of an imminent new period . . . It was inevitable that the encounter of 1915 would be repeated in 1922.

> Mussolini, Speech to the Senate, 15 December 1931

The Fascist State is a will to power and to government . . . Fascism is opposed to Socialism . . . and analogously it is opposed to class syndicalism.

> Mussolini, *Dottrina del fascismo*, 1932

He who has iron has bread; but when the iron is well tempered, he will also probably find gold.

> Mussolini, Speech in Bologna, 25 October 1936.

Neutral?

At the time of the international diplomatic crisis of July 1914 Mussolini was the leading propagandist of the revolutionary wing of the PSI and, since December 1912, editor of *Avanti!*. Under his tutelage the paper's distribution had doubled to between sixty and seventy-five thousand daily, with some issues reaching 90,000 and even 100,000 copies (Farinelli, Paccagnini, Santambrogio, Villa, 1997: 239–40). In the same period, PSI membership had increased from 20,459 to 47,724, and with a decidedly anti-militarist programme the youth section, led by Amadeo Bordiga, stood at over 10,000 members (Tranfaglia, 1995: 10–11). Not surprisingly, therefore, with the Austrian ultimatum to Serbia known among the public, and with the war drums beating, Mussolini declared on 26 July that the Italian working class would give 'not a man, not a penny!' and that it would spill 'not one drop of blood' for a cause 'that has nothing to do with it'. He demanded a declaration of absolute neutrality from the Italian government and warned that if this were not forthcoming the proletariat would 'impose it by all means necessary' (OO, VI: 287–8). He subsequently issued slogans such as 'Down with the war!', 'Long live the international solidarity of the proletariat! Long live socialism!' (OO, VI: 289, 290–93).

Within little more than a week of Serbia's 25 July rejection of the Austrian ultimatum, German backing of Austro-Hungarian intransigence turned the Balkan crisis into a European war triggering a chain reaction of invasions dominated by the German offensive against Belgium and France. Yet one nation that was fully implicated in the balance of power hung back: on 3 August Italy announced its neutrality. Mussolini had therefore got his wish. But all was not quiet in the socialist camp. On 19 August the Prefect of Milan wrote to the Ministry of the Interior concerning a socialist youth meeting which had been held two days previously. While participants had voted down a motion calling for volunteers to help Italy's 'Latin sister' (i.e. France), a pro-war current had, the Prefect claimed, left its mark on the participants, who had gone home with an sense of 'unease' (ACS, A5G, b. 107, fasc. 225, s.fasc. 25, doc. 133). It is difficult to know how much credence to lend to the Prefect's report. Either way, Mussolini seems not to have been influenced at this stage by any such pro-war sentiments. On the contrary, in a letter of 3 September to PSI Secretary Costantino Lazzari he averred that Francophilia was beginning to have 'a devastating effect' among socialist ranks, and that this 'risks lumping us in the same basket as the warmongers!' (OO, VI: 442). The PSI's 21 September anti-war *Manifesto*, which was drafted by Mussolini and co-signed by the reformist parliamentarians, asserted a 'profound antithesis between war and socialism'; war, it stated, amounted to 'the annihilation of individual autonomy and the sacrifice of freedom of thought to the State and militarism' (OO, VI: 366–8). On 25 September Mussolini suggested that two months of 'warmongering campaigns' by subversives and radical democrats meant that tacit PSI disapproval of the war was no longer enough. He demanded that workers' organizations furnish *Avanti!* with 'an affirmative or negative reply as to whether it is a good thing or not for Italy to maintain absolute neutrality'. The undoubtedly positive response to this plebiscite was to be thrown in the face of those who had 'renounced their ideals of yesterday' (OO, VI: 369).

It should be noted, however, that it was Mussolini, and not the Italian proletariat, who here posed the question of intervention or neutrality. Indeed, Mussolini had begun to question socialist anti-militarism even before the outbreak of the war. In November 1913 he founded a periodical, *Utopia*, in which he expressed his own (as distinct from the PSI's) views more freely, including on war. In the May 1914 issue he published an article by Sergio Panunzio in which the revolutionary syndicalist argued that a war would create a revolutionary situation and that 'who cries *Down with war!* is thus the most ferocious conservative' (Panunzio, 1914a).

Correspondence between Mussolini and Panunzio in May 1914 reveals that Mussolini personally identified with this thesis (Perfetti, 1986: 157–8). In August Mussolini, this time as editor of *Avanti!*, refused to publish an article by Panunzio. It is likely, according to Francesco Perfetti (1986: 145–7), that the piece in question was the same one published by Mussolini in the August–September 1914 issue of *Utopia*, in which Panunzio argued that 'we need to universally follow the only admissible logic: the logic of war' (Panunzio, 1914b). In a series of anonymous 'war notes' written between 3 and 11 August, again in *Utopia*, Mussolini offered no serious opposition to the war. The notes of 6 and 8 August rejected the general strike in the event of an enemy invasion and argued that to effect territorial changes, 'and not only "peripheral" touch-ups', it would be necessary 'to "blow up" Austria-Hungary' (OO, VI: 321–5). In an 8 September letter to his friend Cesare Berti, he seems to have hinted that he was in fact keeping his real opinions on the war under wraps. Referring to a misunderstanding over a bill of exchange for which he had acted as guarantor and which he mistakenly thought Berti had already paid off, Mussolini wrote: 'You too have adopted my system: you have many things to tell me, but . . . you keep them in your pen' (OO, VI: 442). Furthermore, excusing himself for reasons of illness Mussolini did not go to Lugano, Switzerland, for the 27 September meeting of socialists from neutral countries. The final resolution, whose compromise content was reasonably foreseeable given that the meeting was attended by Italian reformist parliamentarians and maximalists, and by German- and French-speaking Swiss socialists, rejected the concept of national defence in capitalist regimes and saw all the belligerents as involved in inter-imperialist rivalries. It did not even mention the Austrian attack on Serbia or the German invasion of Belgium, let alone stigmatize them (Valiani, 1977: 65–8).

Something was clearly amiss, and things began to come to a head on 4 October when Giuseppe Lombardo Radice, a university lecturer in pedagogy who had recently left the PSI over its neutrality, reported in a conservative newspaper that he had been having an epistolary exchange with a key PSI figure. The unnamed person, who was in fact Mussolini, had assured him that if Italy went to war against Austria there would be '"no obstacles from the socialists. No revolts, no strikes in case of mobilization"' (Lombardo Radice, 1914). On 7 October an open letter to Mussolini from pro-intervention anarchist Libero Tancredi was published in another conservative newspaper. It accused the *Avanti!* editor of being 'a man of straw' (*un uomo di paglia*). This term implies someone who lends his name to positions which are not his, while leaving it to others to express what he truly believes (Zingarelli, 2000: 1,251, 1,968). Tancredi stated that Mussolini had spoken of the classes that would need to be mobilized for intervention and had said he would fight with enthusiasm in a war against Austria-Hungary. The *Manifesto* of 21 September and the proletarian 'referendum' of 25 September were, for

Tancredi, complete hypocrisy; while the 'illness' that had prevented Mussolini from going to Lugano was, he claimed, just one in a long stream of imaginary maladies invoked by Mussolini to avoid speaking at neutralist meetings (Tancredi, 1914).

In a press interview of 6 October Mussolini revealed that he was the socialist about whom Lombardo Radice had written. He stated that 'the truth of the matter is that from the beginning of the war . . . socialist neutrality has been affected by a clear as day "partiality": it has always been "conditional" . . . Sympathy for France, hostility towards Austria' (OO, VI: 376–9). In his replies to Tancredi he defended himself only against the accusation of two-facedness without challenging the central thrust of Tancredi's polemic (OO, VI: 381–5, 386, 388–92). Finally, on 18 October Mussolini published a long and crucial article that urged the PSI to redefine neutrality, replacing an absolute principle with a contingent and tactical policy – 'active and operating neutrality'. He claimed that he was not asking the party to change position, but to draw the right conclusions from the partiality towards the Entente which, as far as he was concerned, it had always held (OO, VI: 393–403). Not the PSI, but Mussolini could indeed be found, from the very beginning of the conflict, dividing the belligerent blocks into defenders and offenders, between those who tried to stop the war and those who wanted it. In a speech of 29 July he expressed total perplexity at the mere suggestion that Italy would 'give its children to Austria against Serbia or against France' (OO, VI: 290–93). On 1 August he praised British Foreign Secretary Sir Edward Grey for doing 'everything humanly possible' to avoid the generalization of the conflict (OO, VI: 294). Three days later he made it clear that Germany's demand for free passage through Belgium was a 'pan-Germanist' plan that Belgium could not accept (OO, VI: 297). Between Germany and Belgium, therefore, he was not neutral. On 5 August he extended the same distinction to France (OO, VI: 305–6). On 1 September he claimed that the PSI and *Avanti!* 'continue their propaganda for neutrality and against the war, conceding only one hypothesis: a war required to fight off a possible invasion' (OO, VI: 349), a thesis which he had also expounded as early as 3 August (OO, VI: 295). By 18 October his recognition of Italy's 'right' to mobilize in order to 'defend' its neutrality was now understood as the right and necessity to 'practically oppose' the invasion before it happened, that is 'to free ourselves "in advance and for always" from such possible future reprisals' (OO, VI: 393–403).

Hence the article of 18 October 1914 was not a sudden shift from neutrality to a call for preventive war, but a coherent drawing together of a latent pro-intervention argument which had pervaded Mussolini's writings since the beginning of the conflict. Before deciding to reveal his pro-war position he had no doubt been awaiting the outcome of events on the Franco-German front, an issue which came to a head in early September at the Battle of the Marne, when Anglo-French troops halted what to that point had been the seemingly unstoppable German offensive into Belgium and then northern France. Indeed, in his article of 3 August one argument he gave in favour of 'neutrality' was the possibility of an Austro-German victory on all fronts (OO, VI: 295). A letter of 28 August to parliamentarian Mario Piccinato warned against the 'risk' and 'danger' of propaganda for war against Austria-Hungary and Germany (OO, VI: 441). Rather, as he wrote to Mario Missiroli, a journalist friend, on 26 August, 'Italy cannot but wait and prepare itself' (OO, VI: 440–41). To what degree, however, did the 'socialist revolutionary' Mussolini's 'neutrality' and interventionism, Austrophobia and Francophilia differ from the policy of Italy's rulers? And with what consequences for understanding the nature of Mussolini's political trajectory?

Mussolini, Mazzini and the Conservative Élites

It should be noted that the government also awaited the outcome of the Marne battle before definitively deciding to prepare for war (Salandra, 1928: 173–4; Albertini, 1951, Part 2, Vol. I: 333–45; Malagodi, 1960: 21–2). Italy's coalition with Austria-Hungary in the Triple Alliance, in force since 1882, had come under serious strain during what by 1914 had been a fifteen-year antagonism marked by suspicions, jealousies and rivalries over influence in the Balkans. This increasingly anti-Austrian foreign policy had been accompanied during the same period by a gradual realignment with France (Serra, 1950; Chabod, 1952: 19–49; Askew, 1959; Vigezzi, 1969: 3–52; Bosworth, 1979; E. Gentile, 1990, Ch. 8; Ruffo, 1998). In short, Mussolini's political stance between July and October 1914 saw him aligned with the Italian State on the key issues of foreign policy. Adventitious convergence and nothing more? The confusion of the times? Or real political alliance with Italy's rulers? One way of exploring this further is to ask about Mussolini's and the State's respective approaches to domestic policy in relation to Italian intervention. Antonio Salandra, who became Prime Minister in March 1914, saw a war regime as an ideal opportunity for re-establishing liberal-conservative values around a strong and anti-popular political centre. He wanted to free himself from ongoing dependence on the parliamentary majority headed by Giovanni Giolitti and to reverse the progressive political integration of the labouring classes that had underlain Giolitti's premierships. Salandra claimed in his memoirs that this was because parliamentary democracy stood 'in irreconcilable contradiction with the authority of the State' (Salandra, 1928: 201–15). As we have seen, Mussolini's 21 September *Manifesto* referred to the 'profound antithesis' between war, the State and militarism on the one hand, and socialism on the other. Did his openly declared interventionism now imply adherence to Pro-State and anti-socialist militarism?

During a meeting in Bologna on 19 and 20 October it became clear that the vast majority of the PSI leadership did not accept Mussolini's interpretation of 'neutrality'. At the 19 October session Mussolini insisted that if his motion for active and operating neutrality were not accepted he would resign his post as *Avanti!* editor. This he did after the ballot of the following day in which his motion received only one vote (his). On 15 November 1914 newspaper stalls were selling the first edition of Mussolini's own newspaper, *Il Popolo d'Italia*. On 24 November the PSI expelled Mussolini at a meeting of the Milanese section. His paper was deemed to be in open conflict with the party on a life and death issue and to be a treacherous attempt to split the working class. Before expelling him, however, *Avanti!* had asked 'Who's the paymaster?' (Lazzari, 1914). The answer is that while, as relatively recent research has confirmed, Mussolini also received support from government-backed sources in France (Nemeth, 1998), it is now undisputed that his main technical and administrative help came from Filippo Naldi, managing director of the Bologna-based newspaper *Il Resto del Carlino* (De Felice, 1965: 269ff; Valiani, 1977: 71 and n. 130 for bibliography; Bosworth, 2002: 105–7). In August 1909 *Il Resto del Carlino*, which to that time had supported the moderate policies of Giolitti, came under the control of Bolognese agrarians. Following the socialist success in the Emilia region in the October 1913 general election, the paper went into crisis. It was saved by Naldi who introduced large sugar-producing concerns from Turin. These became the majority (60 per cent) shareholders as part of their endeavour to gain greater control over the Italian press with a view to generating pro-nationalist opinion (Malatesta, 1977: Part 2, Ch. 1). Through Naldi's connections, Mussolini's paper was supported by the Agenzia Italiana di Pubblicità, which in turn was backed by a number of industrialists and arms manufacturers all pushing for Italian intervention (De Felice, 1965: 276ff). Not only were they interested in expanding foreign markets and fields of investment for Italian capital, and in releasing Italian capitalism from dependency on Germany, but they were also concerned to impose a strong war regime in the factories, a strategy which would *perforce* require a definitive weakening of the PSI's influence among the labouring classes (Webster, 1975: Ch. 5; Gibelli, 1999: 26–8).

It is arguably the case, however, that Mussolini did not share the goals of his main financial backers, and that while he may have differed with the PSI leadership he nevertheless remained on fundamentally socialist and democratic terrain. Indeed, Mussolini claimed in the inaugural article of *Il Popolo d'Italia* that the paper was 'independent, extremely free, personal, *mine*. I'll answer only to my own conscience and to nobody else' (OO, VII: 5–7; Mussolini's italics). A commission of enquiry into the 'Mussolini case', made up of socialist members of the Milan council, concluded in February 1915 that Mussolini was indeed free to write what he wished in *Il Popolo d'Italia* without prior sanctioning from his backers (De Felice, 1965, Appendix: 684–8). Mussolini's own writings lend weight to this finding. In that same inaugural article he specified that he had 'no aggressive intentions' against the PSI, and 'Socialist daily' in fact appeared as the main subtitle of the newspaper. Moreover, on 23 November he wrote a polemic against the very bastions of Italian imperialism who were propping up his paper, arguing that 'the whole nation is in the hands of a small financial-industrial oligarchy based primarily on the steel industry'. This oligarchy was among what Mussolini referred to as the 'internal enemies of the freedom of the Italian people' (OO, VII: 29–31). The political independence of *Il Popolo d'Italia* seems also to have come at an economic price: archive documentation of unclear origin reveals that in April 1915 the paper was in 'a dreadful state', needing 20,000 lire per month to survive and taking in only 1,000 lire from advertisements (ACS, Min. Int. Dir. Gen. Ps, Div. AA. GG. RR., *Stampa italiana*, F1, 1890–1945, b. 20, fasc. 40.43, 'Il Popolo d'Italia', doc. 104). From February 1915 Mussolini had to appeal to sympathetic readers for financial support (OO, VII: 187–8).

But a major clue to the relatively independent voice which *Il Popolo d'Italia* provided Mussolini lies in the title of the new paper, which recalled *L'Italia del Popolo* of Mazzini (De Felice, 1965: 276, n. 1). If Mazzinianism now defined Mussolini's position, he was on track for a collision with Italy's ruling conservative élites, and this in fact transpired. Following the death of Foreign Minister Antonio di San Giuliano on 16 October, Salandra temporarily took over the foreign affairs portfolio. On 18 October he made his infamous speech to Foreign Ministry functionaries in which he nakedly declared the need to act with 'a spirit emptied of every preconception, of every prejudice, of every sentiment which is not that of the exclusive and unlimited devotion to our Fatherland, of *sacro egoismo* for Italy' (Salandra, 1928: 377–8). On 19 November Mussolini declared *sacro egoismo* to be 'unacceptable for the socialist proletariat' (OO, VII: 13–15). This was because, as he claimed in a public speech of 13 December, 'the law of solidarity cannot stop at competitions of an economic nature, but goes beyond these' (OO, VII: 76–81). In late December he negatively compared *sacro egoismo* to the greater sense of duty and sacrifice with which Mazzini had pushed previous generations into war. Mazzini 'knew well that war was sacrifice, blood, ruin, destruction'; but he also knew that 'every generation has its ineluctable duties to carry out'. Salandra's *sacro egoismo*, on the other hand, was 'the selfishness of the well-to-do classes, of the Triple Alliance-loving Senate, of the temporal Pope, of the contraband bourgeoisie' (OO, VII: 97–110).

On 5 November Salandra ceded the Foreign Ministry to agrarian conservative Sidney Sonnino, who proceeded to navigate a profitable course for Italy in the turbulent waters of the European war. Formal negotiations between Italy and Austria-Hungary for territorial compensation under Article VII of the Triple Alliance treaty began in the second week of December 1914. The details of these negotiations have been examined elsewhere (Valiani, 1966b) and need not concern us here. They are characterized by the fact that they had little chance of success if only because neither side was seriously committed to reaching an accord. Italy's discussions with London, on the other hand, were defined as 'serious' even before they got underway (Vigezzi, 1961: 427). As we saw in Chapter 1, the resultant Pact of London conflicted with the aspirations of southern Slavs, who in a 7 December 1914 declaration had announced their intention to create a union of Serbs, Croats and Slovenes on the ruins of the Austro-Hungarian Empire. In late April 1915 they founded a Yugoslav Committee in London, an initiative which sought to influence the Great Powers into recognizing an independent Yugoslav state (Vivarelli, 1991, I: 172–3). Mussolini's writings and speeches during the period of Italian neutrality reveal far greater proximity to the Mazzinian and 'Yugoslav' theses than to Sonnino's peculiarly Austrophile version of Italian imperialism. In contrast to the latter perspective, Mussolini argued in January 1915, in markedly Mazzinian terms, that Italy had to intervene in the war for 'international and human ends', which meant 'contributing to the break-up of the Austro-Hungarian Empire, the oppressor of nationalities and the bulwark of European reaction' (OO, VII: 139–41). In March he dealt with the theme of Italy's 'mission' in the world with direct reference to Mazzini. According to Mussolini, Italian unification saw Italy find its 'place' in the world; but every 'place' created a new 'hierarchy of forces' which required a redefinition of one's 'place' and hence of one's 'mission'. The 'mission' implied in this newly conquered 'place' (when, as Mussolini augured, Italy broke with the Triple Alliance) was quoted by Mussolini from Alfredo Oriani's *La lotta politica in Italia* (1892): it was the tradition of the French Revolution, democratic politics, the destruction of the Austro-Hungarian and Turkish Empires, the liberation of the Slav peoples and the completion of Italy's national-territorial tasks with the conquest of Trento and Trieste (OO, VII: 253–5). On 19 May he referred to the Serbs as 'the Piedmontese of the Balkans', by this meaning that he recognized in Serbia the driving force of Balkan unification. 'Not only this', he stated, 'but Italian intervention guarantees their independence, it guarantees Great Serbia a vast outlet onto the Adriatic. With Austria-Hungary crushed, Serbia will have nothing to fear for its national independence' (OO, VII: 398–400). Not for nothing, then, did the nationalist imperialists accuse Mussolini of being 'up to his neck in democracy' (Pancrazi, 1914). For his part, Renzo De Felice defined *Il Popolo d'Italia* as 'the most important organ of revolutionary interventionism and, substantially, also of democratic interventionism' (De Felice, 1965: 288).

However, other evidence suggests that the nationalists' and De Felice's interpretations are too one-sided. First, Corrado De Biase has convincingly shown that the 'democratic' conception of intervention pursued by republicans and revolutionaries eventually conflated into Salandra's *sacro egoismo*. He suggests that this occurred by virtue of the national terrain on which those democrats ultimately placed the meaning of Italy's impending campaign (De Biase, 1964). It should be noted in this regard that already on 23 August, hence long before Salandra's *sacro egoismo* speech, Mussolini argued that the anti-war abstract 'principle' of the PSI needed to be distinguished from what he termed the 'reality' of the 'national' terrain (OO, VI: 335–7). In a speech of early September he reminded listeners that 'we are socialists, and, from a national point of view, Italians' (OO, VI: 361–3). On 25 October he rejected the label of 'nationalist', but nevertheless defined his position as 'national' (OO, VI: 420–23). In November he asked if in the future there might not exist a non-internationalist socialism which would act as 'a point of equilibrium between nation and class' (OO, VI: 427–9, 430–32).

Secondly, following the 19–20 October Bologna encounter Mussolini claimed in the press that he had left his job at *Avanti!* because he had been looking for a debate in the PSI and could not get one (OO, VI: 409–12, 413–15, 443). This was clearly false, since despite his protestations to the contrary (OO, VI: 424–6) Mussolini had in fact made a take-it-or-leave-it ultimatum when proposing his pro-war motion. When the PSI subsequently asked him to explain the origins and nature of *Il Popolo d'Italia*, rather than comply and defend his position in the party Mussolini affirmed, the day before his expulsion, that a man like him could 'never submit supinely to the will of those at the head of the docile socialist herd' (OO, VII: 32–4). He began to hint at the dubiousness of *Avanti!*'s funding, insinuating that the paper had 'its little and big secrets' (OO, VII: 25–7). At the 24 November meeting he claimed that he had a right to an explanation for the expulsion, even though it was already quite clear at that stage why he was being expelled. A letter of 26 November from the Prefect of Milan to the Ministry of the Interior confirms that Lazzari nevertheless reminded him there and then of the issues at stake (ACS, A5G, b. 107, fasc. 225, s.fasc. 25). The day after that meeting Mussolini repeated that 'the right to defend myself . . . was violently denied to me' (OO, VII: 45–6); again this was an untrue affirmation, since despite the meeting's boisterous character Mussolini was allowed to speak and actually spoke (OO, VII: 39–41). We are faced, in other words, with the proposition that Mussolini's manoeuvre at Bologna and his subsequent accusations and insinuations reflected the fact that he had already engaged in a public propaganda campaign *against* Italian socialism and that, together with the campaign for Italian intervention, it is this which defines the character of *Il Popolo d'Italia* on its foundation.

Finally, in the August–September 1914 issue of *Utopia* Mussolini published a long letter from *Il Resto del Carlino* correspondent Mario Missiroli. Missiroli argued that in order to pursue its own imperialist project in the Mediterranean, Italy should stay in the Triple Alliance, while Austria-Hungary should remain intact in order to defend Italy against Slav expansionism. The war, in his view, would result in 'the predominance of one race over another'. He argued that 'the error of democracy consists precisely in holding that liberty is the loosening of ties between State and citizen: on the contrary, these links need to be destroyed'. By this Missiroli did not mean an anarchist-type freedom of the individual from the

State, but a conflation of the former into the latter so that 'every citizen feels the State, *the whole State*' (Missiroli's emphasis). In his introduction to Missiroli's letter, Mussolini claimed to have a number of differences with the author, but he did not specify what these were. What he did do, however, was to applaud the 'fresh originality' of Missiroli's letter and the 'magnificent impetus of the passionate scholar who investigates wider horizons' (OO, VI: 326–30). Fine praise indeed for an imperialist, racist and anti-democratic thesis. Deep ambiguities therefore characterized Mussolini's 'Mazzinian' interventionism which the founding of *Il Popolo d'Italia* consecrated, and it is to an analysis of their fuller implications that we now turn.

Reinventing Mazzini

Two formally distinct schools of nationalist thought predominated in Europe from the eighteenth century up to the First World War. One was closely identified with France, and pointed to the nation as a contract of individuals based on rights and freedoms. The other derived primarily from Germany and saw the nation as an a priori immutable and eternal product of nature which could not be put to the test of plebiscites and human will (Tamborra, 1963). Mazzini's understanding of nationhood betrayed elements of both these trends. Without liberty, for Mazzini there could be no nation. The latter, in his view, was a common principle developed in a common experience and tradition; it was primarily a faith and a duty, of which territory was but an expression. While, to be sure, he argued that Italy's borders had been clearly defined by nature, he did not subordinate human will to geography, but understood these boundaries to be a guarantee against Italian usurpation of other peoples' rights and freedoms. Since Fiume and Dalmatia fell outside these borders, he argued that they should be conceded to the Slavs as part of a future Yugoslav federation, and he did not push for Italian domination in Istria, hoping instead that the inhabitants there would one day unite with Italy of their own accord (Chabod 1961: 71–2, 78, 80–4). Be that as it may, Mazzinian thinking could not avoid the underlying problems associated with the geographical understanding of nationhood, and most particularly those arising when the transition from the abstract 'nation' to the geo-political 'nation state' has to be effected in ethnically mixed zones. When claiming that Italy's borders had been 'traced by the hand of God', Mazzini downplayed the contradictions in his Deity's handiwork by underestimating the German-speaking majority in South Tyrol. He favoured Italy in areas where linguistic borders did not coincide with strategic ones, but disallowed France's strategic claims to Nice and Austria's to Trieste. Moreover, Mazzini's claims to Malta, Corsica and Nice all conflicted not with his arch-enemy Austria – the defeat of which was so closely identified with his crucial category of Italy's international humanitarian 'mission' – but with Britain and France (Chabod, 1961: 217; Mack Smith, 1994: esp. Ch. 19).

Adherence to Mazzinianism was not, therefore, synonymous with political and programmatic coherence. It was, rather, an easily adaptable system of ideas open to varying interpretations. On 28 November 1914 Mussolini argued that victory over Germany would create the conditions in which 'peoples will be reconstituted within their natural borders' (OO, VII: 54–5). What did this imply? Were all peoples outside their 'natural borders' to return home? And if so, was this to be by forceful expulsion if they in fact wanted to stay where they were? Or perhaps the presence of an ethnic majority or even minority in a given territory defined the 'natural' characteristics of that territory? Either way, Mussolini certainly held some racially informed notions of what lay at the heart of conflicts between nations. In late December he referred to the 'irrepressible dispute between races' and to the 'eternal dispute between Latins and Germans' (OO, VII: 97–110). Two weeks earlier he had argued that national consciousness and culture were an expression of a nation's recognition of its own economic interests over against those of other nations, all of which led to the 'closing in' of the 'psychological and moral unity' of peoples (OO, VII: 76–83). In short, a nation's perception of itself issued from its negative perception of the external other. Moreover, in an article of 14 February 1915 Mussolini wrote that, in the event of war, 'it is necessary to win but more important to fight'. His point was that 'the titles of nobility and greatness of peoples' were achievable only 'with the blood of armies'. Avoiding intervention in order not to lose a whole generation of youth 'may keep Italian mothers happy' but at the cost of 'humiliating a people'. By 'demonstrating to the world that she is capable of making war, a great war: I repeat: a *great war*' (Mussolini's italics), Italy would 'cancel the ignoble legend that Italians can't fight' (OO, VII: 196–8). On 6 March he wrote that war 'tempers' a people in a 'burning forge', and that this had pride of place over 'all other necessities of an economic, political, territorial and military character that are used to justify and speed up intervention' (OO, VII: 235–7). Were the rights of other peoples to be subordinated, in a decidedly non-Mazzinian fashion, to Italy's drive for Great Power status?

On 24 January 1915 Mussolini was involved in a debate at the founding meeting of the *fasci d'azione rivoluzionaria*, nuclei of self-proclaimed revolutionary inter-ventionists. A motion was passed which stated that national problems needed to be resolved in Italy and elsewhere 'for the ideals of justice and liberty for which oppressed peoples must acquire the right to belong to those national communities from which they descended' (OO, VII: 308–9). It is noteworthy, however, that the *fasci* meeting did not then define its territorial aspirations in relation to the topic of 'descent'. Commenting on the proceedings, Mussolini wrote that 'the difficult question of irredentism was posed and resolved in the ambit of ideals of socialism and liberty which do not however exclude the safeguarding of a positive national interest'. Hence claims to 'positive interest', even when undefined, could be made on the basis of 'ideals' of 'justice' and 'liberty'. Mussolini affirmed that 'it would not have been completely superfluous to specify and delimit our irredentism from the territorial point of view', since in this way irredentism would not 'collapse into nationalism or imperialism'. But he then argued that the issue of territory was in any case 'a "subordinate" question which does not remove the importance and value of the fundamental principle [of the motion]' (OO, VII: 150–53). He therefore based himself on the very 'principles' and 'ideals' which the motion had posited in place of stating its territorial ambitions, and which he himself had argued to contain nationalist and imperialist implications.

The practical consequences of this became apparent when, on 29 January, Mussolini responded to a letter from Giuseppe Prezzolini, former editor of the intellectual review *La Voce* (and of whom more presently). Prezzolini had argued that for economic, commercial, ethnic, ideal and national reasons Italian claims in the Adriatic should include Fiume. Mussolini wrote that while at the *fasci* meeting he had said nothing on Fiume, this did not mean that he was ignoring the question: 'I thought someone else would have spoken on the argument to convince me; but that didn't happen, since the issue of irredentism was brought onto the terrain of ideals.' However, Mussolini then accepted Prezzolini's claim to Fiume, specifying, however, that this was 'more for the second order of ideal reasons . . . than for reasons of an economic character' (OO, VII: 156). Hence Mussolini explained his non-commitment on the Fiume question by making reference to the *fasci* affirmations of 'principle' and 'ideals', and then made a territorial claim to Fiume precisely on the basis of those 'ideals'.

Mussolini's claim to Trieste was anything but trouble-free, and even involved potential conflict with the Slavs. In March he expressed not so much joy as concern over Russia's victory at Przemysl. This contradictory sentiment was due to the fact that a Russian 're-evaluation of the Serb point of view – already in part accepted by the Russian press – could cause serious embarrassment for Italy' (OO, VII: 283–5). Yugoslav Committee representative Frano Supilo's busy itinerary had in fact brought him from London to Belgrade to Petrograd where he received support (albeit ambiguous at that point) for Southern Slav claims to Trieste (Boro Petrovich, 1963). Mussolini argued that Russia's support for Southern Slav claims was also the expression of 'pan-Slav politics' and went on to state that Trieste 'must be, and will be Italian through war against the Austrians and, if necessary, against the Slavs' (OO, VII: 290–93).

With Fiume and Trieste on the annexation list, Mussolini turned to Dalmatia in an article of 6 April. He claimed that even a majority of Italian speakers was 'not a good enough reason to claim exclusive possession of *all* of Dalmatia' (Mussolini's emphasis). Here a concession on one issue (Italy could not claim all of Dalmatia even if it had had a majority Italian-speaking population there) was a territorial claim on another (Italy was entitled to parts of Dalmatia because there were Italian-speaking populations to be found there). He in fact had 'no objections' to Italy claiming a vast section of the Dalmatian coast and the whole of the Archipelago. 'Italian cities' in Dalmatia were required as Italy's 'stepping-stone' to 'economic and cultural expansion' in the Balkans once the war was over (OO, VII: 308–9). All this means that his 24 January assertion to the effect that the war was for 'the liberation of the unredeemed peoples of Trentino and Istria' (OO, VII: 139–41) left open the unmentioned possibility of territorial claims to the latter which, it will be remembered, did not form part of Mazzini's national vision. Wherever there were 'Italians', there was Italy.

Not that Mussolini's territorial ambitions were limited to those areas where ethnic Italian speakers were present. He saw the Entente as a vehicle for Italy's territorial aggrandizement, and for this reason he was keen to see Italy declare war not solely against Austria-Hungary but also, and in fact primarily, against Germany (OO, VII: 136–8, 202–4, 298–300, 301–3, 320–22). In an article of 4 March he explained that 'to those who accuse us of being "hypnotized" by the Adriatic . . . we reply that while war against both of the Central Powers can give us exclusive dominion in the Adriatic, it also places us side by side with the Triple Entente in the Mediterranean basin, looking towards the east, where Italian expansion can find vast and fertile soil for its energies' (OO, VII: 232–4).

What was to be the internal social corollary of this open-ended programme of territorial expansion? And what, more specifically, was the role Mussolini ascribed to 'Mazzini' in the formulation of this vision? Mazzini's notions of society and politics were of a mystic and ethereal character. While he saw the working class as a significant new force in history, he was keen to offset its moves towards independent political organization, imploring it, in his *I doveri dell'uomo* of 1860, to subordinate its material wellbeing to its 'duties' (Mazzini, 1961: 191–203). As regards the peasantry, Mazzini certainly endowed it with a great revolutionary potential (Mack Smith, 1994: 278ff), though he saw it as limited by its desire for social and economic betterment and as therefore closed to his impervious mystic patriotism. In his *Interessi e principii* of 1836 Mazzini wrote that 'to instill a single principle into the soul of a people or in the mind of its educators and its writers will be far more valuable for that people . . . than the presentation of a whole list of interests and rights to each individual' (Mazzini, 1961: 83). Anyone who thought of mobilizing peasants or workers around their economic aspirations was, for Mazzini, a base materialist and potential dictator. Materialism, he opined in his *Questione morale* of 1866, was an 'old historical phenomenon inseparable from the agony of a dogma' (Mazzini, 1961: 162). A keen adversary of Marx, he opposed non-religious, non-mystic, and class conflict socialism, this contrast being conceived of as a type of cosmic battle of spirit over matter and liberty over tyranny (Mack Smith, 1994: 271ff, 277ff). The mobilization of the masses would, he averred in *Interessi e principii*, occur by an inculcation of 'faith' which, 'revealing itself in the acts [of small groups of conspirators]', would 'set forces in motion' (Mazzini, 1961: 83).

There is an uncanny similarity between Mussolini's and Mazzini's socio-political terminology and method. In January 1915 Mussolini argued that the primary task of the *fasci* was to create a pro-war state of mind among the working masses via 'many words, but more important again gestures and examples' (OO, VII: 139–41). He wrote in March that in the period of the Risorgimental wars a 'sleeping people' was 'shaken' by Mazzini and other patriots and 'dragged to the battlefields with the virtue of the word and with the even more efficient and persuasive one of example' (OO, VII: 275–7). The point here is that, like Mazzini, Mussolini's proposals for popular participation in the war contain a socially conservative thrust in that they substitute gestures and words for mass political mobilization and far-reaching social reform, which in the Italy of the day undoubtedly amounted to land reform, especially given that the majority of the Italian Army would be made up of peasants. Also like Mazzini, Mussolini saw the leaders of socialist organizations as dogmatists and enemies of free thought. He argued in December 1914 that the PSI's rejection of the war derived from its adoption of an 'analytical category' when, according to Mussolini, the outbreak of the conflict had put an end to 'everything that was solid, fixed, what we believed to be dogma' (OO, VII: 97–110). Mussolini placed Mazzini at the top of a list of French, Russian and English libertarian, anarchist and utopian socialists ranging from Proudhon to Bakunin to Fourier, to Saint Simon, to Owen. He cited these in order to show how pro-intervention socialists like himself were roaming in 'the field of unconfined spirit' and were in favour of 'infinite liberty!' to 'repudiate Marx' and 'return to Mazzini' (OO, VII: 150–55).

However, Mussolini's adoption of anti-dogmatic 'free thinking' was not, as he suggested, a consequence of the outbreak of the European war. In November 1908 he wrote a review of the work of Friedrich Nietzsche, praising the German philosopher's thinking precisely because, as he saw it, it lacked a system, or what he declared to be 'all that is rotten, sterile and negative in all philosophies'. Mussolini described the Superman as Nietzsche's 'greatest creation' and 'the hope of our redemption' (OO, I: 174–84). This suggests that when, in 1914–15, Mussolini wrote or spoke of 'Mazzini', the 'Mazzini' in question had been re-elaborated through the grid of the otherwise unmentioned a-moral Nietzschean Superman. Hence the social issues associated with Mazzini would take on an entirely new significance in congruence with the expansionist war for which Mussolini campaigned. Three considerations add weight to this hypothesis.

First, in the 1908 review Mussolini argued that the Nietzschean ideal would only be understood by 'a new species of "free spirits"' who would be 'fortified in war'. The 'free thinkers' or 'unprejudiced spirits' which Mussolini associated with his

1914–15 'return to Mazzini' are arguably, therefore, the *Freigeist* which Nietzsche first developed in 1878 in his *Human, all too human*, and which was developed fully between 1883 and 1885 in the figure of his Superman of *Thus spoke Zarathustra*, the book reviewed by Mussolini in 1908. Secondly, in calling for war against Germany and Austria-Hungary it is unlikely that Mussolini would have argued for a 'return to Nietzsche' in his 'anti-dogma' crusade against the PSI. By pointing to figures such as Proudhon, Bakunin and Owen, Mussolini clearly played on the fact that all of these figures were located within Entente countries and within the 'anti-dogma' petty bourgeois socialist tradition. Nietzsche, on the other hand, had the double disadvantage of being non-socialist and a German. Finally, Mussolini's refusal to raise the slogan of land reform is commensurate with Mazzini and Nietzsche; both of them rejected appeals to what they saw as the low materialist morality of the masses, and both were easily adaptable to Mussolini's understanding of Italian intervention as based on something other than a necessary mobilization of the peasantry around the concrete socio-economic issues which directly concerned it.

This distortion of Mazzini can be said, therefore, to have issued from the impact of power reproduction processes on symbols and representations, or what in our Introduction we defined as ideology. Other evidence supports this interpretation. In 1909 Mussolini wrote about the work of French 'revolutionary syndicalist' Georges Sorel, himself greatly influenced by Nietzsche. In his *Réflexions sur la violence* written in 1905 Sorel argued that the myth of the general strike derived its strength from the power of the images of an undefined future that it provoked among the proletariat. The myth would create a continued state of proletarian class consciousness in readiness for a Napoleonic-style battle to the death with the bourgeois adversary (Sorel, 1999). However, in Sorel's myth the proletariat, as Italian Marxist Antonio Gramsci noted, has 'no active and constructive phase of its own' (Gramsci, 1979: 127). While Sorel adopted formally revolutionary proletarian terminology replete with references to Marx and Engels, this lack of political independence and strategy for the working class strongly suggests that his myth was in substance a call on what he saw as a degenerate and fearful bourgeoisie to augment *its* class consciousness and to make no reforming concessions to workers.

This indeed is how Mussolini interpreted it. In his review of Sorel's book Mussolini argued that working-class beliefs in democracy and socialist reformism could only find their material origins in 'bourgeois degeneration' while 'we syndicalists . . . don't want to inherit the patrimony of the bourgeoisie in a period of decadence'. It was therefore necessary for the bourgeoisie 'to reach the apex of its power' to only then fall under the fatal blow of the working class. The function of 'proletarian violence' was that of 'forcing capitalism to remain ardent in the industrial struggle and to concern itself with the productive function'. Mussolini berated what he called 'this fearful, humanitarian, philanthropic bourgeoisie . . . , this good-hearted bourgeoisie which makes useless charity instead of accelerating the rhythm of economic activity' (OO, II: 163–8). Thus long before the outbreak of the Great War Mussolini had been looking to capitalist forces as the kernel of his vision of 'socialism' while contemporaneously challenging a fundamental tenet of Mazzinian ideology, namely humanitarianism. Indeed, in his review of Nietzsche's work he likewise argued that one obstacle to the Superman's ambitions was the fact that the 'common people' were incapable of understanding the necessity of a 'greater level of wicked deeds' due to their being 'Christianized and humanitarian'. Most importantly, in an article written a month before the review of Sorel's book, and in which he fused Nietzsche with syndicalist theory, Mussolini argued that 'men' were required to keep alight the mythical flame of the general strike (OO, II: 123–7). It is legitimate to conclude, therefore, that buried somewhere not too deep below the surface of Mussolini's pre-1914 socialism lay a recognition of himself as a Nietzschean Superman, understood as a self-appointed mobilizing functionary of a weak-willed bourgeoisie which was failing to stand up to the proletariat and its political and economic organizations.

This is why it is crucial to note that a similar distortion of Mazzini through the Nietzschean grid lay at the heart of nationalist imperialist ideology as formulated by Enrico Corradini in the decade leading up to and including 1914. Corradini argued in 1914 that liberal values had created the conditions for the class struggle where 'the foreign voice of Karl Marx drowns out the Italian voice of Giuseppe Mazzini' (Corradini, 1925: 255). To remedy this, he had argued in 1911 in favour of a lay theocracy as the national ideal: 'The religious devotee knows that every act must answer to God, and therefore tries to do good deeds according to the will of God ... In a similar fashion, by explaining that certain acts of theirs must answer to the nation so that the latter can fulfil its task, national consciousness can and must activate in citizens the sentiment of duty and thus the way of discipline' (Corradini, 1925: 115). Yet while his terminology was more or less unvaried with respect to Mazzini's, Corradini's notion of religious 'devotion' and 'mission' could be seen developing in a moral scale going from the individual to the nation via the family, at which point the discourse halted. Corradini argued in 1905 that to go beyond the nation towards the rest of humanity was not possible because 'at present an organic body ... like the individual, the family, the nation ... and whose name is humanity does not exist, and will not exist even in the future' (Corradini, 1925: 43).

Why this alteration? A central theme to Corradini's schema was Italian industrialization. This was not to issue from a radical transformation of social relations in Italy, and one can scour Corradini's writings and speeches in vain for any such notions. For Corradini, rather, speaking in 1909, industrialization was inseparable from 'an industrial imperialism which today appears the definitively modern form of imperialism and which tomorrow will be only the first step of new military, political and general imperialisms'. In his view, however, Italy lacked 'a will to imperialism' and hence needed to develop a spirit 'which is precisely of peoples in whom the vigour of life is naturally joined with the will to make the first part of world history and not the last' (Corradini, 1925: 86–7). Clearly, there was no place for Mazzinian humanitarianism in this project. Corradini made no bones about his desire to transfer national wealth towards the financial and industrial oligarchies, important sectors of which propped up his political movement. When the latter's newspaper, *L'Idea Nazionale*, was transformed into a daily in 1914 its board of directors consisted of Corradini and four industrialists, one of whom was Dante Ferraris, president of the car and arms manufacturer Fiat and of the employers' federation Lega Industriale (De Grand, 1978: 51). Corradini placed no limits on Italian expansion, seeing open-ended territorial demands as an opportunity for the State to impose greater internal repression and increased military spending (De Grand, 1971: 403). The high point of the domestic dimension to this policy was the destruction of the economic and political organizations of the working class. Again in 1909 Corradini declared his movement to be 'in antagonism with socialism and in accordance with the clear indications of the historical period' (Corradini, 1925: 86). With direct reference to Sorel he called that same year for a revolutionary stand-off between bourgeoisie and proletariat: 'What solidarity, what peace, what social legislation! War, war between the classes!' (Corradini, 1925: 86). A politically and economically defeated workers' movement was to accept its role as part of what he often called a 'proletarian nation' in struggle with 'the great bourgeois, banking, mercantile and plutocratic Europe' (Corradini, 1925: 100, 221).

The theme of 'men', or even a 'man', which, as we have seen, Mussolini had stressed as part of his pre-war redefinition of the task of socialist leaders, had also been elucidated in politico-cultural circles close to Mussolini and, for that matter, Corradini. Writing in Corradini's *Il Regno* in 1904 Prezzolini argued that the pusillanimous bourgeoisie needed to realize that the class struggle was a two-way affair. To stand its ground against socialism it needed to physically rearm (Prezzolini, 1904b). While arguing that the repressive apparatus of the State was an instrument at the bourgeoisie's disposal (1904a), Prezzolini insisted that what was needed was 'direct action on the part of the despoiled class'. By the latter he meant not landless peasants or unemployed farmhands but the bourgeoisie and the agrarians who were to form an anti-socialist alliance: 'We need to begin to act and to finish asking the State to act on our behalf.' The mass base of this direct confrontation with socialism was to be found 'above all among the organizers [of society]'. At the head of this armed middle- and lower-middle class intelligentsia was to stand 'an example and a voice: that is, *a man*' (Prezzolini, 1904c; Prezzolini's italics).

True, Prezzolini eventually dissociated himself from Corradini's *Il Regno* and founded *La Voce* in 1908. But this practice of separation was old, and rather unconvincing, hat. In 1903 Prezzolini initiated the periodical *Leonardo* with another intellectual, Giovanni Papini. In an article of that year Papini called for an 'intellectual empire' and the 'imperialist ideal' as distinct from what he declared to be Corradini's conception of force as 'essentially material and exterior'. However, he concluded his piece by affirming that his thesis was 'not a statement of unfriendliness' towards the nationalists (with whom his article was effectively trying to engage), but an expression of 'the need for separation'. He specified that while Corradini was an adversary of modern civilization and democracy, 'we too are ferocious enemies of such things'. Thus when he declared to Corradini that 'we are not and will not be with you' (Papini, 1903a) it is difficult to imagine who exactly he thought he was fooling. When Papini was not using *Il Regno* to reiterate his anti-socialist discourses already expounded in *Leonardo* (Papini, 1903b), he was using it to restate Corradini's theories concerning the relation between class and nation, the centrality of the bourgeoisie as the ruling class, and the need to recognize that 'the army is the most important organ we possess' (Papini, 1904b). He also expressed his conviction that the Catholic Church was a bulwark of conservatism which the 'great party of the bourgeoisie' could use to its favour (Papini, 1904c).

Prezzolini played a similar double game. Writing in *Il Regno* in 1903 he used his own name to repeat exactly the same themes he had dealt with as the more 'philosophical' 'Giuliano il sofista' in *Leonardo*: namely, 'however reduced the bourgeoisie is, however beaten it is' that 'it still has a long way to go' (Prezzolini, 1903). Neither did *La Voce* represent a definitive rupture with Corradini. Prezzolini's considerations in 1910 on the formation of the nationalist imperialists into a political organization were not only not negative, but he even claimed credit for himself and Papini for what he saw as the positive side of Italian nationalism, that is 'the concern for economic and cultural interests' (Prezzolini, 1910c). *La Voce*'s original 'opposition' to the Italian 1911 invasion of Libya was based not on anti-imperialist considerations but on the lack of fertile soil in Libya and on a rejection of the bad taste of Corradini's war rhetoric (La Voce, 1911a, b). An editorial in fact announced the review's discipline, insisting that once war had started all internal opposition, especially socialist opposition, was to cease (La Voce, 1911c). *La Voce* conceded freedom of action to the government and hoped that Italy would go to Tripoli 'with honour' (La Voce, 1911d). Prezzolini resigned as chief editor in March 1912. However, on his return to the helm in November of that year his rhetoric was a testimony to the influence of his mentor: 'And war elevates all hearts! One cannot but feel, in these days, the greatness of war. How happy I am to have been born in a generation which was the first to reject the commonplaces of pacifism, when to speak of the valour of war seemed a heresy!' (Prezzolini, 1912). When war broke out in 1914 Prezzolini again resigned as editor of *La Voce*. Dazzled by Mussolini's ability to hatch a new paper from nought, he went to work for *Il Popolo d'Italia*. Referring to Mussolini in an open letter to his former colleagues he wrote: 'Do you know that he is a "man"?' (Prezzolini, 1914). Prezzolini had found his 'man'.

Fascists, State and Society: the French Connection

In a 1917 letter to Prezzolini, Mussolini cited *Leonardo* and *La Voce* as lying at the core of his own political-cultural formation (E. Gentile, 1999: 107). In 1909, during his period in the Trentino, Mussolini promoted *La Voce*, and with the highest of praise for Prezzolini, Papini and *Leonardo* (OO, II: 53–6). Even before the war, then, Mussolini was profoundly influenced by the anti-liberal, anti-socialist cultural avant-garde, itself open to Corradini's nationalism. True, while Corradini, Prezzolini and Papini were celebrating the Libyan war, on 18 November 1911 Mussolini was sentenced to one year's imprisonment for his opposition to it (of which he served four months). Arguably, therefore, the influence of these circles was at that stage still somewhat limited. Yet it should be noted that Mussolini was arrested precisely for his agitations in favour of a 'general strike' against the war, terminology which in his Sorelian vocabulary meant anything but a generalized downing of tools, as we have seen. Furthermore, from his prison cell Mussolini began a biography, noting that he had been born on 29 July 1883, that is 'when the sun had been in the constellation of Leo for eight days' (OO, XXXIII: 220). This was clearly an ambitious petty bourgeois intellectual who had a strongly individualist sense of his own importance. While it cannot have been an easy stretch, the prison time did him no harm in terms of publicity, immensely aiding his popularity among radical socialists and hence his 'revolutionary' (but as we have seen ideologically pro-capitalist) campaign against socialist reformism at the PSI's Reggio Emilia congress of July 1912 and, from there, his ascension to the position of chief editor of *Avanti!* (Bosworth, 2002: 83–9).

That said, Richard Bosworth is undoubtedly right to warn against the danger of overstretching the evidence in favour of interpreting Mussolini's pre-1914-war political culture as already marked by national socialism (Bosworth, 2002: esp. Chs 2–4). But Bosworth does not then identify the point at which this political culture crystallized into fascism. Indeed, he is convinced that Mussolini's entire political career was caught up in a 'structure', substantially devoid of 'intention' and hence marked by the absence of any real network of guiding principles and ideas. He thus underestimates the role which the Great War might have played in forging Mussolini's pre-war pot-pourri of latent nationalism and rhetorical 'socialism' into a system of ideas and related practical consequences identifiable with fascism (O'Brien, 2002b). While, to be sure, the name of Corradini does not appear in Mussolini's writings before an article of 26 August 1914, and even then only for purposes of polemic (OO, VI: 339–43), on the basis of the foregoing analysis it is legitimate to hypothesize that a Corradini-type renewal of political authority and State legitimacy lay at the heart of Mussolini's advocacy of intervention in the European war.

Mussolini was keenly aware of the radical divide between State and society which had issued from Italian unification. The latter had in fact been effected from above by the ruling élites of the penninsula in alliance with the monarchy of Piedmont. In December 1914 he referred to the State's 'organic incapacity' to resolve 'the fundamental problems of our national existence' (OO, VII: 72–5). This was true from various points of view. The ruling élites had always seen the masses of workers and peasants as a threat to the State which the founding fathers of unification had taken so many pains to bring into being. An at times sincere desire to oversee improvements in the living conditions of the masses was overwhelmed by a more ardent ambition to defend at all costs the economic and political interests of the dominant classes through violent State repression of popular protest. This strategy had most recently marked the turn-of-the-century governments of di Rudinì, Pelloux and Saracco (E. Gentile, 1990: Ch. 1). The Piedmontese Constitution of 1848, which was imposed on the rest of Italy between 1859 and 1861, certainly recognized individual and collective liberties, including a free press and the right of association. But its clauses then made these rights dependent on laws outside the Constitution itself, a flexibility which allowed collusion between political élites and the military resulting in the arbitrary (but perfectly legal) imposition of martial law in cases of civilian disorder. In 1898, and again in 1902, strike threats by railway and telegraph workers saw those sectors militarized and hence subject to the military penal system (Violante, 1976). This approach failed, however, to guarantee either social order or an expanding internal market in the wake of a major take-off in the Italian economy beginning around 1894. This goes a good way towards explaining the rise of Giolitti from 1901 onwards. Giolitti inaugurated pro-worker social reform, decreased State repression against strikes for higher wages, and expanded suffrage. His concessions were nevertheless made possible by the economic boom, and from the outset they met with resistance from the power interests upon which they tended to impinge (E. Gentile, 1990: Ch. 2). Moreover, the Italian economy was marked by sharp crisis and increasing unemployment from 1907 onwards, and by 1914 Italy had succeeded only in laying important infrastructural foundations, but not in reaching full industrialization (Cafagna, 1970). By that year GNP per capita was only half that of Britain and only two-thirds that of Germany (Procacci, Gv., 1997: 3). Statistics for 1911 show that 38 per cent of Italians were still illiterate, and in some areas of the peninsula illiteracy was almost total. Between 1912 and 1913 over 1.5 million people emigrated (Corner, 2002: 20–21). The vast majority of Italians continued to identify primarily with their local town (*paese*) and not their nation. Even when universal manhood suffrage was first applied in the elections of October 1913 the results still reflected the lack of national integration: no peasants were either present or represented (Bosworth, 1983: 89). The Giolittian experiment had evidently reached objective limits within the existing socio-economic and political frameworks, and it was upon these contradictions that the far right drew in order to challenge the inadequacy of Giolittism to prepare Italy to stake its place in a world marked by inter-imperialist rivalry.

As regards national rites, ceremonies and cultural representations, it was not that the liberal State had ignored such questions following unification. Along with the celebration of the Constitution of 1848 there were attempts to glorify the 1870 incorporation of Rome into the Kingdom (Caracciolo, 1996). However, there is no evidence to suggest that the State seriously interested itself in the creation of a system of national worship (E. Gentile, 1993: 5–25). A massive renaming of streets after the leading figures of the Risorgimento was undertaken in the first two decades of national life, but this seems to have been the outcome of local initiatives by patriotic mayors (Rafaelli, 1996). Also, the national flag, a tricolour which originally aspired to the democratic values of the French Revolution, was soon incorporated into the individual materialization of national unity which was the Soldier-King (Oliva, 1996). Stamps and postcards were not utilized to diffuse the incarnation of Italy in the allegory of the turreted lady (as they were in France with Marianne); rather, in accordance with an authoritarian vision in which the consensus of the masses was deemed unnecessary, the Italian ruling élites saw to it that the Monarchy, and not Italy as such, was exalted in an affirmation and reaffirmation of dynastic power (Gibelli, 1998: 94–5). Italy, in short, would not enter the European war with a *union sacrée*; there would be no generalized mobilization of pro-war sentiment around national traditions, founding myths or political institutions. Indeed, on the eve of the war popular anti-State sentiment was as widespread as ever. In June 1914 demonstrations against militarist celebrations of the Constitution were met with brute force by the authorities. This resulted in a general strike and the proclamation of independent republics in areas of Emilia and Romagna during the so-called 'Red week'.

For Mussolini, this entire inheritance represented a grave danger for the efficacy of the imminent Italian campaign. He argued in December 1914 that '"peoples and States" have everywhere realized a fusion into a block of 'national unanimity"', and that 'the distinction between governments and governed is no longer possible' (OO, VII: 72–5). But, he stressed in April 1915, 'there has been no moral preparation. Worse, the government has not wanted it and has impeded it' (OO, VII: 311–13). Yet the only war possible in modern times was, in his view, a war 'felt by the people, made by the people, through the State' (OO, VII: 341–3). France represented an important reference point for Mussolini, as witnessed by the striking straplines placed on the front page of *Il Popolo d'Italia* in November 1914. In the top left-hand corner was written 'He who has iron has bread', a dictum attributed to the French insurrectionist socialist Auguste Blanqui. In the top right-hand corner,

Napoleon Bonaparte was quoted as saying 'Revolution is an idea which has found bayonets'. A daring interpretation of these subtitles could be that Italy's agrarian question ('bread') would be resolved following industrialization ('iron') to be achieved not by an internal social revolution but via victory in the war ('bayonets'). This process was to be overseen by a strong and ostensibly *super partes* State (Napoleon) but with the indispensable aid of men of action (Blanqui), whose heroic, individualistic gestures would, much like Mazzini's, be presented as a mobilizing surrogate for the raising of issues of a socio-economic and political nature that might concern those mobilized. Before examining Mussolini's other uses of French history, let us first explore the role of the men of action between State and society in the context of the 11 April 1915 interventionist demonstration in Milan.

This latter initiative was countered by the PSI. Police intervened, killing one man, Innocente Marcora, an electrician. Mussolini was absolutely furious. He argued that the State's violence had been 'cold and meditated' (OO, VII: 329–31), and an examination of the archive documentation relative to the causes of Marcora's death suggests that he was absolutely right (ACS, A5G, b. 107, fasc. 225, s.fasc. 23). Marcora's death united interventionists and neutralists in a mass one-day stoppage and demonstration in Milan called for on 14 April. Mussolini supported the demonstration as did the *fasci d'azione rivoluzionaria*, who were referred to by Mussolini as the 'fascists' (which he put in inverted commas). On 14 April he argued that the demonstration had been called in order to 'safeguard the fundamental rights of citizens, and to "protest" against systems which must cease once and for all'. He called for the 'transformation or breaking up of most of the State machine' (OO, VII: 329–31). To begin with, the Police Commissioner and Prefect of Milan both had to pack their bags (OO, VII: 332–4). However, Mussolini's portrayal of himself as being in conflict with the repressive apparatus of the State needs to be treated with caution. For one thing, it will be noted that the above quotation sees the word 'protest' in inverted commas. Indeed, the defence of citizens' democratic rights was not the main reason for the participation by the 'fascists' in the 14 April demonstration. Mussolini wrote that 'it doesn't take much to understand that the people of Milan did not direct its protest against the State, but against a special organ of the State: the police'. By their presence the 'fascists' guaranteed the demonstration's 'absolute apolitical character' in relation to neutrality or intervention (OO, VII: 332–4). Mussolini argued that police violence '"sabotages" the regime and digs the grave of the institutions better and quicker than any ... subversive' (OO, VII: 329–31). Mussolini and the 'fascists' were therefore primarily present as self-appointed representatives and defenders of State authority, but from *within* society and, where necessary, in tactical disagreement with the State on how best to achieve this.

Mussolini's dependence on France and its history included no small amount of references to republicanism. In November 1914 he argued that the war would

'perhaps see a few more crowns fall to pieces' (OO, VII: 39–41). On 7 April he
inveighed not only against *sacro egoismo* and against Salandra's élitist secrecy but
against the King who was described as a pro-German 'Philistine' (OO, VII:
311–13). The following day he accused the Monarch of being 'foreign' and
'neutral'. Mussolini reminded Vittorio Emanuele III that Camille Desmoulins had
once exclaimed that '"In 1789 only twelve of us were republicans"', then adding
that only three years later 'the Monarchy fell under the guillotine' (OO, VII:
314–16). Interestingly, however, in all of Mussolini's other anti-royal articles from
the period of Italian neutrality the King was always given one last chance to see
the interventionist light (OO, VII: 22–3, 97–110, 139–41, 142–8, 220–21, 243–6,
386, 389–90). Against this constantly renewed stay of execution, in December
1914 Mussolini joked about the beheading of Louis XVI and Charles I. He also
opined that by virtue of the war 'Russia will be overturned . . . in its feudal and
Tsarist scaffold'. But he mentioned nothing about the inevitable proclamation of
an Italian republic or the erection of a gallows in Rome. The full consequences of
his 'republicanism' were, therefore, only really applicable to Russia and the
Central Powers, the latter being described as 'feudal nations' at war with the 'democratic nations' (OO, VII: 96–110). It is of crucial importance, therefore, that
another French theme accompanied Mussolini's rhetorical attacks on the Italian
Monarchy. On 16 April he remarked that should certain 'cowards' and 'fomenters
of panic' insist on 'serving up – either in public or in private – their lugubrious
prophecies', there was 'a very simple way to reduce them to silence', and 'even in
this case we are inspired by the example of republican France' (OO, VII: 335–7).

The full import of this allusion to Jacobinism can be best tackled if we take into
consideration Mussolini's July 1915 characterization of that phenomenon as 'the
vanguard of the bourgeoisie' (OO, VIII: 74–6). But this was not the only definition
of which he was aware. He had argued in 1909 that 'the proletariat is not Jacobin'
and for this reason 'it is probable that on its triumph a period of persecutions and
red terror will not follow' (OO, II: 123–8). In his article on Sorel that same year
he noted that the revolutionaries of 1793 carried out 'savage acts . . . when they
had power in their hands and were able to use it to oppress the vanquished' (OO,
II: 163–8). For Mussolini, then, Jacobinism involved persecutions and terror, and
was a bourgeois revolutionary phenomenon. Gramsci observed that in the Italy of
the day Jacobinism was understood as 'the particular methods of a party and government activity which [the Jacobins] displayed, characterized by extreme energy,
decisiveness and resolution, dependent on a fanatical belief in the virtue of the programme and those methods'. However, he also noted that the programmatic and
repressive dimensions to Jacobinism had become separated. A 'Jacobin' was now
any politician who was 'energetic, resolute and fanatical, because fanatically convinced of the thaumaturgical virtues of his ideas, whatever they might be'
(Gramsci, 1979: 65–6). In this regard, it should be remembered that while

Mussolini applied a revolutionary democratic characterization to the war, he had no programme of democratic social reform for Italy, while as regards the overthrow of 'feudal' systems he limited this to the imminent transformations to be wrought on the Central Powers and Russia by the conflict, as we have seen.

It stands to reason, therefore, that his application of 'Jacobinism' to Italy must have implied distinctly repressive measures as part of a programme for social conservation in and through expansionist war. Repression would not be used against reaction to defend a threatened revolution, but against those who challenged the powerful and their drive towards, and pursuit of, imperialist war. In a word, socialism, redefined as counter-revolutionary 'reaction', was the object of this 'Jacobin' ardour. In November 1914 Mussolini referred to the PSI leaders as 'my enemies' (OO, VII: 35–7), and assured his readers that he would fight them 'with all my energy' (OO, VII: 42–3). Following the socialist call to oppose the 'fascist' demonstration on 11 April Mussolini wrote that 'if the war liberates us from a PSI which has become reactionary, then long live the war, let it be welcome and let it come soon' (OO, VII: 317–19). Indeed, of Mussolini's 160 articles, speeches and interviews published between the founding of *Il Popolo d'Italia* and Italian intervention, eighty-six (53.7 per cent) are either directly or indirectly in confrontation with the PSI and/or *Avanti!* (OO, VII: 5–7, 9–11, 16–17, 18–19, 20–21, 22–3, 24, 25–7, 28, 32–3, 35–7, 38, 39–41, 42–3, 45–6, 47, 49, 50, 52, 56, 57–8, 59, 60–61, 84–5, 91–3, 94–6, 111, 113–15, 117–19, 120–2, 126–8, 129–32, 133, 134–5, 139–41, 142–8, 149, 150–53, 154–5, 156, 157–9, 160–62, 163–5, 166–70, 174–5, 176–9, 180–82, 183–4, 185–6, 193–5, 211–12, 213–16, 219, 220–21, 222–4, 243–6, 261–3, 264–7, 268–9, 273–4, 278, 280–82, 285, 286–9, 290–93, 294–6, 301–3, 304–7, 317–19, 326–8, 335–7, 344–8, 349–52, 353–5, 356–8, 359–63, 367–9, 382–3, 384–5, 387–8, 389–90, 391–2, 396–7, 398–400, 401–5, 409–10, 414–17). All of this lends weight to Trotsky's view that fascism 'contains a reactionary caricature of Jacobinism' (Trotsky, 1971: 282).

But as with the pre-war anti-liberal and anti-Parliament political culture of the right-wing nationalists, Mussolini's 'Jacobinism' also took the form of anti-Giolittism. His invective reached boiling point when, following the revelation in parliament on 7 May that Italy was preparing to enter the war, Giolitti, who had retreated to his residence in Piedmont, returned to Rome on 9 May, suggesting, through this action, that the neutralist option was still on the table. Over 300 of his parliamentary supporters left calling cards in his Rome residence as a symbolic expression of solidarity. On 13 May Salandra tactically resigned as Prime Minister, effectively daring Giolitti to use his parliamentary majority to guarantee that Italy would stay out of the war. In Rome that same day the right-wing nationalist poet Gabriele D'Annunzio announced that 'if inciting citizens to violence is a crime, I will boast of this crime, assuming sole responsibility for it . . . All excess of force is legitimate, if it prevents the Nation from being lost' (D'Annunzio, 1915: 73–4).

Interventionist protests of between 5,000 and 30,000 people took place all over Italy, Giolitti being the common target of their slogans. A significant number of prefects' reports shows that these demonstrations were formed mainly by the petty bourgeois intelligentsia and students, who for the most part supported intervention for reasons of expansionism and Great Power politics (Vigezzi, 1959; 1960). On 11 May Mussolini demanded that parliamentary deputies be 'handed over to a war tribunal'. He argued that 'for the health of Italy a few dozen deputies should be shot: I repeat *shot* in the back' (Mussolini's emphasis), and some ex-ministers (unnamed) 'sent to jail for life'. By returning to Rome Giolitti, in his view, had 'sabotaged the spiritual preparation of the Nation for war' (OO, VII: 379–81). Three days later Mussolini stressed that 'if [Giolitti] triumphs along with [his] red scoundrel accomplice . . . Italy will be thrown into the most profound convulsion of her history. An epoch of individual and collective retaliations will begin. The traitors will pay for their crime in blood . . . We cannot ease up when the enemies spy and pursue. We must confront them head on and, whatever the price, rout them' (OO, VII: 387–8). Giolitti declined the invitation to form a government, claiming in his memoirs that a person opposed to the war could not assume the premiership at that time (Giolitti, 1967: 542). The King thus reinstated Salandra on 16 May, and the Parliament, including Giolitti and his followers, voted in favour of war credits four days later. But this did not satisfy Mussolini's 'Jacobin' thirst. On 24 May he accused the socialists of being 'people who work for Austria-Hungary and Germany', veritable 'traitors' because they had made 'continuous propaganda which for months and months has been aimed at depressing the energies of the army and the nation'. He argued that while there was still time for 'individual salvations' this was on the understanding that 'for the Party it's over'. On only one condition could Italian socialism be saved: 'if the Austrians reach Milan'. In the meantime, he once again evoked the need for 'firing squads' for 'traitors and *cowards*' (OO, VII: 414–17; Mussolini's emphasis).

It should be noted, however, that it was not only through newspaper attacks that Mussolini was prepared to practice and encourage anti-socialist 'Jacobinism'. In an article of 23 February 1915 he ridiculed the neutralist rallies of 21 February, arguing that they had failed completely (which was not true: they were well attended; see Valiani, 1977: 102). He attributed this to absenteeism and to the fact that 'while for a whole week *Avanti!* had sneered at the "lean ranks of the fascists"' the latter had nevertheless 'intervened everywhere'. Their 'debut' had been 'brilliant' and the neutralists had been 'dispersed' (OO, VII: 211–12). The fascists showed that they did not fear 'neutralist violence' and had managed here and there 'to impose on the demonstration a precisely opposite character to the one hoped for by the PSI' (OO, VII: 219). In a report of 1 February 1915 to the Ministry of the Interior, the Prefect of Bologna observed that at a meeting of 30 January the local *fascio* had passed a motion which deplored socialist talk of resorting to the general strike in case of Italian intervention. The motion affirmed that 'the Socialist Party tries to distort the general strike – an essentially revolutionary arm in the hand of the international proletariat for its social and political claims – to the benefit of the political and militarist tyranny of the German Empires'. The motion promised to 'impede, with all means necessary', what it termed 'the planned hypocritical and cowardly betrayal' (ACS, A5G, b. 89, fasc. 199, s.fasc. 14). This terminology is identical to section III of the programme of San Sepolcro which, taken to its logical conclusion, resulted, as we saw in Chapter 1, in the physical attack on the socialist demonstration and the *Avanti!* offices in April 1919. To be sure, much of this, including Mussolini's claims in late March 1915 regarding the further dispersal of neutralists by what he termed 'patrols' (OO, VII: 294–6), may have been exaggerated. But inserted as it is in a broader system of imperialism, war, anti-socialism, social conservativism and the reproduction and reinforcement of State authority, it is recognizable as fascism, in however embryonic a form.

Moving Statues

It should nevertheless be remembered that while Mussolini and *Il Popolo d'Italia* provided a point of reference for the *fasci* interventionists, Mussolini was not the key inspiration for the pro-war movement. He was present as a participant at the 5 May demonstration in Quarto, a coastal town in Genoa, while the central figure, D'Annunzio, spoke at the unveiling of a statue sculpted by Enrico Baroni and dedicated to the departure of Giuseppe Garibaldi and 1,000 redshirts from that town in 1860, an event which would lead to the conquest of Sicily by late July and, by October that same year, to the annexation of the whole of the Italian south to Piedmont. The figure of Garibaldi had long since lost its solely democratic and republican implications. These could certainly play their part in culturally mobilizing disparate forces for intervention: Garibaldi signified war when war was called for; he signified energetic voluntary action in pursuit of the completion of national unity in the context of internationalist and humanitarian ideals. But Garibaldi was also readily identifiable with other themes such as patriotism and with the obedience to the Monarchy that he himself had expressed when ordered to halt his and his volunteers' advance in the Trentino in 1866 (Isnenghi, 1982). Originally designed to represent solely Garibaldi, Baroni's monument was later reworked to incorporate the strength, muscularity and masculinity of a hefty working man. The finished product was a composite of labour, Risorgimental values and national aggrandizement which together evoked a productive myth in which the proletariat was absorbed into the nation. All it needed was the poetic word to bring it to life, and this D'Annunzio provided in a spectacular display of individual charisma and gestures combined with the religious terminology of fire, water and faith to forge a cross-class community ready to push abroad in a poetically charged harmony (D'Annunzio, 1915: 18; Gibelli, 1999: 54–64).

Like D'Annunzio, Mussolini was capable of dabbling in terminology which could weave together symbols of blood, death and resurrection into a nationalist, imperialist and anti-socialist discourse. He could also rework the symbol of Garibaldi so that it conformed to an imperialist strategy. He claimed on 31 December 1914, in an article entitled 'Blood which unites', that the Garibaldine volunteers fighting in the Argonne showed 'socialist and neutral Italy' the way of 'duty and sacrifice' (OO, VII: 112). On 8 January the death in the Argonne of Bruno Garibaldi, grandson of the Risorgimento revolutionary, was said to have 'annihilated' the PSI's authority. The dead Bruno was still living and 'when the dead come back to life, there are those living who must die'. Hence 'your time is up, oh socialists of Italy' (OO, VII: 120–22). With the death of Costante Garibaldi, another grandson, again in the Argonne, Mussolini argued in March 1915 that the 'holocaust of blood' had 'sealed a fraternity of spirits and of sentiments which remains unaltered, profound and immutable'. With reference to the fact that, following the dissolution of the Garibaldine Legion in France, Peppino Garibaldi, yet another grandson of Garibaldi's, and other Garibaldine volunteers had enrolled in the *fasci d'azione rivoluzionaria*, Mussolini proclaimed: 'Garibaldine volunteers, your task in France is over. We await you in Italy. The Nation recalls you. It recalls you to fight the internal and the external enemies' (OO, VII: 250–51). And as regards speaking in front of statues of Garibaldi, Mussolini had done so on 31 March in Milan at an interventionist demonstration, declaring that 'at the foot of this Monument we reaffirm, yet again, our will for war' (OO, VII: 297).

An examination of *Il Popolo d'Italia* shows that a lot of space was given over to D'Annunzio's Quarto speech and to the pro-war demonstration in general. Yet Mussolini's short 6 May article on the event dedicated not one word to D'Annunzio. Mussolini, rather, was awaiting 'the word from Rome' (OO, VII: 366). The same can be noted of the previous day's article: Mussolini focused on Salandra's decision not to go to Quarto (OO, VII: 364–5). Again, not a word about the poet. Jealousy and rivalry? Perhaps. But it is clear that Mussolini placed emphasis on politics and State authority, whereas D'Annunzio, according to George Mosse, was somewhat blind to political reality since he subordinated politics to symbols and beauty, and to a mystical understanding of his own powers (Mosse, 1987: Ch. 4). What if Mussolini could further invert the D'Annunzian hierarchy of myth and politics in order to project a new type of State–society rapport from within the national experience of war? As the cannons opened fire, Mussolini's chance came.

–3–

Mind and Matter
May–November 1915

Above all, Fascism, in so far as it considers and observes the future and the development of humanity quite apart from the political considerations of the moment, believes
neither in the possibility nor in the utility of perpetual peace. It thus repudiates the doctrine of Pacifism – born of a renunciation of the struggle and an act of cowardice in the
face of sacrifice. War alone brings up to their highest tension all human energies and
puts the stamp of nobility upon the peoples who have the courage to meet it. All other
trials are substitutes, which never really put a man in front of himself in the alternative
of life and death.

Mussolini, *Dottrina del fascismo*, 1932

Cadorna, Mussolini and the Italian War Plan:
Resurrecting the Bayonet

As a wartime journalist, editor, newspaper owner and male citizen eligible for military service, Mussolini had a direct interest in military plans, operations and the
manner in which the war would be conducted. What was the nature of Italian war
doctrine and how did Mussolini relate to it? On 21 August 1914 the Chief of
General Staff of the Italian Army, Luigi Cadorna, issued a circular to army commanders entitled *Memoria riassuntiva circa una eventuale azione offensiva verso
la Monarchia Austro-Ungarica durante l'attuale conflagrazione europea*
(USSME, 1929: Appendix 1). This war plan foresaw an attack against Austria-
Hungary along the ninety kilometres of border stretching from the Julian Alps
along the river Isonzo and the Carso down to the sea. A further memo of 1
September 1914 entitled *Direttive* and another of April 1915 entitled *Varianti alle
direttive del 1 settembre* extended the front of potential offensive warfare to a 600
km arc along the north-central and north-eastern frontier (USSME, 1929:
Appendices 2 and 3 respectively). This massive dispersal of forces is incompre-
hensible when one considers that the Austro-Hungarian Army had recovered from
the Russian onslaught of the previous autumn and had sacrificed territory along
the Italo-Austrian political border to maximize defensive advantage in moun-
tainous terrain. In his post-war account of his period as commander of Italian
forces, Cadorna asked readers to note that the *Memoria riassuntiva* 'was written

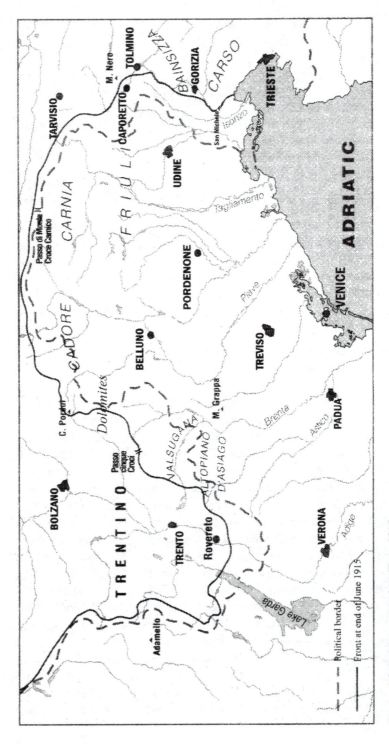

Figure 3.1 Italo-Austrian front June 1915
Source: adapted from Isnenghi and Rochat (2000), page 148.

on 21 August, when we had no experience of the European war, when, that is, the war had not yet become immobilized in the trenches of the western front' (Cadorna, 1921, I: 95). Yet it is evident from the foregoing exposition that the war plan of August 1914 was not subsequently modified to take account of the difficulties of offensive warfare revealed at Ypres in October–November 1914 and during the Franco-British offensives in 1915 at the Noyen Salient, between Rheims and Verdun, and at Neuve Chapelle. Cadorna knew of the defensive predominance of modern firepower on the western front, since his observers on both the German and French sides of the lines had conveyed this information (Rochat, 1961).

But Cadorna also made anachronistic tactical miscalculations. In an officer-training circular published on 25 February 1915 he argued that infantry coming face to face with enemy artillery during an assault was to continue moving forward without seeking protection, since in this way losses would be 'very much lower than those which would occur by hesitating or retreating'. This no doubt explains why the whole of the second part of the circular is dedicated to a detailed exposition of the manner in which the nature of the ground to be crossed, and not enemy or domestic artillery and machine guns, determined the speed of the advance. While Cadorna formally accepted the need to co-ordinate artillery, infantry and machine guns, the circular has no discourse on the division, the army unit in which infantry and artillery were in fact united and co-ordinated. The fact is that Cadorna saw officers' morale and the bayonet as of greater significance than modern firepower. He insisted that 'it is indispensable [for the officers] to maintain faith in the offensive's success and in the efficiency of the bayonet; to infuse this faith in the men and to drag them fearlessly through the zone stormed by enemy projectiles in order to conquer the laurel of victory' (Cadorna, 1915: 19, 20, 27–8, 31–5, 37–45, 50). In short, soldiers were to duck and dodge enemy shells and machine gun spray as they headed for the real purpose of combat, which was to stab the adversary with a piece of metal attached to the end of the rifle barrel. Like the majority of European commanders Cadorna was off the mark by approximately sixty years. Already in the American Civil War (1861–65) frontal bayonet assaults had shown themselves to be no match for the muzzle-loading rifled musket. Subsequent military developments produced a battlefield dominated by breech-loading rifles, machine guns and above all artillery, both field and heavy, which used high explosive shells. The result was a concentration and destructiveness of firepower that made offensive warfare extremely difficult, large-scale frontal infantry assaults redundant, and hand-to-hand combat a minor feature of war rather than a decisive factor (Howard, 1976: Ch. 6; McNeill, 1983: 190–93). What, then, is the broader significance of Cadorna's dogmatic insistence on the offensive?

According to Jack Snyder, the training and duties of army commanders can sometimes leave them examining international relations from a narrow military perspective in which war is seen as an inevitable part of life. When suspicion of what others are up to is applied to war planning, the outcome can be a push for preventive war. The consequent offensive war plan allows commanders to structure their armies better by deploying them along pre-established lines of advance. Defence, on the other hand, while certainly more easily organized, allows politicians to enter the fray. Offensive doctrine thus becomes inseparable from the military's operational autonomy, which in turn is often the reflection of a desire to safeguard institutional interest (Snyder, 1984: Chs 1 and 8). This analysis finds resonance in Cadorna's doctrine, since he firmly believed that the military should be left free to implement strategic plans without meddling from politicians and government to whom he attributed all Italy's lost wars, including the disaster of 1866 (Rocca, 1985: Chs 1–3). However, Snyder's stress on the schism between military and political spheres arguably underplays the possible relation between offensive doctrine, political strategy and ideology. While Clausewitz appears twice in Snyder's book, the Prussian theoretician's considerations do not weigh upon his methodological framework. Halfway into writing up his posthumously published (1832) *Vom Kriege*, Clausewitz reached the conclusion that there could be no purely military dimension to war making and strategy, as in the last analysis politics was the determining factor. Clausewitz also argued that how a society wages war reflects the structure of that society and its core values. This is because interacting social forces impose their logic both on the aims of the war and the intensity with which it is conducted (Clausewitz, 1993: esp. Book 8).

Indeed, Cadorna may have continually assailed politicians, but this was itself from a right-wing political standpoint. In his war memoirs, for example, he quoted the nationalist imperialist Alfredo Rocco on the weakness of the State's authority (Cadorna, 1921, I: 8, 29). Cadorna claimed that by the turn of the century the army was being sneered at by citizens who had too many democratic rights, while the right of the army to shoot on insolent and disrespectful crowds had been diminished. Civilian recruits had brought democratic presuppositions to bear on relations with their superiors, for example, denouncing the latter for mistreatment instead of respecting military discipline whose code was 'the superior is always right especially when he is wrong'. Like the nationalist far right (but not only), Cadorna pinpointed what he called the 'Giolittian dictatorship' as the main root of the evil. He claimed that on taking over the army in July 1914 he found it in a dismal material and psychological state, and he blamed this on the Parliament which in his view was more concerned with the national budget than with what he termed the 'national interest' (Cadorna, 1921, I: 4–33). However, statements such as these only show the degree to which Cadorna's military thinking was propped up by systematic resort to undocumented anti-popular accusations, blatant falsity, denial of objective information and methodological limitations all imposed by reactionary social and political interests. Between 1900 and 1914 politicians voted 23.7 per cent of the national budget to the armed forces and this does not include the thousand million lire for the Libyan war. Under the 'Giolittian dictatorship' the army received more money than ever: between 1913 and 1914, when Italy was in the throes of a grave economic crisis, Giolitti handed over 502 million lire against the 284 million the army had received between 1899 and 1900. The Italian Army in 1914 was a well-armed, well-manned and extremely well-financed fighting machine, and could spend its money as it saw fit. Its 'difficulties' were due to the fact that it was an overstretched instrument of external expansion and internal repression (Rochat, 1991: Ch. 4).

If the content of Cadorna's 1915 training booklet finds resonance in Snyder's understanding of the offensive cult as deriving from the military's push for operational and institutional autonomy, it is equally true that the self-rule enjoyed by the Italian Army was the expression of a tactical price paid by the ruling conservative élites in order to guarantee their alliance with the military in defence of common class privileges. In exchange, the army invariably supported the conservative and nationalist right (Rochat, 1991: Ch. 1). Cadorna's doctrine of the offensive can therefore be defined as a militarist ideology. By this is meant that it emphasized the necessity of hierarchy and subordination, physical courage and blind obedience as social values in a situation where war was deemed a natural part of human existence, and where long lists of dead soldiers (the inevitable outcome of men exposed to well-placed machine guns and light field and mountain artillery) were considered as indicators of national determination and the right to Great Power status (Howard, 1976: 212; 1992: 225). A recent reassessment of the meaning of the 'Cult of the Offensive' before the First World War concludes in favour of the need for commanders to rhetorically emphasize human will over technology in order to raise it to a level where it might be comparable to material factors (Echevarria II, 2002). The argument is unconvincing, and anyway is certainly not applicable to the Italian case. The ultimate scope of Cadorna's military ideas cannot be divorced from the strategy of Italian monopoly capitalists and their agrarian and political allies to use Italian intervention in the war for purposes of territorial aggrandizement and internal anti-democratic reaction.

Even before Italian intervention, Mussolini displayed some interest in the military conduct of an eventual armed conflict. On 24 January 1915 he declared: 'I believe if it comes to war the greatest freedom should be given to the General Staff. Lawyers who practice politics will have to keep quiet, as all wars in which there is rivalry between the political and military authorities are lost' (OO, VII: 142–8). On 14 February he insisted on the need for an unremitting offensive, suggesting that when politicians and diplomats kept out of military affairs 'soldiers . . . stop only when they have reduced the enemy to impotence' (OO, VII: 196–8). The Cadorna line was here repeated almost verbatim. And like Cadorna, Mussolini made a fetish of the bayonet. On 29 April he wrote that 'the formidable mallet of Italy's one and a half million bayonets' would 'beat without truce and without pity' until the mortal blow had been delivered to Germany (OO, VII: 356–8). Following D'Annunzio's speech at Quarto, Mussolini warned the government to leave aside its diplomatic manoeuvres and 'entrust the lot of Italy to the bayonets of its soldiers' (OO, VII: 366). When Salandra had been reinstated on 16 May Mussolini could inform the 'Italian bayonets' that 'the destiny of the peoples of Europe is, together with that of Italy, entrusted to your steel' (OO, VII: 396–7).

What of other weapons? In his polemic with Mussolini in October 1914 (see Chapter 2) Libero Tancredi pointed out that the editor of *Avanti!* had said privately that the Italian '91 rifle was a good weapon, a point which Mussolini confirmed in his reply. Like the French Lebel and the German Mauser, the Italian '91 breech-loaders could fire up to twenty rounds a minute at a distance of up to 3 km. In short, these rifles were just one of the many reasons weighing *against* the frontal bayonet assault. In his November 1914 polemic against the steel monopolists Mussolini noted a shortcoming in the supply of the Déport cannon (OO, VII: 29–31), a French light field model produced under licence in Italy. He did this, however, without specifying the weapon's calibre, which in this case was 75 mm. No other references to this or any other light field cannon can be found in Mussolini's writings or speeches before his departure for the front in September 1915. All we find, rather, are some fleeting references to a German mortar. On 1 December 1914 he furnished readers with the name and address of Emilio Kerbs, a German journalist who had supplied information to the Wolff'sches Telegraphen-Bureau (the semi-official German news agency) regarding the financing of *Il Popolo d'Italia* by the French. Mussolini justified his intimidating act by claiming that 'it is as well in these days . . . of the 42 [cm] mortar to know the exact address of the Prussians' (OO, VII: 62–3). In his speech of 13 December he argued in favour of the historical relativity of firepower by noting that 'the war machines of the ancient Romans are the ancient equivalent of the present day 42 [cm] mortars' (OO, VII: 76–81). We must wait almost five months before being reminded once again that during its invasion of Belgium and France the German Army had banked on 'the efficiency of the famous, but not for that reason less hypothetical "420" [mm] mortars' (OO, VII: 367–9).

It is evident that Mussolini's reference to the 42 cm mortar was in the form of a jingoistic catchphrase, and was not based on any real knowledge of the piece. The mortar in question was without doubt the Krupp 420 mm heavy howitzer, more commonly known as Big Bertha, used to devastating effect in the German assault on the fortresses of Liège in August 1914. The point, at any rate, is that precisely because it was a very important and powerful siege weapon Big Bertha was not the first concern of soldiers attacking enemy trenches. These were far more likely to be killed by the cross-spray of machine guns (about which Mussolini said or wrote nothing), or the bombardment of light field artillery such as the 75 mm (which Mussolini discussed only algebraically and arguably not at all), or by the enemy equivalent of the Italian '91 rifle (a weapon which Mussolini appreciated but whose contemporary significance he clearly did not understand). Thus with no serious knowledge of developments in military technology, Mussolini largely supported the basic approach of Cadorna to the organization and conduct of warfare, namely military autonomy from political control and unbridled offensive warfare as corollaries of a right-wing nationalist programme of external expansion and internal anti-democratic reaction. How did he address the outcome of Cadorna's opening offensive and subsequent manoeuvres before his own call up in late August 1915? And what impact did these operations have on his understanding of modern war?

Mussolini's Missing War, May–September 1915

Cadorna's initial operation beginning 24 May, commonly known as the *sbalzo offensivo*, achieved little. For the Italian 4th Army's advance through the fortified Dolomites to have had even the remotest chance of success, huge quantities of heavy artillery would have been needed. But on intervention Italy had just over 2,000 pieces of artillery and only 192 of these were of medium and only 132 of heavy calibre. Like the French, Italy had a preponderance (1,797) of 75 mm light field pieces. Siege artillery was in place only on 5 July and even then was shy of a battery. In any case, the army as a whole was not fully mobilized until 15 June (Pieropan, 1988: Ch. 4; Isnenghi and Rochat, 2000: 145–51; Schindler, 2001: 41–5). On 13 June Cadorna decided to switch all attention to the river Isonzo, transferring seven reserve divisions to that area. For their part, the Austrians had tactically withdrawn to the east bank of the river between Gorizia and the sea. Exceptions to this were the bridgeheads at Gorizia and, further north, Tolmino. These two strongholds now represented the defining feature of the Isonzo front, the one at Gorizia becoming Cadorna's primary objective. He paid particular attention to the Oslavia–Podgora trench system and the Mount San Michele–San Martino del Carso line, which reinforced the north and south of the Gorizia bridgehead respectively. Four offensives were unleashed on the Isonzo in 1915: 23 June–7 July, 18 July–4 August, 18 October–4 November and 10 November–2 December. These were marked by the inability of Italian 75 mm light field artillery to seriously damage enemy barbed wire trench protections, and by the ability of by now experienced Austro-Hungarian soldiers, having absorbed the brunt of the artillery bombardment, to return quickly to defensive positions to meet the frontal assault. Between June and December 1915 Italy had over 130,000 casualties in return for irrelevant territorial gains which did nothing to remove the Gorizia bridgehead (Pieropan, 1988: Chs 7–12; Isnenghi and Rochat, 2000: 162–5; Schindler, 2001: Chs 3–6).

Mussolini observed the initial confrontation, up to and including the Second Battle of the Isonzo, from an unchanged position as journalist and political activist. Between 24 May and 2 September (the day on which he published a farewell article as he downed pen and headed for the front) he published sixty-four articles and one letter in *Il Popolo d'Italia*. These allow us to assess what became of his interventionist ideas, political language and military theories, and to explore the extent to which he used the war to experiment with a national-religious type language that could give greater political substance to the D'Annunzian nationalist-imperialist aesthetic.

Eleven articles (16.9 per cent) were dedicated to Italy's war (OO, VIII: 3–4, 17–19, 23–5, 71–3, 79–82, 87–9, 97–9, 128–30, 138–40, 186–8, 291–2), though of these only two made (fleeting) reference to Italian operations on the Isonzo (OO, VIII: 87–9, 97–9). A third reference to Isonzo operations appeared (again fleetingly) in an article dedicated to the Russian front (OO, VIII: 40–22). Against this, twenty-six articles (40 per cent) were devoted to war issues outside the Italian theatre (OO, VIII: 8–10, 20–22, 26–9, 33–6, 37–9, 40–42, 43–6, 58–61, 65–8, 69–70, 74–6, 100–101, 106–8, 134–7, 141–4, 150–51, 152–4, 155–7, 158–60, 161–2, 163–7, 168–70, 171–3, 175–7, 178–80, 189–91). If we add to the latter the eight articles on German social democracy (OO, VIII: 5–7, 11–15, 47–9, 50–54, 62–4, 84–6, 181–3, 184–5), the total number of pieces not dealing with Italy rises to 52.3 per cent.

A language of national renewal through blood and sacrifice, death and resurrection appeared in seven pieces, or 10.7 per cent of the total (OO, VII: 418–19; OO, VIII: 30–32, 90–91, 92–6, 97–9, 195–6, 291–2). Of these seven pieces four had an anti-socialist thrust (OO, VIII: 30–32, 90–91, 92–6, 291–2): 'Blood is blood', affirmed Mussolini on 20 June, 'and too much has been spilt to be able to go on speaking of a future of universal brotherhood.' The nation, referred to as the 'hard and solid terrain of the race', had been 'revivified' through the blood of its sons, and for this reason 'international socialism is a corpse' (OO, VIII: 30–32). The interventionist demonstrations of May were a key indicator of national renewal for Mussolini, a theme which he touched upon in six articles and which on some occasions he linked to anti-socialism. He argued on 20 July, for example, that 'the purification of Italy' was begun by 'the marvellous days of May' which also marked 'the last step of the official Socialist Party towards putrefaction' (OO, VIII: 92–6; see also VII: 418–19 and OO, VIII: 55–7, 74–6, 79–82, 90–91).

Anti-socialism was in fact a key component of this bulk of material. Of the sixty-five pieces seventeen (26.1 per cent) were engaged in polemic with the PSI (OO, VIII: 30–32, 55–7, 77–8, 83, 90–91, 92–6, 102, 103–5, 109–11, 112–14, 115–17, 118–27, 131–3, 145–7, 148–9, 174, 192–4), and if we add to these the eight articles dedicated to attacks on German social democracy the total rises to 38.5 per cent. A total of thirty articles were written before the Second Battle of the Isonzo and it is revealing that when the anti-German, Balkans and eastern front articles from this period are combined they account for seventeen of those thirty articles, or 56.7 percent (OO, VIII: 5–7, 8–10, 11–15, 20–22, 26–9, 33–6, 37–9, 40–42, 43–6, 47–9, 50–54, 58–61, 62–4, 65–8, 69–70, 74–6, 84–6). But during the Second Battle of the Isonzo the polemic against the PSI replaced the predominant focus on the war outside Italy of the articles written before the battle and accounts for eleven of the eighteen pieces written during this time, or 61.1 per cent (OO, VIII: 90–91, 92–6, 102, 103–5, 109–11, 112–14, 115–17, 118–27, 131–3, 145–7, 148–9). In the period following the Second Battle of the Isonzo, Mussolini returned to the form and content of his articles prior to that offensive. A heavy emphasis on foreign issues, amounting to thirteen out of seventeen pieces, equivalent to 76.5 per cent (OO, VIII: 150–51, 152–4, 155–7, 158–60, 161–2, 163–7, 168–70, 171–3, 175–7, 178–80, 181–3, 184–5, 189–91), was accompanied by only one article dedicated to the home front war regime (OO, VIII: 186–8). The absence of language of national religion once again correlates with the reduction of the anti-socialist content to the articles which amount to five of the seventeen pieces (OO, VIII: 148–9, 174, 181–3, 184–5, 192–4).

A provisional conclusion from the above is that as a distant observer Mussolini was unable to reconcile his politico-military preconceptions with the reality of the war on the Italian front, notably the stalemate, about which he had little to say. As a response to the stasis he focused on the eastern front, the Balkans or Germany (with whom Italy was not at war). But ignoring the Italian front did not mean that Mussolini was not influenced by events unfolding there. Anti-socialism, present in Mussolini's discourse since October–November 1914, radically intensified during the Second Battle of the Isonzo. Anti-socialism was also linked to national-religious terminology which itself was bound up in a system of terrain and the renewal of the 'race' (*stirpe*) through sacrificial and cleansing blood. He certainly recognized that 'the war's long delay in the trenches has completely altered the character of the war itself', and argued that 'an army of heroes is doomed to disaster if it doesn't have munitions' (OO, VIII: 23–5). However, missing from his discussion was the concept of artillery and he in fact dealt only with bullets (*pallottole*).

Finally, Mussolini responded in seven of the sixty-five published pieces (10.8 per cent) to accusations concerning his absence from the front (OO, VIII: 16, 77–8, 83, 109–11, 145–7, 148–9, 192–4). Moreover, of the three letters written in this period, including two not published until the 1950s (OO, VIII: 291–2), all mentioned the same theme. It was a touchy point. But why was Mussolini not at war? He claimed he had been refused as a volunteer because he was liable for imminent call up (OO, VIII: 16). Archival evidence of unclear origin nevertheless suggests that in 1915 Mussolini consciously sought to be exempted from military service through the good offices of Bissolati. The latter refused, however, saying that those who preached war should go and fight it (ACS, SPDCR, b. 98, fasc. X/R 'Bissolati Leonida'). At any rate, Mussolini now had a chance to prove his detractors wrong. He was going to the zone of combat which he had to all intents and purposes excluded from his writings of late May to early September 1915. Any abstract considerations surrounding the war's technological character and related tactics would have to be re-examined in the concreteness of industrialized mass death. Or would they?

Mussolini was called up on 31 August 1915. He left *Il Popolo d'Italia* in the managerial hands of Manilo Morgagni (Bosworth, 2002: 114) and former syndicalist Giuseppe De Falco, who had become chief editor on 12 March 1915 (OO, VII: 252). Mussolini was now free to switch his attention to the daily representation of his combat experience in a war diary, which he wrote for contemporary publication in *Il Popolo d'Italia* and which was republished in volume form in 1923. When the latter volume appeared it was with the addition of some non-diary material, the clarification of real names with respect to some originally used initials, the specification of dates (Mussolini sometimes only used the day) and one or two minor (but not for that reason insignificant) cuts from the *Il Popolo d'Italia* version. Unless otherwise stated, all quotations are from the 1923 publication. Alex Aronson explains that the desire to have one's diary published reflects a psychological urgency to remain visible to a public which is to draw lessons from the internal retreat which the diary represents (Aronson, 1991: 102). Hence while Mussolini's diary shared the common feature of all diaries in that it was a means through which the author's identity could be reconstructed (Didier, 1976: esp. Ch. 2; Aronson, 1991: Ch. 6), the fact that it was written for publication strongly suggests that Mussolini intended using it as a vehicle for self-promotion and self-projection on a new plane. Through the diary Mussolini literally wrote himself into the war. It thus becomes the key source for understanding his response to the conflict and the way he applied and adapted his political ideas and language in relation to his personal experience of combat. The remainder of the present chapter will examine the first section of the diary (9 September–16 November 1915) with the following questions in mind. Did Mussolini's language of national religion intensify with respect to the May–September articles, and if so in what context and for what reason? How did Mussolini relate to the men and the officers? Did he reassess his position on offensive doctrine and arms and munitions in the war of attrition? Finally, what was the ideological nature and function of the war diary?

Baptism on the Isonzo

Having done is military service with the Bersaglieri between 1905 and 1906 (De Felice, 1965, Appendix: 665–7), Mussolini was assigned to the same corps as a private in the 33rd battalion of the 11th regiment. The Bersaglieri corps was formed in Piedmont in 1836 for the purpose of upsetting the enemy with accurate marksmanship and speed, defending mountain positions, protecting retreats and assisting in ambushes. These tasks were symbolically represented in the distinct design of the corps' hat: in particular its wide brim had been devised to prevent soldiers from dosing off on the ground, whereas the plumes were for camouflage behind trees and bushes from where the soldier was to leap unexpectedly (Anon, 1976: 1–9). To be sure, by 1914 all this had long since formed part of a mythical cachet. For one thing, the tasks of the Bersaglieri were by then indistinguishable from the infantry in general, particularly as regards the task of domestic policing (Rochat, 1991: 45–50). For another, entrenched stasis and long-range weapons had necessitated the abandonment of decorative luxuries in battle, since these rendered the soldier unnecessarily visible and more easily picked off. In the opening phases of the Great War, for example, many a Frenchman had paid with his life for the fancy red stripe down the side of his trousers (Keegan, 1999: 85). Likewise, the plumes in the Bersaglieri's hat had become a dangerously outdated nicety, useful only as a component of dress uniform, whereas the wide brim was clearly not indicated for cramped trench conditions. Even so, the 30 kg backpack was not the only weight carried by Mussolini as he headed for the front: he also bore a symbolic baggage the significance of which he would have to reassess in the context of trench warfare immobility.

Mussolini was positioned on the far northern sector of the Isonzo front in the area between Monte Nero and the Iavorcek, approached via Udine and Caporetto (see Fig. 3.1). On arrival at Udine, on 13 September, Mussolini noted 'interminable supply trains immobile along kilometres and kilometres of track'. He commented: 'What an enormous amount of effort is required to supply and provision a fighting army!' The following day he again observed 'interminable lines of trucks and lorries of all types coming and going incessantly ... One has the impression that the war is near.' Then: 'The sound of cannon thunder reaches us from afar. I love this life of movement, rich with great and humble things.'

Already, then, Mussolini had begun to observe the enormous quantities of supplies needed to put and keep a modern army at the front. He had also heard the sound of the weapon that was predominating in the present war. Yet he was still immersed in a concept of 'movement'. As he was moving forward on 15 September he passed through San Pietro Natisone, one of seven towns on the Italian side of the border where Slovene was spoken. Then he approached the old border, noting that the Italians were beginning to make themselves at home: 'The Austrian road signs have gone.' However, the removal of signs did not alter the contradiction underlying the Mazzinian conception of Italy's frontiers. Once beyond the old border, in the village of Robich, Mussolini asked a boy his name. '"Stanko"', replied the boy. '"Then what?"' asked Mussolini inquisitively. But the boy did not reply. Mussolini was then informed that the boy's surname was Robancich. 'A decidedly Slav name', wrote the diarist. Mussolini's investigation into the local population finished without further comment. How did he give expression to the new but contradictory Italy emerging in this early phase of the war? Having passed through Caporetto he reached the river Isonzo on 16 September and wrote: 'The Isonzo! I have never seen clearer waters than those of the Isonzo. Strange! I knelt upon the cold water and drank a sip with devotion. Sacred river!'

According to anthropologist Arnold Van Gennep, events such as this represent the first of three phases of rites of passage. Following a baptismal separation from a profane and impure world, the initiate goes through a period of trial on the margin (liminal phase) without which he/she cannot be integrated (or reintegrated) into the community. When the water used is not ordinary but sacred (as it is in Mussolini's definition of the Isonzo) initiates are accepted into a religious fraternal order (Van Gennep, 1981: 10ff, 55, 66). Mussolini, too, characterized the community into which he had entered as a religious-fraternal one, though he was keen to establish that the religion in question was of a secular type. He had a long-standing aversion to religion and the Catholic Church, the most recent expression of which was his anything but commiserating comment on the death of Giuseppe Sarto, Pope Pius X, on 20 August 1914 (OO, VI: 333). In a diary entry of 19 September he reported how his captain referred to war as '"the most sacred and most bitter of duties a citizen has towards the Nation"' and how another spoke of '"the religion of duty!"' The religion of duty and sacred devotion to the nation: Mazzini is present in all but name. On 19 October Mussolini observed that 'Father Michele, the regiment chaplain, has arrived. But he's itching to be off.' He wrote on 1 November that 'it has been announced that Father Michele will say mass to the Command. But from my company nobody moves.' The day after he asked: 'Are these men religious?' and answered: 'I hardly think so. They swear often and with pleasure. They almost all carry a medal of a saint or the Madonna, but this is equivalent to a lucky charm. It's a type of sacred mascot.' The evidence supports Mussolini's representation of the soldiers' approach to religion. Despite claiming later that they were for the most part satisfied with their wartime work, chaplains were actually convinced that, with the exception of the Alpini, soldiers were not particularly religious. The men swore a lot and at times this had an anti-clerical and even anti-God content. As regards Father Michele's uneasiness, chaplains in fact spent little time among the men, and were often in a hurry to get away from the front lines. They ran through confessions and were seen by the soldiers as malingerers (Morozzo della Rocca, 1980: esp. Chs 1, 4 and 5).

The religious-fraternal Mazzinian community of Mussolini's war diary was one in which class distinctions and military rank were disappearing. On 19 September he wrote: 'I note – with pleasure, with joy – that between officers and soldiers the most cordial camaraderie reigns.' Officers were 'more . . . like brothers . . . than superiors'. In his first morale-boosting talk that same day the captain assured the men that in him they would find '"not only a superior, but a father, and a brother"'. Mussolini observed: 'You can speak with an officer without having to stand to attention.' The uniform was 'almost abolished'. Captains and lieutenants, and especially non-commissioned lieutenants, underpinned the fraternal and popular nature of the warrior community: 'With these officers', he again stated on 19 September, 'anyone who speaks of a reinforcement of militarism with the inevitable Italian victory is living in another world.' This was because the present war was 'made by peoples and not by traditional armies'. Indeed, 'the enormous majority of Italian officers have come, with mobilization, from civilian life. All the subalterns are non-commissioned lieutenants or junior grade lieutenants and they fight and die valiantly.' The evidence bears out Mussolini's observations. Of the 45,000 officers available in August 1914, about 20,000 were non-commissioned, and in 1914 almost all of these were lieutenants or junior lieutenants (Rochat, 1991: 114–15). For Mussolini, the large presence of this socio-military stratum meant that the fraternal warrior community was underpinned by consent rather than coercion. On 30 September he defined one captain as 'a man who knows men, a soldier who knows soldiers. He doesn't need to resort to disciplinary measures to make sure that everyone carries out their duties.' On 14 November a lieutenant admonished a private who was complaining about the cold. Mussolini wrote that even so the officer adopted a 'subdued voice', recognized the cold was unbearable and sought a change of guard, which was duly conceded by the captain. All this contributed to the fact that, as Mussolini wrote on 16 October, 'nobody says "I'm going back to my home town"; what they say is "I'm going back to Italy". For perhaps the first time Italy appears as a sole and living reality, as the common Nation, in the consciences of so many of its sons.'

To what degree did the experience of combat in the second phase of Van Gennep's schema correspond to the Isonzo baptism and its fraternal communal corollary? The baptismal ceremony at the Isonzo was not the only community-forging ritual of its kind. The following day, 17 September, a soldier was injured by an enemy shell. Another shell detonated near Mussolini, covering him and others with leaves and earth. That evening Mussolini noted that they had been 'baptized by the fire of cannon'. Unlike its ritual cousin on the Isonzo, this baptismal ceremony was more overtly associated with the forging of a fraternal community: on 19 September Mussolini wrote that 'the life of continued risks binds our spirits together'. Brotherhood produced from this type of experience is what during the Second World War American psychologists and sociologists noted as the 'small group' or 'buddy' syndrome. Acts of group solidarity, loyalty towards fighting comrades and fear of letting others down are crucial in generating group cohesion and improving military performance (Stouffer, 1949, II: 118–27). Anthropologists see the phenomenon as a 'kinship morality'. This goes beyond 'fictive brotherhood' (such as adoption) and conflates kinship and friendship into what Meyer Fortes called 'amity'. The fraternal order becomes a peculiarly morally charged one in which the readiness to risk one's life for one's 'kin' is informed by the desire to guarantee the continuation of the social order in-the-

making (Fortes, 1969: 110). Joseph Henderson relays that individual altruistic gestures and the renouncing of all personal ambition during the liminal phase are
symbolic of death as a necessary prelude to rebirth (Henderson, 1984: 32).

Mussolini's war diary reveals elements of these socio-psychological and anthropological categories. We read how on 18 September in the heat of rifle and
machine gun exchanges 'the fire is of an infernal intensity', with the real (rifle and
machine gun) and metaphorical (hell) functions of 'fire' here at work. Right at that
point, following a cry of "'Hit the deck! Hit the deck!'" Mussolini wrote: 'But I
must get up and give my place to an injured soldier whose arms have been shat-
tered by the explosion of a bomb.' He then took a blanket and covered the soldier,
letting the reader know in passing that the blanket was his own (*la mia coperta*),
that the weather was cold and hence that he was making a personal sacrifice.
Mussolini also made the confrontation with death necessary for the return to life.
On 10 October he noted that 'today, for the first time, my life was in danger'. He
had in fact narrowly escaped being struck by flying shrapnel. An identical event
occurred on 17 October, and Mussolini kept count: 'For the second time in seven
days I have run the serious and immediate risk of death.'

Mussolini was not documenting only his own experiences of war. The inter-
mingling of the real and symbolic confrontation with death was the experience of
the entire warrior community. This he demonstrated with particular reference to
injuries. On 19 September he wrote of a soldier who, despite having had a leg torn
apart by a bomb, had a 'serene face and delicate profile. He asks for a sip of coffee.
A cigarette. And they carry him away.' The following day a corporal fell into
Mussolini's arms. The diarist wrote: 'He is only injured. His face is covered with
dust and blood. The injuries are on his legs . . . He is calm, tranquil. Not a cry, not
a moan. He keeps it in like a good soldier.' On 9 October: 'There is an injured man
of the 8th company being carried on a stretcher. A bullet hit him while he was
warming himself at the fire. He hums and smokes.' In summing up his impressions
of his various contacts with the injured men, and how they made light of their
injuries, Mussolini wrote on 18 October: 'This is the product of the environment
in which we live. No injured soldier wants to appear weak and afraid at the sight
of his own blood in front of his comrades. But there's a deeper reason. You don't
moan over an injury when you run the continued risk of death. The injury is the
lesser evil.'

Injury was therefore a surrogate for death and hence for rebirth which could
only come through death. This interpretation is confirmed by an article written by
Mussolini on 24 March 1915, in which he quoted the poet Enotrio Romano as
saying that behind Giuseppe Mazzini "'a dead people placed itself'", to which
Mussolini added that the Italian people 'slept a profound sleep, like that of death'
(OO, VII: 275–7). In the war diary entry of 2 November we read: 'If old Enotrio
Romano came back to the world and saw these men who are marvellous in their

tenacity, in their resistance, in their abnegation, he would not say as he once said: *Our Nation is contemptible!'* (Mussolini's italics). Enotrio Romano was the pseudonym which the poet Giosuè Carducci (1835–1907) used for his ardently impatient patriotic works. The two poems quoted by Mussolini are from the collection *Giambi ed epodi* (1867–72). The first is from the sonnet 'Mazzini' (c. 1870) in which Carducci referred to the third Italy (after Rome and the Communes) as a cemetery (Carducci, 1959: 171–3). The second quotation is from the ode 'In morte di Giovanni Cairoli' (1870). This poem is strongly Jacobin in its accusations against Italy's 'traitors and cowards', and melancholic over Cairoli's death in 1869 (due to wounds received in 1867 in the Papal territories), not to mention the incompleteness of Italian unification (Carducci, 1959: 89–99). Carducci was strongly anti-clerical, since he saw Papal power as an obstacle to national unity (Salinari and Ricci, 1975: 799–832). But while his Mazzinianism and anti-clericalism were also key elements of Mussolini's war diary, unlike the world of *Giambi ed epodi* Mussolini's diary reveals a fully realized Mazzinian Italy reborn in the confrontation with death.

What role did Mussolini ascribe to himself in this symbolic universe? In an article published in *Il Popolo d'Italia* six weeks before Italian intervention he wrote:

> Spread out through the divisions of the army, the 'interventionists' will spur on the others, and will be the best soldiers because they know the 'reasons' why the war is being fought. Given the essentially rural composition of the army, the infusion of 'idealist' elements will without doubt have positive repercussions on the outcome of the war. (OO, VII: 323–5)

The army considered such proposals to be dangerous. On 10 June 1915 Vittorio Zuppelli, Minister for War since 10 October 1914, ordered all army, division and regiment commanders to ban revolutionary propaganda in the trenches and to keep a close eye on Mussolini in particular (De Felice, 1965: 319–20). On 20 September 1915 Mussolini reported in his war diary how his colonel sought to isolate him with an administrative job (which he declined). What, though, did Mussolini's pre-intervention proposals for enthusing the peasant soldiers amount to in practice?

On 17 September he was marching under shell fire for the first time, 'encouraging those who are near me'. He wrote that following this a soldier from 'the lowest plains of [northern] Italy', hence a peasant soldier, approached him and said: '"Signor Mussolini, since we have seen that you have much *spirit* (courage) and have led us in the march under grenade fire, we wish to be commanded by you"' (Mussolini's italics and parenthesis). If examined through the grid of sociological categories, and in particular Max Weber's understanding of the charismatic leader, this small incident may be quite revealing. For Weber, charismatic leadership is a form of authority which differs radically from scientifically verifiable bureaucratic leadership and from traditional leadership which derives its authority from the past. It is legitimated by the followers after they have received some sort of proof of the qualities of their prospective leader through a heroic, supernatural or superhuman act (Weber, 1968, I: 241–2). Both the heroic act on Mussolini's part and the recognition of this on the part of the peasant soldier have clearly occurred in the above incident. Other factors justify interpreting this episode along these lines. On 15 October Mussolini informed his readers that 'in war, money is frowned upon. Whoever has any sends it home.' This finds direct resonance in Weberian theory, according to which the charismatic community is one which is 'specifically foreign to economic considerations' (Weber, 1968, I: 244). Also, the peasant soldier who addressed Mussolini did so using the first person plural. He was therefore speaking on behalf of a wider group of soldiers which formed the social base of the charismatic relationship.

We have so far isolated what for anthropologist Clifford Geertz is the role of religious symbols in fusing the worldview of a community with its ethos. By 'worldview' is meant 'the picture [it has] of the way things in sheer actuality are, [its] most comprehensive ideas of order' (Geertz, 1975: 89). Mussolini's war diary community saw itself in essentially Mazzinian terms, as a fully realized lay religious national community which had been resurrected to life from the ashes of the old, 'dead' Italy. By 'ethos' Geertz means 'the tone, character, and quality of [the community's] life, its moral and aesthetic style and mood' (Geertz, 1975: 91). The war diary community's ethos was its group solidarity, its morally based kinship which was emotionally charged by the common danger of death and the readiness to sacrifice for one's brothers in arms. Mussolini was recognized by the peasant soldiers as the charismatic champion of their cause and all of these themes were crystallized in the baptism ceremony on the Isonzo.

Problematic Passages: Charisma, Myth and Ideology

However, other processes are at work in the diary which suggest that Mussolini's portrayal of a fraternal warrior community is somewhat forced. For example, Mussolini's claim to the effect that the soldiers had finally come to recognize themselves as part of Italy can be seriously questioned. As Antonio Gibelli has argued in his analysis of peasant soldiers' letters, the likelihood exists that a peasant soldier's reference to 'Italy' was decidedly confused. 'High Italy' was used by peasants for areas close to or beyond the old pre-war border, while the term 'Italy' was applied to that part of the country which was not the front (Gibelli, 1998: 148ff). Moreover, in the handful of diary entries preceding the Isonzo baptismal ceremony we find little or nothing corresponding to an ideal fraternal order. At most we have a declaration that the morale of the troops in the barracks is 'not negative' (9 September); a court martial (11 September); a pep talk by the lieutenant colonel which was so paternalistic that it even offended Mussolini (12 September); and a near fight among the soldiers themselves (16 September). An examination of this fight reveals that it was over the fact that two gunners were telling other soldiers that the war was going badly for Italy and the Entente. Mussolini wrote that the two soldiers 'shut up in time', thus avoiding 'an energetic beating'. Actually, they avoided not only that: a relatively minor case of diffusion of 'false and alarming news' could warrant, say, four months' hard labour in a military prison (Forcella and Monticone, 1998: 138). The point, at any rate, is that the incident revealed a lack of internal harmony and hinted at physical violence. In this regard it is important to note that rites of passage can be interpreted as the symbolic means through which a society makes sense of, and controls, the danger inherent in the transition from one social state to another (Brain, 1977). A reassessment of the central role of Mussolini in the rite of passage underlines the full implications of this 'danger' for understanding the ideological character of the war diary.

To begin with, there are a number of important divergences between Mussolini's charismatic community and persona on the one hand, and Weber's typology on the other. For example, the description of a court martial in the entry of 11 September demonstrates a legal-rational structure, whereas for Weber a charismatic community 'is specifically irrational in the sense of being foreign to all rules' (Weber, 1968, I: 244). Moreover, missing from the relationship between Mussolini and the peasant soldiers portrayed on 17 September as recognizing his heroic qualities is a fundamental component which renders that relationship charismatic in the strictest Weberian sense. For Weber, in genuine charisma the recognition by a following does not constitute the foundation of legitimacy; rather, the recognition is a *duty* for those who have been called, by virtue of the appeal and the proof, to recognize the genuineness of the charismatic authority and to act accordingly (Weber, 1968, I: 242). With the peasant soldiers we see only faith in the heroic leader. On 2 November Mussolini noted that the peasant soldiers accepted the war 'as a duty not to be discussed'. He mentioned also that he had 'never heard them speaking of neutrality or intervention' and was convinced that 'they are unaware of the existence of these words'. In short, the soldiers' response to the call up was no doubt that of anti-war peasants unable to give an organized response to the State's imposition of universal military service. Their sense of 'duty', if one can call it that, was decidedly passive and was not connected to Mussolini's charisma.

It might be argued that we are stretching Weber's model beyond its limits, in that for him the charismatic leader is an 'ideal type', an abstract amalgam of the characteristics of any number of individuals which serves not as a reflection of social reality but as a heuristic means against which reality can be measured (Weber, 1968, I: 4ff). However, the above inconsistencies may derive from the anachronistic nature of Weber's model itself. It has been argued that the German sociologist too readily applied his pre-industrial and anti-bureaucratic abstract model to what he himself considered rational and bureaucratic capitalist times, thus over-stressing the potentially revolutionary character of modern charisma (Ake, 1966/67; Oomen, 1967/68). For Gramsci, individual leaders, however charismatic, are subordinated to the political organizations in and through which modern day social forces pursue their interests. This means that, when they do appear, charismatic individuals function to keep their following within politically controllable confines (Gramsci, 1979: 129–30). Arthur Schweitzer argues that it is through the perception of a modern charismatic leader's 'revolutionary' heroic gestures and actions that the basis for political stabilization or even reaction is laid (Schweitzer, 1974); meanwhile according to Carl Friedrich charisma is not a type of *leadership* at all, but a type of *power* (Friedrich, 1961), whereas Weber's methodological ide-alism led him to focus on the charismatic *individual* as distinct from the *message* conveyed through charisma (Ratnam, 1964; Cohen, 1972).

It might be further objected that we are not privy to what went on in the minds of the peasant soldiers in relation to Mussolini's charisma and a sense of 'duty'. But the significance of social relations represented in a text lies not in their histor-ical truth or falsity, 'but in how they contribute to the fashioning and perpetuation of a particular process of signification' (Eagleton, 1976: 74). Crucial here is the concept of ideology, as defined in the Introduction, and its relation to the repre-sentation of lived relations. According to Louis Althusser, 'the form in which we are made to see ideology . . . has as its content the "lived" experience of individ-uals' (Althusser, 1971: 204–5). From this point of view, Mussolini's war diary is a mythopoeic construction of charismatic power presented as a real life relation with the peasant soldiers, while *Il Popolo d'Italia* is the vehicle through which the message conveyed through charisma – that is a politically passive form of popular mobilization which does not impinge upon dominant social and political relations – entered the social realm in more or less real time (the section of the dairy under examination was published in six batches, on 28, 30 December 1915 and 1, 3, 5, 9 January 1916). Is this how Mussolini understood his charismatic function?

An examination of the 21 September diary entry suggests that it was. On that occasion Mussolini transcribed a letter he had received from a worker soldier whom he had met while marching to the front. Clearly politically self-mobilized, the worker (who described himself as such) wrote about the struggles between neutralists and interventionists and claimed that when the war broke out he con-sciously linked '"thought to action"'. Recalling his meeting with Mussolini he concluded: '"You left me your signature, but more than that I feel in my heart and in my soul a living light and happiness which I will never forget and which will accompany me until the completion of the Nation's destiny."' The worker's duty-bound recognition of Mussolini's charismatic qualities was clearly more in line with Weber's understanding of the charismatic relationship. However, what the soldier said about 'the struggle between neutralists and interventionists' remains a mystery, since Mussolini edited it out of his transcription. Mussolini also skipped over what had been discussed at their encounter. Furthermore, the worker soldier's literacy, his expressed thirst for knowledge and his awareness of political and class consciousness were of little concern to Mussolini who when speaking of him used the same paternalistic terms adopted for the peasants on 17 September when they asked to be led by him, that is *'Sancta simplicitas!'* (Mussolini's italics). Mussolini referred to the 'moving simplicity' of the worker soldier's letter, which he described as typical of the 'humble soldiers of Italy'. In short, the politics of social class in relation to the war was removed by Mussolini so as to arrive at the real point of this diary entry: his own charisma and its mesmerizing but politically innocuous effect on the worker soldier.

Another example is the entry of 31 October 1915 in which Mussolini reported a conversation he had with a soldier who had been abroad and since returned to Italy. He did not say why or when this soldier returned. He may have been one of the approximately 5,800,000 counted in the 1911 census as living in the Italian diaspora (Salvetti, 1987: 287, n. 23) and who had since returned home for one reason or another. Alternatively, he may have been among the approximately 500,000 men who between August and November 1914 returned to Italy following the 6 August 1914 decree which demanded that those subject to call up make their way home. However, almost all of the latter were from Europe (Salvetti, 1987: 283), whereas the soldier mentioned by Mussolini had spent six years in North America. In any case, despite writing on 1 November that among the soldiers in general 'there are those who are more alert and cultivated. They are those who were abroad, in Europe or America', Mussolini did not accredit this prodigal son of Italy with any such intelligence. The soldier in question declared himself republican and Mussolini asked why. '"Because I was in New York"', replied the ex-emigrant. Mussolini commented: 'The fact of the matter is that he doesn't even know the meaning of the word "republic". He's also almost illiterate.' Yet Mussolini did not explain the meaning of republicanism to that soldier. He merely added that the soldier was courageous and that 'his slanging matches with his stretcher bearer colleague keep the rest of the brigade's spirits up'.

It does not matter that this latter example does not involve the effects of Mussolini's personal charisma on the 'republican' soldier. What counts is that this incident confirms the nature of the *message* transmitted via charisma when it does appear: namely Mussolini was not concerned to encourage the political self-mobilization of soldiers from the labouring classes having assumed their passivity in advance. In particular, his own ambiguous position on the Monarchy (see Chapter 2) meant that he was not going to get bogged down in discourses about republicanism. His charisma served as a mobilizational substitute for discussion with worker and peasant soldiers about the war's social and political significance for them *as* peasants and workers. Hence while the war diary represents social relations as spontaneously lived, they are in fact a construct of ideology. To what degree did this ideological project find resonance in the liminal phase of the rite of passage?

The Margin Revisited: Awaiting the Offensive

We saw earlier that Mussolini ascribed a central place to injured soldiers in his literary construction of an Italy reborn in the real and symbolic confrontation with death. Of the ninety countable injuries men mentioned in his war diary between September and November 1915 (others are quantified as 'a few' or 'many' and are therefore excluded from our calculation), seventy-three (81.1 per cent) were from artillery, twelve (13.3 per cent) from bullets and five (5.5 per cent) from hand bombs. We need not for the moment draw any conclusions from these figures. First, rather, it is important to note that the early war diary entries confirm Mussolini's lack of knowledge of the weapon which predominates in the above figures – artillery. On 13 September he wrote of 'a cannon of spectacular proportions' without, however, specifying its calibre. Four days later he heard shells whistling through the air and only described their 'formidable' character, not their type. Things began to change on 20 September: 'Climbing back up the hill, I pass near the kitchens. There is an enormous unexploded 305.' Even greater aptitude is evident by 14 October when he heard 'twenty strikes of the [Austrian] 280' after which he stated that the daily firing of the Austrian 'cannonette' (*cannoncino*) meant that 'it has become familiar to us: it's a 75 mm mountain cannon.' In the entry of 18 October his expertise was undoubted:

> There go our 75s. They have a hissing sound and a dry and angry explosion. The 149s are powerful. The detonation of their shells is almost jovial in its profundity. The 210s have a brief and muffled roar. Then there's our rather nice 305. It comes from afar, from beyond the mountains, like a pilgrim. It passes over our heads slowly and solemnly. You can follow it along its journey with your ear. The parting blow cannot be heard so far off is it, but we hear its arrival. The explosion of an Italian 305 makes the mountains tremble.

By 25 October he could add to the list: 'Guns of all calibre types are in function: 65, 75, 155, 280.'

Again, we need not for the moment conclude anything from this and will proceed, rather, to bring these considerations to bear on the categories of movement and death. In the very first war diary entry (9 September) we discover not only that 'nobody can say' where the soldiers were going, but that 'this doesn't matter. The essential thing is to move.' Knowledge of what one was doing in the war was here subordinated to movement towards undefined destinations. We have no overt mention in this section of the war diary of the vast territorial claims which Mussolini argued for before Italian intervention. Elements of a Mazzinian irredentist war are present, for example in the chorus of a soldier's song transcribed on 14 October which went: "'Trento and Trieste, I will take you back.'" As regards deaths, there is nothing akin to mass industrialized extermination in this section of the war diary. In Mussolini's account there are twenty-nine countable deaths (again, there were more, but as with injuries these are specified as 'a few' or 'many'), of which artillery was the biggest single cause, accounting for ten. Mussolini accorded a privileged position to the dead in his war diary. On 18 September he noted that four or five crosses of a collective grave bore no names: 'Poor dead', he wrote, 'buried in these impervious and solitary mountain ranges. I will carry your memory in my heart forever.' Crucially, too, on 19 September the company captain said: "'These lands were and are ours. We have re-conquered them. Not without spilling blood. Just this night a bloody Austrian mine buried many of my Bersaglieri.'" Blood, death and vague territorial discourses ('these lands') are here combined, pointing to the possibility that unspecified territorial expansion lies at the heart of the present and future kinship morality of the idealized warrior community being forged in the second phase of the rite of passage. What evidence is there for this?

The theme of 'movement' is central here. In the early war diary entries, when the concept still prevailed as Mussolini was on the move from the rear to the front and from mountain to mountain, trench life formed part of the forging of national spirit. In the 19 September entry we read that:

> When, in Italy, one spoke of trenches, thoughts ran to the English ones in the low plains of Flanders, furnished with all the comforts, not excluding, or so it was said, heating systems. But ours, here, 2,000 metres above sea level, are rather different. We're talking about holes dug in the rocks, dugouts exposed to bad weather. Everything provisional and fragile. It's truly a war of giants that the extremely strong soldiers of Italy are fighting.

But by early October Mussolini had come to realize that this was a war of stasis, a fact of life which conflicted with his overriding concern to see an offensive get underway. On 8 October he was convinced that 'an advance is imminent', but with no prospect of this in the immediate offing we discover a more negative side to trench life. He wrote on 11 October that 'life in the trenches is the natural life, primitive. A bit monotonous', and the following day he remarked that rain and fleas were 'the real enemies of the Italian soldier'. Against this, word of possible manoeuvres was said to reanimate the soldiers. On 13 October Mussolini wrote that 'news is spreading among the squads that soon there will be "action". The news does not depress, but raises spirits. It is the prolonged inaction which unnerves the Italian soldier. Better, infinitely better, to be *firing upon* than to be *fired upon*' (Mussolini's italics). In the same entry Mussolini transcribed a passage from a Bersaglieri song which called on the traditional plumes in the corps' hat to 'kiss my burning cheeks . . . and repeat to me: Forward! Forward!' But it was the Italians who were subject to enemy fire, and on 17 October Mussolini documented:

> High calibre [enemy] artillery causes less victims, perhaps, than those of medium or small calibre, but it exercises a depressing influence on the spirit of the soldiers. The infantryman feels disarmed, impotent against the cannon. When artillery strikes our position, everyone is like a condemned man. The whistle announces the projectile and each soldier asks: 'Where will it explode?' Against the cannon no defence is possible, beyond, that is, the 'shelters' which are not very deep and even less solid. They are stones piled together with sods of earth. You must remain immobile, count the hits and wait for the bombardment to finish. The cannon also upsets the soldier for another reason: the type of injuries it produces. Rifle or machine gun bullets do not mutilate in the same way as the projectile of a cannon.

In a rather contradictory fashion, therefore, the modern technology required for national regeneration and community building through the 'baptism of fire' and the confrontation with real and symbolic death through injury was the same technology that was contemporaneously depressing the morale of the men and impeding the 'movement' required to achieve a resurrected nation. How did this tension in Mussolini's text fare in the context of the Third Battle of the Isonzo?

On the day the offensive began (18 October) Mussolini wrote:

> The advance seems imminent. It's symptomatic! The Bersaglieri don't say 'combat', 'action' or 'battle'; no: they say 'advance'. It seems that for them it is already axiomatic, intuitive, necessary that one of our battles resolves itself in an advance. It isn't always like that. But the general and singular use of the term is another symptom of the spirit of aggressiveness that animates the Italian soldiers and their certainty of victory.

We are now well and truly out of the ambit of a supposedly spiritual, fraternal, self-sacrificing, altruistic and anti-militarist community and have entered one in which victory was to issue from an offensive which in turn was to be fuelled by a 'spirit of aggressiveness'. Mussolini noted how, against the depressing effects of enemy cannon, the sound of Italian guns made the Bersaglieri 'jump with joy'. But his optimism was soon belied. On 21 October Mussolini and his fellow soldiers were still undergoing 'long hours of waiting and immobility'. Two days later he completely overturned his earlier positive assessment of trench life, and now unequivocally expressed a growing conviction that the war of stasis and attrition undermined the recomposition of the soldiers into a new, idealized military community premised on the triumphant offensive:

Our war, like that of all the other nations, is a war of position, of attrition. A grey war. A war of resignation, of patience, of tenacity. By day you stay under the ground: it's only by night that you can live a bit more freely and tranquilly. All the decor of the old type of war has disappeared. The rifle itself is about to become useless. Enemy trenches are assaulted with bombs, with deadly hand grenades. This war is most antithetical to the 'temperament' of the Italians.

A detailed history of the Bersaglieri makes no mention of Mussolini's regiment in the fighting during the Third Battle of the Isonzo (Sema, 1997: 57–60). The official regiment diary counts 134 casualties (AUSSME, entries of 21 October–4 November inclusive), which is 0.2 per cent of total Italian losses in the offensive. With nothing to show for present military operations Mussolini reminisced on 2 November about the past, and in particular about the 11th Regiment's August 1915 conquest of the Plezzo basin and then Plezzo itself:

In the first months of the war, the Bersaglieri crossed the border, with songs on their lips and with fanfare heading the battalions. After two months rest at Serpenizza, the order to continue the advance finally came, and, despite a whirlwind of enemy cannon fire, the Bersaglieri quickly conquered the Plezzo basin and dug in 400 metres beyond the city which the Austrians then almost completely destroyed with grenades. Whenever the Bersaglieri narrate the episodes of that offensive, the satisfaction and enthusiasm of the conquest still vibrate in their words.

Rounding up all these considerations, and adopting literary-critical terminology supplied by Terry Eagleton (1976: 89), we could say that an aesthetic mode of presentation, in this case the original positive estimation of trench life, was forced to cede to the predominance of stasis. Mussolini's text rediscovered its lines of meaning, or resolved its 'problem', only by finding a 'solution' which, in reassessing trench life as negative, revealed the ideology of which the diary was an expression and which it was in turn reproducing. Dominant social and political relations were to be reaffirmed via politically passive, charisma-based mass mobilization and territorial expansion premised on a successful offensive. The nature of this authorial strategy is further evidenced by the fact that while Mussolini was prepared to negatively reframe his previously positive assessment of trench life, he did not use his increased knowledge of the power of modern artillery to alter his pre-war position on offensive warfare. Rather, he reaffirmed those assumptions by citing the excruciating effects of artillery as the fulcrum of his symbolic system of national rebirth through the spilling of blood, the incurring of serious injuries, the sacrifice of life and the nation-forging effects of emotional bonding deriving from the shared confrontation with real and symbolic death in the liminal phase of the rite of passage.

Mussolini, the NCOs and Ideology

As we saw earlier, Mussolini argued that it was the officers, and in particular captains, lieutenants and non-commissioned lieutenants, who provided the cement of the fraternal order and guaranteed its popular, anti-militarist, socially horizontal and fraternal character. It should be noted, however, that in August 1914 in the fighting forces almost all captains (4,042) were professional soldiers as were 6,978 subalterns (Rochat, 1991: 114). These were therefore going to bring their army values, and not their civilian ones (as argued by Mussolini), to bear on their conduct when commanding men at war. If at all, the latter values would be brought by the NCOs. What, then, was the sociological composition of captains, lieutenants and non-commissioned lieutenants? And to what worldview did they generally adhere?

It has been estimated that between 1898 and 1915, 49.4 per cent of men who graduated from the artillery and engineering military academy in Turin were from the middle bourgeoisie or the nobility, though at that stage the latter's social condition was for the most part equivalent to the former's. The 43.3 per cent of graduates whose social position was undefined were also most likely middle class in social status if not in economic condition (Langella, 1988). Career officers were therefore primarily bourgeois, urban and linked to industry, commerce and public functions (Rochat, 1991: 33–5). These considerations are generally valid both for the Turin academy and for the school of infantry and cavalry in Modena, which produced the majority of officers. In the latter case, however, the years between 1904 and 1910 witnessed a decrease in the city component (pay was better in the industrial sector) which accounts for what was a rise in the admissions from the south of Italy from 30.06 to 34.12 per cent. However, this 'southernization' of the army, so central to John Whittam's thesis concerning the army's mental obtuseness and aversion to change in the lead up to the First World War (Whittam, 1977: Ch. 10), while certainly evident before 1914 was not in fact completed until after the European conflagration (Balestra, 1993).

But, even assuming a radical decrease in the aristocratic social component with respect to the bourgeoisie, this did not signify either social or ideological democratization of the Italian army. The exclusion of the labouring classes was guaranteed by the educational requirements and the unaffordable fees. Also virtually excluded, therefore, was the petty bourgeoisie, since salaries of council or bank clerks were equivalent to the costs of military college courses (Maciulli, 1993a). Only 7.3 per cent of graduates from the Turin academy between 1898 and 1914 are thought to have been petty bourgeois, almost all of whom were from families of State employees (Langella, 1988: 329). Grants certainly existed for less well off families, but these were almost always given to sons of army or navy officers, sons of State bureaucrats who had been killed in action or sons of war medal holders.

In short, the army chose who received the scholarships and did so using criteria of professional corporatism, patriotism, loyalty to the King and the reproduction of the military caste and its values (Maciulli, 1993b: 559). Hence as Piero Del Negro argues, there was no co-existence of 'aristocratic' and 'democratic' models in the Italian Army, *pace* Whittam. The officer corps formed part of the conservative and reactionary bourgeois-aristocratic bloc represented by the executive power and headed by the King (Del Negro, 1979; 1988).

Nothing much alters when we assess the politico-military culture of the non-commissioned lieutenants and junior lieutenants. The literature of this category reveals not a guarantor of the war's popular character, but a profoundly paternalistic and self-centred stratum which saw itself as the fount of all knowledge and the patient sufferer of the shortcomings of all and sundry. Our knowledge of the military experience and perceptions of the peasant and worker soldiers is limited by the fact that our image of them is based on information passed on by NCO writers (Isnenghi and Rochat, 2000: 269ff). The peasant soldier is generally portrayed as 'naturally' resigned because the NCO saw himself as a 'natural' mediator with the 'natural' right to demand submission to his orders which he himself had been ordered to administer. We are dealing with what Mario Isnenghi has called the 'myth of subordination' or the 'ideology of resignation', a 'dehistoricization' process whereby the 'static vision of social relations' held by the High Command was rationalized and then reproduced by its NCO representatives on the ground (Isnenghi, 1970: Ch. 3).

There is evidence in Mussolini's war diary to suggest that he was one such medium through which the professional officers' static vision of social relations was filtered. In the entry of 3 October he was ordered by his captain to rewrite a resolution which the captain himself had drafted and which eulogized 'the spirit of comradeship' between old and young soldiers in his company. The resolution in question said that the comradeship was functional to the '"vision of those shining ideals of Nation and family, which will in their turn be the most appropriate prize for the sacrosanct duty performed."' To diffuse family, nation and duty slogans was the reason why, on 12 April 1915, Cadorna had readmitted the clergy to the army after its expulsion between 1865 and 1878 (Morozzo della Rocca, 1980: Ch. 1). The captain's motion amounted to the same programme. In the note which he wrote to Mussolini informing him not just to redraft the original resolution but how to redraft it, we read that this was to be '"in the way most felt by [the soldiers'] simple and good spirit."' Paternalistic (the soldiers' 'simple and good' spirit) and socially conservative perspectives ('shining ideals', not social reform, would be the prize for duty) originating in the military caste were here passed down the ranks by and through Mussolini. And Mussolini concurred with the resolution's content: 'I ask myself: "But isn't [the captain's resolution] already beautiful? What can I say that could improve on it?" However, I obey.'

Two questions arise here. First, is it possible that Mussolini's cultural and political detachment from the men was counterbalanced by full identification with the junior officers? Secondly, if he was to all intents and purposes an 'officer' even though officially a private, how did his literary construct of his own charisma correspond to the junior officers' approach to mobilization?

The answer to the first question is affirmative. Mussolini in fact applied to become a non-commissioned junior lieutenant and from his war diary we know that he was called to officer training school on 6 November 1915. But the entry of 14 November reveals that he was ordered to go back to the front with no explanation and no promotion. In a 13 January 1916 letter to Salandra, Zuppelli informed the Prime Minister that he had been furnished with documentation relative to Mussolini's 'deplorable' past as a political militant (ACS, PCM, *Guerra Europea*, b. 19, fasc. 4, s.fasc. 1, prot. 4). Mussolini nevertheless paid little heed to his objective rank, locating himself squarely in the socio-military ambit of the junior officers, and they in turn recognized him as one of their own. On 19 September: 'Some officers want to meet me. Here's junior Lieutenant Giraud. Young and valorous . . . "I'd like to have you in the seventh company", Giraud tells me.' On 22 September: 'Captain Mozzoni calls me to his tent. I find Lieutenant Fava of the 27th battalion with him. Long, friendly conversation.' Mussolini and his newspaper campaign for intervention had found resonance among precisely this sector. On 16 September: 'A medical captain seeks me out among the ranks. "I want to shake the hand of the Editor of *Il Popolo d'Italia*."' Three days later: '"Is Bersagliere Mussolini here?" "I'm Mussolini." "Come here, I want to embrace you." And we embrace. It's Captain Festa of the 10th company of the 157th infantry . . . "Your newspaper campaign for intervention honours you and Italian journalism."' A couple of lines later a southern university student affirmed: '"Who would ever have thought that I'd find myself with Mussolini as a private! I'll write to my father about it immediately. He often spoke to me about you."' On 30 September: 'I brought some back issues of *Il Popolo d'Italia* to Captain Mozzoni, since he asked me for them.' On 24 October Mussolini was called to an officer's tent and invited to remain for dinner: 'Restaurant menu: "Rice, roast meat, omelette, fruit, dessert. Wines: Chianti and Grignolini in bottles."'

Coming now to the second of the above questions, an analysis of the mobilizational methods of the officers reveals an absence of socio-political discourse and a role for abstract, demagogic or tear-jerking speeches, and the recounting or carrying out of valorous feats. This practice permeated down through the ranks. On 19 September Mussolini wrote that the major gave a morale-boosting talk which was 'affectionate and touching'. The captain's talk which followed was 'frank and emotional' and 'touched the depth of our hearts'. The captain in fact spoke to the soldiers of the '"memorable gestures"' of the regiment to which they belonged. That same day Mussolini wrote of a meeting with a junior lieutenant who began to narrate how he had taken command of a '"furious battle which lasted 20 hours"' and which had wound up as a '"deadly and indescribable man-to-man."' On 16 September we read of an 'afternoon of chat. Episodes of war. Unanimous exaltation of the Alpini.' Mussolini identified with corporals and sergeants in the same way, and they, too, furnished accounts of valour. On 8 October: 'I meet up again with Lieutenant Fava who introduces me to the captain of his company, Jannone. Friends from other battalions – as soon as they hear of our arrival – come looking for me. Corporal Major Bocconi . . . Corporal Major Strada . . . Corporal Giustina Sciarra, from Isernia, comes looking for me as he wants to meet me.' In an entry of 18 September 1915, we read: 'This morning they divided us into the three companies of the battalion. The operation was long. Some corporals and sergeants helped us pass the time by recounting glorious episodes of the 11th Bersaglieri during the first months of the war.' And when, on 29 October, Mussolini himself called for propaganda among the soldiers, he limited this to 'communications from our Army and those of the allied nations, together with a few articles and accounts of valorous episodes, with a view to keeping morale high among the troops'.

To conclude, it has been argued that in the modern world the aesthetic may serve an ideological function by producing an 'ineffable reciprocity of feeling' which 'encode[s] emotive attitudes relevant to the reproduction of social power' (Eagleton, 1986: 75, 95). The section of Mussolini's war diary examined in the present chapter had precisely that function. The inception of the new, indicated by the symbolism of the Isonzo baptismal scene and by the creation of an idealized military community in this opening phase of the war, was only apparent, and the existing social and political system was in fact left untouched. What Gramsci described as the 'nerveless', 'dispersed' and 'crisis-ridden' basis for the emergence of modern charismatic and mythical mobilizing figures – in this case the transitional 'danger' represented by anti-war sentiment among the men or possible peasant and worker demands for social change in exchange for risking their lives – was rechannelled into, and ostensibly contained, by the symbolic world of the rite of passage. Together with appeals for futile offensive operations, feeling was evoked as the lowest common denominator to deal with military stasis, the warfare of attrition, the destructive power of artillery and, most importantly, as a surrogate for democratic discourses among peasant and worker soldiers. Where the 'new Italy' was to differ from the old one was in its territorial enlargement, and indeed the baptismal ceremony on the Isonzo took place in newly conquered territory. But another important rupture with the past was that the socially hierarchical, paternalistic and profoundly conservative worldview of the Italian State was not to be imposed solely using force. Rather, the warrior community hinged on the emotion-based self-mobilization of captains and non-commissioned lieutenants and, most importantly, on the charismatic figure of Mussolini himself. This emotionally and symbolically charged but socially and politically conservative nation at war was then presented to readers of *Il Popolo d'Italia* as a spontaneously lived and functioning series of social relations which had been passively accepted by soldiers from the labouring classes. In turn, the readers of *Il Popolo d'Italia* appear to have been from those very sectors of the middle and lower middle classes that provided the junior officers of which Mussolini was one in all but name.

–4–

Digging In
November 1915–June 1916

For all measures, even the most difficult, that the Government will take, we will place the following dilemma before the citizens: either accept them out of high patriotic spirit or have them imposed.

Mussolini, Reply to the Minister for Finance, 7 March 1923

Consent is as variable as the sand on the sea shore . . . Posed as axiomatic that all government measures create malcontents, what will you do to prevent the disquiet from spreading and representing a danger for the solidity of the State? You will avoid it by resorting to force.

Mussolini, *Forza e consenso*, March 1923

No hierarch is he who does not know how to go down among the people in order to glean its sentiments and interpret its needs.

Mussolini, Speech at the Foro, 28 October 1937

Home Front, November 1915–February 1916

On 24 November Mussolini developed a viral infection (or so it is presumed, since this remains an open question, for which see O'Brien, 2002a: 13, n. 48) and was transferred to the military hospital in Cividale where he remained for thirteen days, upon which he was transferred to Treviglio (about 60 km from Milan) for further treatment. He had therefore left the front line community and was distant from the final spasm of the Fourth Battle of the Isonzo. Mussolini was granted a month's convalescent leave to expire on 16 January. He did not, however, reach the front until 11 February. The period between 16 January and 11 February has never been adequately accounted for, though it seems that Mussolini spent some time in a Bersagliere depot on the way back to the front (Pini and Susmel, 1953, I: 306). Once back in Milan, he swapped the war diary for commentaries in *Il Popolo d'Italia*. The paper, for which circulation figures are not available, apparently remained on a sound financial basis, as Mussolini confirmed in a 19 January letter to his sister, Edwige (Mancini Mussolini, 1957: 57).

The home front to which Mussolini returned was beginning to confront the military stalemate and dashed hopes of immediate victory. During his sojourn he contributed to the 'war culture' that was created in Italy as in other belligerent societies. This phenomenon emerged as an expression of the 'total' nature of the First World War and the 'brutalization' of conflict which it provoked in the collective imagination as on the battlefield. It was a vision based on a simplified and extreme polarization of the nation and its enemies. At one end of the cosmos stood a negative image of the enemy as an ideological absolute, as the supreme evil, an aggressor, an out and out barbarian and a veritable menace to humanity and to civilization. At the other stood the supreme good, the national collective, the righteous allies and the just war for freedom and national defence. Then there was the obverse of the nation/enemy dichotomy, that is the enemy within, whose scheming and plotting undermined national will and played the game of the external foe. Finally, all this was measured over against sacrifice, defined principally (but not solely) by the suffering and death of the soldier for the salvation of the nation. Hence 'war culture' represented a cultural mobilization, a mustering and focusing of hatred for the enemy and a subsequent and interrelated reinforcement of pro-national and pro-war sentiment and identity (Becker, J.-J., Becker, A., Audoin-Rouzeau, Krumeich, Winter, 1994: 7–10; Audoin-Rouzeau and Becker, 1997; Horne, 1999: 331–3).

To these elements of 'war culture' Mussolini added the voice of the veteran who bore direct witness to the soldiers' sacrifice. He conceptually polarized the external enemy on 24 December by presenting Germany as the real culprit behind the war aims of the Central Powers even though Italy was only at war with Austria-Hungary, and by arguing that any German-inspired peace would be a peace on German terms (OO, VIII: 206–9). Mussolini also developed the subordinate category of allies. In an end-of-year analysis he gave a positive assessment of the Entente in contrast to the Central Powers (OO, VIII: 214–16). As regards the internal enemies, on 27 December he showed his readiness to resort to vitriol to condemn them as traitors. He denounced 'the saboteurs . . . of the national war', warning that 'the impatient should take note and avoid depressing – in any way – the spirit of the nation'. He added that 'we need to put a brake on abstract peace-loving propaganda' which was circulating '*even among fighting soldiers*' (Mussolini's emphasis), and insisted that 'whoever speaks of peace, when the Nation is engaged in a life and death struggle, consciously or unconsciously helps the enemy', and that '*Gémir, c'est trahir!*' (OO, VIII: 210–13).

The background to this last statement is undoubtedly that during the fifteen–day winter leave periods granted after the Fourth Battle of the Isonzo the experiences suffered at the front by officers and men strongly contrasted with the normal bar- and theatre-going activities of the middle classes which soldiers observed in the cities. Soldiers met with statements and questions from people, including loved ones, which more often than not revealed a substantial ignorance of what was happening at the front. Two differing worlds of representation interacted to produce negative effects among both soldiers and civilians. In a circular of 12 January 1916 Cadorna accused the soldiers of spreading bad news, warned that offenders would be severely punished, and even considered suspending leave permits (Melograni, 1969: 95–104). It is difficult to know for sure if Mussolini's 27 December invective was also aimed at the soldiers on leave. Either way, in using the word 'unconsciously' he appears to have extended the olive branch to the internal enemies, suggesting that a window of opportunity was open for them to become aware of the deleterious effects of their actions and consequently to mend their ways. In the same piece he proposed that the government should not resort to openly coercive measures against those who were sapping the national energy but adopt 'purely administrative means'. Alarmists, he claimed, could be silenced by explaining that the lack of major gains was a result of the war's military character, while a purge of the 'Giolittian bureaucracy' would furnish 'the example from above' which would have 'immediate and almost automatic repercussions below' (OO, VIII: 210–13).

Nonetheless, the continued neutralism of the PSI remained Mussolini's principal target. His condemnation of even the most critical elements of German social democracy was a veiled warning that international contacts during the war by Italian socialists would amount to playing the enemy's game (OO, VIII: 206–9). On 4 January he confronted the PSI directly with the impossibility of remaining neutral in an international conflict between democracy and reaction (OO, VIII: 217–19). Four days later he rejected Claudio Treves' theory according to which neither the Entente nor the Central Powers was conducting a democratic war and hence the temporal power of the Papacy would be reinforced regardless of who won. Mussolini accepted, 'for the simple love of polemic', that the war being fought by the Entente was not a democratic one, but then presented Treves with the blunt choice between the two belligerent blocs: 'Is there more "democracy" in the regimes of the Quadruple Entente or the Quadruple enemy?' His point was that should the Central Powers win, the world would return not to the pre-Franco-Prussian war days but to the days before the French Revolution. Again, however, while Mussolini accused the socialists of 'consciously' working to facilitate the victory of the enemy, he added the adverbs 'more or less' and put the word 'worked' in inverted commas, thereby attenuating the accusation. In the main, this article was against the Papacy's neutrality and tried to get Treves and the PSI to draw pro-Entente conclusions from their anti-Vatican standpoint (OO, VIII: 220–23).

The final aspect of the 'war culture' elaborated by Mussolini was the invocation of the front line soldiers as the fulcrum of the national effort. Mussolini projected himself as both embodiment and witness of the soldiers' experience, and of the supreme virtue of sacrifice for the nation that it represented. During his convalescent leave *Il Popolo d'Italia*, as noted, published his war diary. This process, as we argued in the previous chapter, was mythopoeic, deliberately endowing Mussolini with the persona of the front line hero. The process had some effect. Scrutiny of *Avanti!* and *La Stampa* shows that they ignored the war diary. But on 4 January *Il Corriere della Sera*, the leading paper of the Milanese élites and middle classes, quoted two passages from the 18 October entry. One of these pointed to the stoicism of the injured and the other to the elevation of morale on hearing one's own artillery go into action. On 9 January *Il Popolo d'Italia* published two letters, the first of which was from a certain Prof. A. Francisi who on reading Mussolini's war diary claimed to have completed his transition to interventionism. The other was from a soldier on the Carso who had been reading the diary and wished Mussolini well. The following day, Mussolini's paper published a letter from Lieutenant Giraud, Mussolini's direct superior who was out of action through injury and who thanked Mussolini for referring to him in such kind terms. By the same token, however, Mussolini had to defend his construction of a front line persona against sceptics and scoffers. His catholic and socialist opponents naturally seized on anything they could to discredit his military pretensions. For example, in late December *Il Mattino* of Naples (a catholic paper) suggested that Mussolini had been nominated as a junior lieutenant in the territorial militia, had attended officer school, and from there had gone to the front where 'his weak constitution did not resist the discomforts'. It added that he had written an emotional letter to the editors of *Il Popolo d'Italia* lamenting the fact that he had been struck not by the enemy but by a microbe in a glass of water. It finished by announcing that he had been declared unfit for combat and that he would most likely be returning to journalism (Anon, 1915). This attack was responded to by Arturo Rossato of *Il Popolo d'Italia*, who pointed out that Mussolini was and always had been a private. Rossato further emphasized that Mussolini had not been pronounced unfit for further duties at the front and that he had never written a moving letter, as this was not in his nature (Arros, 1915).

Overall, then, Mussolini followed the kind of propaganda drive that he considered himself especially capable of providing to stiffen civilian morale in the face of military difficulties. The demonized enemy within was necessary to stimulate such cohesion, but consensus was also crucial in forging an all-embracing ideology. That this was the case was seen again when, just before reaching his regiment in mid-February, Mussolini read of the incursion over Milan by Austrian aircraft, whose bombs killed a number of civilians. The editors of *Il Popolo d'Italia* had no difficulties identifying the guilty party. In their view, the government of Milan, headed by socialist mayor Emilio Caldara, had basically invited the Austrians in, had insured a major German company before the bombing, and had taken its time before informing citizens of the imminent raid. Mussolini wrote to his colleagues as follows:

That delay of over an hour in the telephone transmission announcing the arrival of the enemy aircraft is mysterious. So too is that *total* insuring of a German company made a few days beforehand ... Let the Germans come ... said and say the *red* neutralists, and the Germans arrive. Wasn't it only yesterday that mayor Caldara absented himself from the opening of the French hospital in Milan? ... [T]he *intimidators*, the *overhead* brigands count on their accomplices who are the *underground* saboteurs of the Nation's energy. (OO, VIII: 298–9; Mussolini's italics).

In reality, telegrams dated 15, 16, 17 and 18 February 1916 from the Civil Commissioner in Milan to the Ministry of the Interior reveal nothing of socialist plotting. They only note the immense participation of citizens and civilian authorities at the funerals of the fifteen dead (ACS, A5G, b. 18, fasc. 31, s.fasc. 1, ins. 19). If anything, the evidence from the press agencies suggests that at 08.30 the Command of Military Division informed the Telephone Office of the arrival of enemy aircraft, but that neither the Prefect, the police, the Mayor nor the fire brigade was subsequently informed in time (see, for example, *La Stampa* of 14 February 1916). Hence the slow response was of military origin. In a letter to Luigi Albertini of 17 February 1916, Colonel Giulio Douhet, a sharp critic of Cadorna who would later pay the price for his insubordination, argued that the defence of the many centres such as Milan was impossible, and that counter-missions by Italian aircraft against Austrian territory were the only solution, along with attacks on the Austrian aircraft as they left Italian territory (Albertini, 1968, II: 473–5). What the air incursions showed, therefore, was that without correct information to hand, Mussolini had a ready-made socialist scapegoat with which to explain away what were in fact serious shortcomings of the military command during an enemy invasion of national territory. And the latter would not be long in coming. In the meantime, Mussolini returned to the war.

Back to the Front: Coercion, Consent and Unholy Waters, February–May 1916

On returning to the front in February Mussolini was positioned in the same sector as in 1915, though further upriver. This area was involved in the Fifth Battle of the Isonzo between 11 and 15 March 1916, carried out in response to French requests for relief following the German attack at Verdun beginning 21 February. Mussolini was not involved in the offensive, since he went on winter leave beginning 2 March and did not return to the front until 23 of that month. In any case, due to bad weather the fifth offensive effectively failed to take off. As regards action, Mussolini was at most engaged in rifle fire exchanges (diary entries of 17, 19, 23 and 26 February). It was, nevertheless, an important period for Mussolini, as on 1 March he was promoted to corporal. The nomination, which he transcribed in his war diary on 29 February, reads as follows: 'For his exemplary activity, high Bersaglieresque spirit and calmness. Always first in every enterprise of work or daring. Heedless of discomforts, zealous and scrupulous in the carrying out of his duties.' Things were even quieter in the Carnia, where Mussolini was stationed from 25 March to 12 November. Fighting in the area between May and June and then in October 1915 had seen no significant gains by either side. When Mussolini arrived, serious operations had long ceased. Mussolini was stationed close to the north-western part of the sector, to the right of the river Bordaglia, with Mount Vas directly in front. On 10 May he recognized that 'this zone is perhaps the quietest of the entire front'. He was not under continuous artillery fire, most of which was going on in the distance, and he was directly involved in small skirmishes in only three entries (6, 15 and 26 April).

An important theme emerging from these militarily placid pages is Mussolini's ongoing concern with the rapport between coercion and consent in the reconstruction of the nation, an issue which had so marked his home front journalistic endeavour in the winter of 1915–16. Straight away on 15 February there is evidence of the army's intensification of repressive measures during a military tribunal. A sergeant was charged with desertion and the prosecutor asked for a life sentence. The tribunal rejected the charge and gave the sergeant twenty years for abandonment of post. A private was then brought before the judges on the same charge, but absolved. This diary entry is similar to the courtroom scene portrayed in the 11 September 1915 annotation, though something has undoubtedly altered in 1916 as regards the prosecutor's demands and the sentences meted out. In 1915 a soldier was accused of abandoning his post, but only one year's imprisonment was requested by the prosecutor and the soldier was acquitted by what Mussolini described as an indulgent, scrupulous and fraternal court. This rising curve of coercion reflected a growing rejection of the war on the part of the men, evidenced by an escalation in the number of convictions for desertions in the Italian Army as the war progressed: in the first year there were about 10,000, while in the second this rose to 28,000 (Forcella and Monticone, 1998: lxxv).

How did Mussolini deal with the rejection of the war on the part of his fellow soldiers? On 25 February he wrote of an attempted evasion of duty. An army doctor told him of a Sicilian soldier who claimed to have been placed under a spell while on leave. The soldier's symptoms were weakness, lack of appetite, pains and homesickness. He in fact came from an area where anti-military sentiment was rife. On the islands and in Sicily in 1914 only four out of twenty-seven provinces reported draft evasion levels *below* the national average (10.4 per cent), as compared to the centre-north where only six out of forty-two provinces reported absences *above* the national average (Del Negro, 1979: 231). According to Antonio Gibelli, the methodological framework in which forms of rejection need to be analyzed cannot, however, be solely that of war. A peasant's escape into anything from abandonment of post to self-inflicted injury is, in his view, better seen as rural rejection of modern society as crystallized in industrialized warfare. Homesickness was one of the forms which this type of rejection assumed, though this involved altogether different symptoms to those such as the melancholy which might arise on being away from home for extended periods. Rather, the normal symptoms fused with the horrors of industrialized warfare to create all types of hallucinations, including the sound of the voices of loved ones in cannon thunder and machine gun fire, or else the appearance of family members as visible images (Gibelli, 1998: 10, 30–34). Mussolini was not a psychoanalyst, but this hardly accounts for the dismissive manner in which he interpreted the Sicilian soldier's symptoms (which he did not detail): 'I understand how a Sicilian suffers from homesickness, homesickness for the sun among so much frost and snow!' Thus in a world where soldiers were 'responding to the collapse of meaning by seeking refuge in nonsense' (Isnenghi and Rochat, 2000: 249), Mussolini's authorial strategy was to remove the theme of refusal, to reject rejection, and to avoid the resort to coercion by making a nonsense out of what in reality was a serious incident, which was easily interpretable as an attempt to evade duty through simulation and thus potentially punishable with death by firing squad (Forcella and Monticone, 1998: 174–8).

Unlike the September–November 1915 or the February–March 1916 diary entries, the March–May 1916 Carnia section of the war diary furnishes no examples of rejection or consensus-building responses to it. Elements of intensified State repression are nevertheless visible. On 7 April Mussolini made a long entry which broke down a company at war into its morale-based components. Of the 250 men, 40 per cent – identifiable with the petty bourgeoisie and the professional classes, plus youth and men who returned from abroad – was said to fight the war willingly. Another 40 per cent accepted it with indifference, while 16 per cent was defined as oscillating between courageous and cowardly. The remaining 4 per cent was characterized in negative terms but as generally unwilling to reveal its point of view for fear of the military code. This is the point. Consensus building was achieved not only by non-coercive methods (heart-warming speeches by officers, accounts of valorous episodes, Mussolini's charisma, making a joke out of rejection of the war) but also by the power of military penal law to which Mussolini alluded.

The lack of action on the high Isonzo and the Carnia between February and May 1916 meant that Mussolini had few if no opportunities to reaffirm and reinforce his qualities as a charismatic hero warrior. On 16 February a peasant soldier came up to him and asked: '"Brother, is it true that we have come here for an offensive?"' Mussolini replied: '"I don't know. And what if we have?"' He urged the soldier to '"be brave"', reiterating that '"I know nothing."' Once again we are here witnessing rejection (the soldier is clearly apprehensive and does not at all relish the thought of a frontal assault), and a proposal for a non-coercive solution to it (firm but friendly encouragement). This incident sharply contrasts with the September 1915 meeting with the peasant soldiers who desired to be led by Mussolini on the basis of their recognition of Mussolini's heroic qualities (see Chapter 3). Moreover, there are no further references to peasants in the February–May 1916 section of the war diary. Worker soldiers appear only in an entry of 1 May, but not in a celebration of the international working-class holiday (which receives no mention). Rather, the reader is presented with the positive effects of militarized labour – a new road open to traffic. The absence of charisma in the February–May 1916 section thus reflects an intensification of the diary's strategy of reframing the nation in conservative social and political terms. Since workers and peasants have been further removed from the diary's social vision, there is no place for charisma in relation to them.

In the Carnia, Mussolini paid particular attention to culturally self-mobilized soldiers. On 30 March there is an account of a Tuscan soldier who had previously been declared a deserter. On Italian intervention, however, he decided for reasons of 'honour' and 'duty' to leave his sweet shop in Richmond, Virginia, and return home to stand a post. On 5 April we read of a Turkish-born soldier who expressed his identity as an Italian 'by race and sentiment' and who had also returned voluntarily to fight for Italy. On 10 April Mussolini transcribed a letter received by a soldier from his brother who had been in Canada and who had not received a reply from the consul to his request to be repatriated on war's outbreak. He therefore joined the British Army. This particular soldier's self-mobilization was based on his disdain for the 'German barbarians'. He declared his readiness to die in battle, hoping first, however, that 'a few Germans will pass through my hands'. Similar reasons for self-mobilization can be found in the 5 April entry where a seaman soldier (who had not returned from abroad) was said by Mussolini to fight the war willingly because he 'hates the Germans'. In all of these instances, political discourse is replaced by hatred for the enemy, issues related to national identity, 'sentiment', and/or military values such as 'honour' and 'duty'. Mobilization is culturally, not politically, informed.

When we examine the élitist corollary of Mussolini's de-emphasizing of the working classes, namely, his relations with the officers, nothing has changed with respect to 1915. Then as now the primary alternative to the harsh world of military justice was the officers. On 21 February a lieutenant recounted to Mussolini how his sergeant had panicked during incoming artillery fire. Rather than admonish the sergeant he stood up on the trench even though surrounded by exploding grenades and shrapnel: "'My fearless gesture encouraged the Bersaglieri more than any punishment or excitation would have done. When I returned soon after, I found sergeant Brenna impassable and fresh among the raging of enemy projectiles.'"

As in the previous year, Mussolini's contacts with the officers are informed by mutual recognition, fraternization, the recounting of valorous episodes, the handing out of copies of *Il Popolo d'Italia*, and a willingness to enter political discourse. One example from each section will suffice here. First the high Isonzo, 24 February: 'I bring a copy of [*Il Popolo d'Italia*] to the battalion commander, Major Tentori [who] recounts the heroic end of a corporal who . . . died saying "I know I'm dying, but I die content for Italy. Long live Italy!" ' Now the Carnia: 'I met the captain commanding the 4th company of sappers. I stayed with him for several hours. His name is Simoni. A Piedmontese, an anti-Giolittian and a fervent interventionist' (10 May). The reason for this ongoing identity with professional and non-commissioned officers while peasants and workers slip into the background is made abundantly clear in the Carnia, when on 3 May Mussolini reported how he had received a copy of Mazzini's writings. He transcribed the following lines from Mazzini's 1832 essay entitled *D'alcune cause che impedirono finora lo sviluppo della libertà in Italia* (Mazzini, 1976: 92–148):

> 'Missing were the leaders; missing were the few to lead the many, strong men of faith and sacrifice capable of wholly grasping the fragmented concept of the masses; capable of immediately understanding the consequences of this and who, boiling over with passion, could then forge these fragments into a sole concept, *that of victory*; who could unite the dispersed elements and find the word of life and order for all.' (Mussolini's emphasis)

Mussolini finished the entry by asking: 'But who among my 250 fellow soldiers knows [Mazzini's writings]?' The answer, of course, is: Mussolini and a handful of self-mobilized interventionists, one of whom gave him the Mazzini volume. Mussolini and the officers are this élite force which had been 'missing' in Italian history to that point. But while, as we saw in Chapter 2, this élitism bears many of the hallmarks of Mazzini's worldview, a further quotation from Mazzini, this time from his 1831 letter to Carles Albert of Savoy (Mazzini, 1976: 38–56), reveals most emphatically that Mussolini and the officers' élitist tasks were not altogether Mazzinian: '"Great things are not achieved with protocols, but rather by gauging one's own century. The secret of Power lies in Will."' Since Mazzini's letter was quite a long one, Mussolini's choice of this particular passage with its implications for the Nietzschean Superman's will to power needs no comment.

There is a further twist to this entry, since it connects directly into other themes related to morale, weaponry and offensive warfare ideology dealt with in the 7 April entry where he had remarked:

> The state of mind globally reducible to the term 'morale' is the fundamental coefficient of victory, and is pre-eminent in comparison to the technical or mechanical element. Who wants to win will win. Who disposes of the greater reserves of psychic and volitional energy will win. 100,000 cannons will not give victory if the soldiers are not

capable of going on the assault, if they don't have the courage at any given moment to 'expose themselves' and face death.

He concluded that in the last analysis the morale of Italian soldiers 'depends on that of the officers who command them', and that morale was therefore good. Mussolini claimed to know this because 'I have "studied" those around me . . . I have "caught" their discourses, isolated their spiritual behaviour in the most varied contingencies of time and place which war imposes on the soldier.' In short, on 7 April he had already been practising the élitist leader task which in his 3 May entry he then fortuitously 'discovered' to be a divination of Mazzini's. The Nietzschean will to power of the 3 May entry was, therefore, the ideology of an élitist group of 'Mazzinian' leaders who would take the fragmented concepts of the vast majority of the soldiers, funnel them into a singular concept of victory, and hence encourage the men to go fearlessly on a frontal bayonet assault against enemy cannon. The ideology of the offensive which in the 1915 section of the war diary was enveloped in the symbolic garb of the liminal phase of a rite of passage is here stated in its non-refracted nudity.

Why? During his movements to and in the Carnia Mussolini encountered numerous rivers, streams and torrents such as the Tagliamento, the But, the Bordaglia, the Volaja, the Fleons (or Degano) and the Dogna. Yet unlike the baptismal Jordan at the Isonzo in September 1915, no sacred qualities are conferred on any of these waters. Since no holy water flows through this territory, it is likely that the territory itself is not sacred. This, then, may explain why in Mussolini's war diary the Carnia does not readily lend itself to symbolic activity, thus providing more unmediated revelations about the socially vertical structures of the war community and its politically and militarily offensive strategy. Further weight is added to this view when we consider that the men who die or who are injured on that territory are reduced to the same non-sacred status as the water. Indeed, of the dead and injured reported in the Carnia between 25 March and 14 May 1916, none are worked into a symbolic system of national rebirth. They are merely reported dead or injured. By contrast, on the high Isonzo, on 15 February, Mussolini reported a visit to the cemetery at Caporetto and noted that on the side of the church wall was inscribed: '"To reclaim the sacred terms which nature posed on the border of the Nation they fearfully faced glorious death. Their generous blood renders sacred this redeemed land."' The Carnia is not conquered territory. This is why it reveals no territorial sacredness, no glorious death, no holy waters and why, therefore, it cannot be worked into a symbolic system premised on an expanded Italy achieved through a victorious offensive and the spilling of the nation's blood on the newly claimed soil. But if territory is so crucial for the construction of meaning in the war diary, Mussolini would soon have plenty of symbolic material upon which to draw. On 15 May 1916 Italy had to come to terms with the fact that its adversary could also carry out offensive operations, and do so, moreover, with a vengeance.

The Austrian 'Strafexpedition'

Austria-Hungary managed to contain the Italian offensives in 1915 while rolling back the Russians in Galicia and eventually defeating Serbia. Yet although armaments were produced in good numbers, food supplies were strained, and it became apparent to Chief of Staff Franz Graf Conrad von Hötzendorf that a negotiated peace on favourable terms was the most desirable outcome. The best chance for achieving this was, in his view, an attack on the Italian front. Concentrating on the Trentino, he hoped to break out onto the plains, cut off Italian forces on the Isonzo, and force Italy to surrender. His personal detestation of Italy, which had intensified following what he saw as its treacherous breaching of the Triple Alliance, underwrote his intention to attack there rather than in Russia, and accounts for the unofficial name given to the May 1916 offensive – *Strafexpedition*, that is punitive expedition.

At least twenty divisions were required to overrun the Italian lines, and German help was therefore needed. However, German Chief of Staff Erich von Falkenhayn reminded Conrad that Germany was not at war with Italy and informed him that he was in any case planning to attack at Verdun. Conrad had to go it alone with between twelve and fourteen divisions. He aimed to unleash a strong diversionary attack on the left in Val Sugana while saving the real offensive for the centre starting from the Folgaria and Vezzena-Luserna plateaus and driving through the Val d'Astico. His intention to begin operations in the third week in March was undermined by the longevity of preparations and by late snow, and the date was therefore moved to mid-May. It was now decided to prepare the ground for the central thrust by increasing the power of the offensive in Val Sugana and by unleashing another massive offensive against the Italian left wing in Val Terragnolo. Two armies, the 11th and the 3rd, were to take part in the offensive. The latter was, in the main, to stay in the background and come up the rear after the XX corps of the 11th Army had broken through onto the plain. Once the transfer of artillery had been completed the 11th Army had 584 small, 174 medium and 58 high calibre pieces in the main theatre, while the 3rd Army had 106 small, 12 medium and 2 high calibre pieces. In the same period the Italian 1st Army, stationed in the area of the imminent attack, had 617 pieces of artillery, many of which were old or overused. The Austro-Hungarians had 300,000 men against Italy's 200,000.

In mid-March Roberto Brusati, commander of the 1st Army, became aware of the danger and on 22 March, while Cadorna was in London for the inter-allied conference (20 March–1 April), sent news to Command Headquarters at Udine of the 'almost certain' attack. He requested more men and materials, and the number of battalions at his disposal subsequently rose from 135 to 199. But sixty-nine of these were stationed between the Stelvio and Lake Garda and hence not in the main offensive's trajectory. As for Cadorna, he was not unduly alarmed by the news. He was planning yet another offensive against Gorizia and saw the Austro-Hungarian build-up as little more than an attempt to divert Italian attention from the Isonzo. He believed that Germany would not enter the war and that the attack could not go ahead with the forces available to Conrad. He knew of Russian preparations for a summer offensive and was further convinced that the two railway lines linking the Trentino with the rest of Austria-Hungary would be insufficient for the transportation of men and materials to the area of attack.

He was mistaken. Cadorna assessed the enemy's intentions by relying too much on Italy's own experiences on the Carso. There, offensives had been clearly limited and Italy had dragged the 149 mm cannons using oxen. In the opening phases of the war, however, Germany had shown the effectiveness of motor traction for the transportation of powerful heavy artillery such as Big Bertha. Cadorna also wrongly assumed that Conrad was privy to his own information about a Russian offensive. Much of this miscalculation was due to the fact that for fear of creating possible successors he had no army group commanders (Trentino–Cadore and Isonzo). He relied instead on a small, insufficiently informed and unauthoritative secretariat headed by Colonel Roberto Bencivenga. A fatal upshot of this bureaucratic centralization was that not only did Cadorna dismiss Brusati's warnings about the enemy build-up, but he was also unaware of the potential disaster inherent in Brusati's dangerous glory hunting and congruent appetite for offensive warfare. Brusati interpreted flexibly Cadorna's 1915 orders to the 1st Army which specified a defensive strategy while allowing limited tactical offensives. He turned permission to rectify the border along tactical lines into an attempt to alter it radically in Val Sugana and Val Lagarina, to come within a stone's throw of Trento and to eliminate the Austro-Hungarian strongholds on the Folgaria and Lavarone plateaus. He had therefore maintained his men in advanced positions which guaranteed neither solid resistance nor adequate reserves. In the area where the main Austro-Hungarian attack was to come (Val Terragnolo–Altopiano di Tonezza–Altopiano dei Sette Comuni), Brusati had fifty-eight battalions in the front line and only fourteen in reserve, *none* of which were between Terragnolo and Tonezza. By 29 April Cadorna was concerned enough to visit the area for the first time since the previous September. He discovered that solely the front line was adequately defended; the second only held at certain points, while work on the third was in its early phases. The fourth line had been adequately defended only on Cima Portule, even though it was the last line of resistance before the enemy reached the plain. But by now it was the beginning of May. The main defence was going to be made on the front lines and with virtually nowhere to run. For his negligence Brusati was sacked on 8 May and replaced by General Guglielmo Pecori Giraldi.

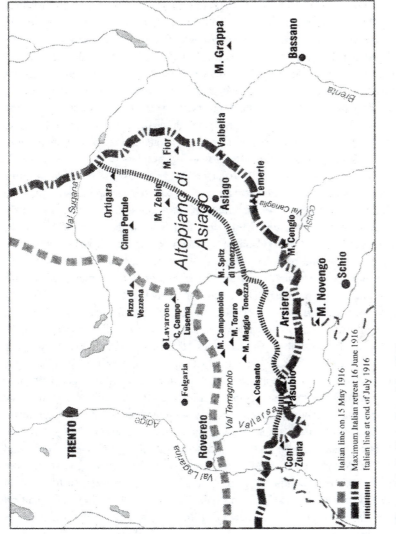

Figure 4.1 *Strafexpedition* May 1916
Source: adapted from Isenghi and Rochat (2000), page 177.

When the attack came on 15 May the Italian front line between Vallarsa and Val d'Astico was crushed by the 11th Army's heavy artillery. The invading forces quickly achieved notable successes in Val Terragnolo and on the Altopiano di Tonezza. Between 15 and 20 May Colsanto, Mount Maggio, Mount Toraro, Mount Campomolòn and Mount Spitz di Tonezza all fell into Austro-Hungarian hands. On 20 May the Austrians threw the 3rd Army into the fray on the Altopiano dei Sette Comuni. Conrad's men occupied Arsiero on 27 May and Asiago on 28. By early June the invaders had penetrated up to 20 km in a line ranging from Val Sugana in the north to the Altopiano dei Sette Comuni (also known as the Altopiano di Asiago) in the centre and, in the south-west, to Val d'Astico, Vallarsa and Val Lagarina. However, at this point the three main Austro-Hungarian commanders differed as to how best to proceed with the offensive, and back-up forces were not numerous. These were symptoms of an attack that was running out of steam. For his part, Cadorna had been working wonders with reserves since 20 May. In the space of two weeks he managed to regroup 179,000 men, mostly from the Isonzo. This was enough for five army corps which made up the new 5th Army.

Italy's numerical superiority became decisive. Conrad's latest offensive in the centre everywhere confronted Italian forces defending the last line before the plain. This situation allowed Cadorna to plan a counter-attack against an unsuspecting enemy on the Altopiano dei Sette Comuni. On 1 June he learnt of the Russian offensive to be unleashed on 4 June, and on 2 June announced that the Austro-Hungarian offensive had been successfully held off. As a matter of fact, the situation was still critical. On 3 June Mount Cengio fell and the grenadiers defending it were forced to retreat to the bottom of Val Canaglia, one stop from the plain. But for fear of Italian counter-attacks the Austro-Hungarians did not push the Cengio victory any further. Conrad's last hope was to conquer Mount Novegno and Mount Lermele but the attack against the former failed between 12 and 13 June, and against the latter on 15 and 16. Cadorna's 2 June bulletin was therefore optimistic, and was most probably aimed at pre-empting arguments which might see the Russian offensive as the deciding factor in the salvation of Italy. A further Austro-Hungarian offensive in the Val d'Astico was aborted precisely because of Conrad's decision to send two divisions of reserves to the Russian front. Moreover, the line reached by Italy following its 'counter-offensive' between 16 June and 24 July was the one more or less left to it after Conrad's 16 June decision to call off the *Strafexpedition* and retreat (beginning 24 June) to a safe line, a manoeuvre once again occasioned by the Russian offensive. Cadorna's 'counter-offensive' only achieved 71,600 casualties in addition to the 76,100 sustained during the enemy offensive. But the invasion had been held off, and Italy was still in the war (Cadorna, 1921, I: Ch. 5; Posani, 1968, I: Chs 11–12; Rocca, 1985: Ch. 7; Pieropan, 1988: Chs 21–22; Herwig, 1997: 204–7; Isnenghi and Rochat, 2000: 176–83; Schindler, 2001: 144–9).

Dealing with Invasion: Reasserting Fascist Authority against the Enemy Within, May–June 1916

The invasion was a political shock to Italy's governing élites, and to Mussolini in his dual capacity as soldier and political activist. Invasion and heavy casualties might have been expected to supply the linguistic basis of a call to popular mobilization against the enemy. The invasion of national territory together with the commission of atrocities against French and Belgian civilians supplied just such a hermeneutic structure for the French in 1914, the nation in arms coming up against attempted violation by the barbarian enemy (Horne, 2000: 73–9). In the Italian case, further material for a mobilization of spirits was ostensibly provided by the anniversary of entry into the war, which fell during the Austrian offensive. In Mussolini's absence, an anonymous *Il Popolo d'Italia* author in fact related the two events. He noted on 24 May that the 'sacred anniversary falls just when the enemy is making its extreme effort', and with a language of 'blood' and 'sacrifice' he managed to connect the real or imaginary sacred union of 24 May 1915 with the same real or imaginary Italy 'still serenely prepared for resistance' and poised for inevitable 'victory'. That same day *Il Popolo d'Italia* printed the text of *Il manifesto dei partiti d'estrema* published and affixed by various interventionist parties and groups which included the *fasci interventisti*. This poster opened by mentioning the invasion which required 'regroupment for the decisive effort'. But Mussolini the soldier remained silent, with no entries in the war diary, which in fact came to a halt after 14 May. The language of offensive as elaborated by Mussolini was clearly inappropriate to the experience of retreat and desperate defence of the national territory. Little or nothing was happening in the Carnia during the invasion: in the month between the beginning of the *Strafexpedition* and the end of the Italian 'counter-offensive' there were no deaths and only one injury in Mussolini's regiment (AUSSME, entries of 15 May–16 June 1916). In a period of military crisis and intense activity from Verdun to the Trentino, for Mussolini to say something from a relatively idle sector would only have further underlined his non-heroic location.

The shock of invasion and near defeat threw the Italian government into crisis. Parliament re-opened on 6 June and after four days of deliberations in which any attempts to raise the *Strafexpedition* were shouted down in a hail of abuse, Salandra had to present budget proposals. He could therefore no longer hold off discussion of the invasion and who was responsible for it. His criticisms that day of Cadorna were, however, half-hearted. He stated that 'if nothing else, better prepared defences would have held off the [enemy offensive] for longer and further from the margins of the mountain zone'. In some respects his pusillanimity is understandable. Already that year Cadorna had scored a heavy victory over the government by successfully ridding himself of Minister for War, Zuppelli, who since 6 January had been criticizing his failed strategy and in particular his dispersal of forces over too broad a front. Cadorna responded to this (and to Salandra's 30 January letter to the King which identified Cadorna's fruitless Carso assaults as the cause of bad morale in the army) by calling on journalist Ugo Ojetti to organize a press campaign which would present him favourably to public opinion. *Il Corriere della Sera*, *Il Secolo*, *Il Popolo d'Italia* and *L'Idea Nazionale* all responded positively. When Cadorna's demands for Zuppelli's removal were resisted by Salandra, Cadorna replied: 'Either Zupelli goes or I go.' Zuppelli resigned on 9 March and was replaced by Cadorna's friend and admirer, General Paolo Morrone. An important precedent thus existed to show how any attempt to challenge Cadorna head-on meant danger for the political assailant. Indeed, not even Salandra's 10 June attempts at semi-diplomacy were enough to save his job, and the government, and he along with it, fell with 158 votes in favour and 197 against (Melograni, 1969: Ch. 3; Rocca, 1985: 140ff).

The crisis leading to Salandra's downfall created a major problem for Mussolini the political journalist. Where did responsibility for the invasion lie? If he attacked Cadorna and the government, this would alter the relationship to the home front that he had defined through *Il Popolo d'Italia* during his winter leave, and even before. In the event, neither he nor *Il Popolo d'Italia* did anything of the sort. Before Salandra's downfall Mussolini wrote nothing, barring a handful of letters, one to Michele Bianchi published in *Il Popolo d'Italia* on 22 May (OO, VIII: 303), one to his brother-in-law dated 1 June (Mancini Mussolini, 1957: 62) and one to his friend Torquato Nanni on 5 June (OO, VIII: 303). As for his newspaper staff, on 18 May they defended Cadorna. A paragraph entitled 'L'offensiva austriaca' is creative indeed: 'The Austrian offensive . . . does not surprise the Italians . . . Our private information on health provisions confirms that the *generalissimo* foresaw and acted, organizing defences and reserves.' Following the removal of Salandra *Il Popolo d'Italia* again focused on defending Cadorna's reputation and, moreover, using Cadorna's theories. In the main article of the 11 June edition it argued that 'if the lack of preparation has been denounced by the High Command, then it must have been determined by political intrusion'. Mussolini's response to the crisis unfolded in a similar vein. The importance of Salandra's fall led him to adjust his creation of a military persona by announcing, on 14 June, that, exceptionally, he would suspend his apolitical role as an ordinary soldier and comment on political events. He wrote a long letter to *Il Popolo d'Italia* in which he expressed his approval of the government collapse. This was because, in his view, 'with the enemy at the door' the resolution to the crisis could only be 'an *interventionist* one' which '*reinforces* and *improves* all of our political and military action' (Mussolini's emphases). But despite this reference to 'political and military action', the letter made no further mention of the military disaster or the responsibilities of the military hierarchy. Salandra was Mussolini's fall guy, though it should be noted that this was only *after* he had fallen. Mussolini took the popular character of the May 1915 demonstrations and pitted it against the élitist cause of Salandra's downfall: 'He had to choose between Parliament and Country, between the discipline of persuasion and that of coercion . . . The people offered itself [in May 1915], but Salandra didn't accept . . . All he had left was the Parliament, where his position was infinitely worse in a hostile and refractory environment' (OO, VIII, 234–7).

This letter-article is proof that despite his silence Mussolini had been watching events closely and chose to move when the military crisis had attenuated and when his comment would ratify a blame which had already been apportioned. But the article is interesting for another reason. Mussolini advocated Bissolati as the new head of government. It was not to be. The 78-year-old Paolo Boselli, a moderate liberal interventionist, formed a government of national unity, which took office on 19 June. Bissolati was given a junior ministry with responsibilities for government relations with the High Command. In a letter to Bissolati dated 20 June, Mussolini suggested that the cause of military failures lay on the home front and that it was *there* that they had to be forcefully resolved. He saw in Bissolati a chance to end a policy which 'by depressing the morale of the country wound up depressing the morale of the combatants, and instead of bringing victory nearer made it improbable or in any case far off'. He asked Bissolati to ensure that the nation be furnished with 'the maximum material and moral war efficiency'. He argued that this would be best achieved 'by limiting – with firmness and severity – the Germanizing not to mention insidious and dangerous peace mongering and by removing – without remission – all those who – out of conviction or inability – are not up to the task' (OO, VIII, 304–5). In short, on account of the invasion Mussolini was increasingly becoming less open to the methods of persuasion vis-à-vis the internal enemy with which he had experimented during his 1915–16 winter convalescence. As with the Austrian air incursions over Milan in February, neither military nor political spheres were primarily censurable; real responsibility lay with the enemy within. At the height of the Austro-Hungarian offensive, the 'fascists' met in congress and drew similar conclusions.

In an unsigned article of 13 May 1916 dedicated to the upcoming national *fasci* congress to be held in Milan on 21–22 May, *Il Popolo d'Italia* argued that the *fasci* were needed in order to accomplish 'the most difficult' task, namely, that of 'paralyzing the daily attempts of neutralists to frighten the nation'. It affirmed fascism's readiness 'to go onto the streets and disperse the hordes of peace criers'. In his introductory address to the 21 May sitting of the congress, reproduced in *Il Popolo d'Italia* the following day, Michele Bianchi remarked that, strictly speaking, the *fasci* should not exist, as once war was declared all dissent was to have disappeared. Since it had not, fascism had been forced to resurface. But that 'fascism' was a less temporary and ephemeral project than Bianchi was suggesting here is seen in the fact that instead of re-emerging to respond to a real threat of neutralism, the congress furnished the conditions for fascism's existence by recreating the neutralist enemy as a mobilizing and self-mobilizing myth even when that enemy was most definitely quiescent (for which see Melograni, 1969: 241–51). While having little to go on as regards the invasion the congress nevertheless had sufficient information (as far as those present were concerned) with which to allot blame: 'Neutralists', it was claimed at the 21 May sitting, were 'spreading false news'. But the false news about events and responsibilities was being spread by Cadorna's bulletins and by the interventionist press, including *Il Popolo d'Italia*, as we have seen. A certain Prof. Lomini, who spoke on behalf of the Turin *fascio*, referred to *La Stampa* as 'a German paper', when an examination of *La Stampa* reveals that unlike, say, *Avanti!* or *Il Popolo d'Italia*, it invariably went uncensored, and clearly, therefore, met with the approval of the military and government authorities. As for Giolitti, the real object of any attack on *La Stampa*, he had retreated from the political scene, and had nothing to say about this period in his memoirs (Giolitti, 1967: 334–5). At any rate, if Mussolini's few comments in this period are anything to go by, proposals for physical confrontation with neutralists were viewed as not strictly relevant to the present at all. They represented, rather, a programme for post-war revenge against socialism. His already-mentioned innocuous 14 June critique of Salandra and his silence over the High Command's responsibilities for leaving the Trentino undefended stood in sharp contrast to his references to 'the Südekumised official socialists'. (Albert Südekum was a German socialist who had visited Italy between late August and early September 1914 as part of a German government propaganda campaign designed to convince Italian socialists that Germany was conducting a war of defence and that Italy should remain neutral. See Valiani, 1977: 45ff). Mussolini further referred to the Italian socialists as 'Croats' and 'agents of the foreigner' with whom 'we will settle accounts after the war'. In a postcard of late June to some citizens from the Romagna he referred, indeed, to the 'terrible day of reckoning' on which 'the *Italian Austrians*' would get their comeuppance (OO, VIII: 305; Mussolini's emphasis).

It is also noteworthy that despite the fact that the enemy was at the door neither Mussolini nor the fascist congress of May felt obliged to introduce a socio-economic and political content to the theme of popular mobilization. The congress was devoid of any social programme, barring Bianchi's call on the bourgeoisie to be grateful to the proletariat after the war. The *Strafexpedition* did not, therefore, provide a basis for challenging the most recent expression of politically backed agrarian conservativism, namely the parliamentary debate of March 1916. Despite being what Antonio Papa describes as 'disturbed and in a certain sense surprised' when informed of the enormous price being paid by the peasant soldiers, the Parliament did not raise the slogan of land reform. The nationalist imperialist Luigi

Federzoni took upon himself the 'moral debt of the nation towards the combatants', while Salandra assured the house rather generically (and hence with no concrete commitment whatsoever) that something should and would be done for the peasants (Papa, 1969: 6–8).

Archive documentation for this period reveals something of the social character of the movement behind the conservative, authoritarian and street confrontation strategy of the fascist congress. In a 3 April letter to the Ministry of the Interior, for example, the Prefect of Ferrara listed the professions of the men who had been chosen to form the leading committee of the local *fascio*. These included a schoolteacher, a technical institute teacher, a law student, an accountant, a lawyer with the title of Cavaliere (a bit like Sir), a railway clerk and a shopkeeper (ACS, A5G, b. 94, fasc. 211, s.fasc. 7). A 14 June letter from the Prefect of Genoa to the Ministry of the Interior reported that of the seventy people who attended a recent meeting the main ones to be noted were lawyers, schoolteachers or university lecturers, and an accountant (ACS, A5G, b. 99, fasc. 215, s.fasc. 9). While it is not clear from these documents whether these sections shared the Milan congress' discussion of street violence (the Ferrara *fascio* reiterated support for Salandra and the Genoa meeting for Sonnino) it is nevertheless the case that, as we saw in Chapter 1, Ferrara was an area in which the middle and lower middle classes had long since struck up an anti-worker and anti-peasant alliance with landowners and the clergy. Bianchi, as we also saw in Chapter 1, was involved in the genesis of that coalition. The *fasci* therefore represented a conservative coalition of middle-class elements, who, while criticizing the State's unwillingness to mobilize popular sentiment for the war, were themselves seeking to bolster State authority and reproduced existing socio-economic relations by redirecting responsibilities for failed mobilization and consequent military disaster onto a mythically aggrandized enemy within. To deal with this enemy in the wake of State frailty, fascists would go onto the streets after the war to confront 'neutralists' – identifiable almost exclusively with the socialists – on what Mussolini promised would be a 'terrible day of reckoning'.

–5–

Disenchanted Warrior
July 1916–February 1917

> The Fascist State does not remain indifferent to the fact of religion in general and to that particular positive religion which is Italian Catholicism . . . The Fascist State does not . . . vainly seek, like Bolshevism, to expel religion from the minds of men. Fascism respects the God of the ascetics, of the saints, of the heroes, and also God as seen and prayed to by the simple and primitive heart of the people.
>
> Mussolini, *Dottrina del fascismo*, 1932

Winter on the Carso, November–December 1916

Once the front had resettled after the *Strafexpedition*, Cadorna oversaw an enormously successful transfer of huge quantities of men, animals, arms and munitions to the Isonzo in July. Between 07.00 and 16.00 on 6 August he unleashed a new offensive against an outgunned enemy who was also short on reserves. Italian infantry captured Mount Sabotino in only thirty-eight minutes. The peaks of Mount San Michele also fell into Italian hands and on 9 August Italian troops finally entered Gorizia. But the enemy fell back on the previously prepared Mount San Gabriele–Mount San Marco–Vertoinizza line. On 16 August Cadorna called a halt to the action. Italy had 51,200 casualties against the Dual Monarchy's 37,500. After this, the Sixth Battle of the Isonzo, Italy felt confident enough to declare war on Germany on 27 August. Despite a revival of Cadorna's credentials both at home and abroad, the offensive's strategic limits were, however, soon apparent. From Mount Santo to Mount Hermada via Mount San Daniele, San Gabriele and San Marco, Austrian defences were even more robust now than they had been at the Gorizia bridgehead. Moreover, the road to Trieste was blocked by the powerful Trstely–Hermada defence line. It was against the latter that Cadorna focused attention in his three 'autumn shoulder pushes' (*spallate autunnale*), or the Seventh, Eighth and Ninth Battles of the Isonzo, dated 14–17 September, 10–13 October and 1–4 November respectively. In exchange for almost 80,000 casualties Cadorna conquered some trenches to the east of Oppachiasela, plus the Nad Logem, the Pecinka and the important strategic positions of Veliki Hribach and the Dosso Faiti. But the road to Trieste remained blocked (Rocca, 1985: Ch. 8, 169–73; Pieropan, 1988: Chs 24, 27, 28 and 30; Isnenghi and Rochat, 2000: 183–90; Schindler, 2001: Chs 8 and 9).

Not even the fall of Gorizia revitalized Mussolini, the muted warrior. In an 8 August letter to the editors of *Il Popolo d'Italia* he declared: 'The news has electrified us' (OO, VIII: 308). His joy was not to last. On 13 August he wrote to his sister that 'the war will continue for the whole of 1917 and this is necessary if we are to win' (Mancini Mussolini, 1957: 65). During the *spallate autunnali* Mussolini wrote only one letter, probably on 29 September (OO, VIII: 308–9) and one letter-article on 28 October which was published on 2 November. In the latter he mentioned the conquest of Gorizia and the declaration of war on Germany as part of what he saw as the more general upsurge in the Entente's fortunes since April 1916. However, the article expressed greater concern over the imminent German victory in Transylvania, and the fear that on account of this the war might be resolved through diplomacy (OO, VIII: 243–7). He wrote nothing about the *spallate autunnali* themselves. On 12 November the pessimistic Mussolini headed home on leave. With what level of credibility would the forlorn warrior tackle the home front? And how, equally importantly, would the home front receive the previously enthusiastic soldier who, while not having died, had almost faded away?

The circumstances surrounding this further withdrawal from the front are dubious indeed. Mussolini had already been on winter leave in March, and it would not be until 1918 that Italian soldiers were granted a second leave period. The fact is that people in high places, especially Bissolati, were doing their utmost, with Mussolini's knowledge, to get Mussolini away from the line of fire and back home to his newspaper (O'Brien, 2002a: 15–16; 2003:14–15). He remained incognito while home, and the four articles attributed to him in this period did not bear his name (OO, VIII: 253–5, 256–9, 260–64, 265–9). But, as in late 1915, his notoriety meant that his political adversaries were keeping a close eye on his movements. *L'Avvenire d'Italia*, a catholic newspaper, published a letter from a real or imagined soldier from Mussolini's regiment who asked: 'Can you, dear *Avvenire*, give me some indication as to the precise whereabouts of corporal Mussolini? Because one thing is for sure: in the front line, with the men of his squad, he is not' (quoted in Anon, 16 December 1916). By late November Mussolini was on his way back to the trenches, this time to the Carso, to where his regiment had been moved in his absence.

The Carso is a vast plateau stretching from Gorizia into Slovenia, characterized by red earth and rugged limestone. Sea climate, for example in Trieste, often reveals continental and alpine characteristics inland and hence rapid decreases in temperature. In winter the area is exposed to the cold and violent Bora wind which can blow up to 120 kph in a constant east-north-east direction due to the pressure between the upper Adriatic and Central Europe. The final section of the war diary begins on 29 November and ends on 22 February 1917. Mussolini was stationed around Lake Doberdò on the Carso for the entire period. For analytical purposes the section can be divided into three monthly sections covering December, January and February. Only the December 1916 section was published in *Il Popolo d'Italia*, in February 1917. This does not mean, however, that the January and February sections will be ignored. While they were not published until the 1923 edition we are interested in the war diary not solely for the way it contributed to ideological processes, but for what it might reveal about the ideological processes of which it was itself a product. In the December section there is an entry for every day and average length is slightly more than 280 words. In January, on the other hand, there are only seven entries, the average length of which is only about sixty words. February witnesses a slight recovery: apart from a major gap from 1 to 9 of that month entries are daily and average eighty words in length. Even before exegesis, these statistics speak volumes: a major expectation was thwarted and the diary expressed this disappointment.

When Mussolini finally located his company on 1 December all was positive: 'Affectionate handshakes. They were expecting me.' The night sky was clear: 'An evening of moon and stars.' He could therefore conclude that 'the "morale" of the Bersaglieri seems elevated, certainly higher than in the Carnia zone. "We have lots of cannons. Advancing will be easy!" A sense of confidence is widespread among everyone.' Later on that night: 'While I write our guns roar without truce . . . I do not know how to summarize my tumultuous impressions of this first day of trench life on the Carso. They are profound, complex. Here the war presents itself in its grandiose aspect of human cataclysm. Here one has the certainty that Italy will pass, that it will arrive in Trieste and beyond!' Good weather; high morale; Italian artillery in action; the Carso; an imminent breakthrough to Trieste: what more could a self-made charismatic warrior hero ask for?

What he wanted was good weather, a theme which in December became a virtual obsession bound up with a more general discourse concerning the morale of the men and military strategy. But the promising night sky did not deliver the goods. On 2 December Mussolini wrote: 'This morning it is raining.' On 4 December: 'Last night, rain. Livid and tranquil morning.' He proceeded: 'The weather is undoubtedly an ally of the Germans. The rain forces us into "postponements" which allow the others to fortify. The rain demoralizes us. We are sons of the sun!' Later on in the same entry: 'A voice: the bombardment for the advance begins tonight. We will see and hear. While I write, on the crest behind us there is a blazing and thunder of cannon fire. Is it the prelude?' If it was the prelude, the composer forgot to follow it up with the opening movement. On 5 December: 'Dark sky and still more livid earth.' That night: 'Bursts of wind and rain.' During the night Mussolini's dugout did not hold up: 'Soaked to the skin, awaiting dawn. Towards Aquileia there is a vast piece of clear sky, but behind us, towards Austria, the sky is pitch black. If only the sun would come out!' Further on in Mussolini's 6 December entry: 'Some sun.' Then: 'From the Gulf of Panzano thick storm clouds are gathering. As long as the sirocco lasts the weather will not improve.' Yet the hope of the offensive was still there behind the clouds. 'Our cannon fire electrifies us. The bombing lasted about 40 minutes. Now it has ceased. Moving from dugout to dugout, I gathered the impressions of my fellow soldiers: "Here the power of the Italians can be seen!" "It's no longer like on the Iavorcek! Now it's their turn to become 'unstuck'!" "They'll have had a good slap in the face!" "The Germans made a big mistake moving, a big mistake!"' Mussolini could conclude a few lines later: 'The voice of our guns: this is all-important for keeping the soldier's "morale" high.' But in the same sentence: 'Sky veiled by mist', on the basis of which a lieutenant told Mussolini that this would put off the offensive. Mussolini therefore wrote: 'Everybody betrays slight impatience, even the most negative! Advance! The battle, with its adventurous and emotional apparatus, and despite its risks, fascinates the soldier. Stasis debilitates. Action refreshes.'

The entry of the following day continued: 'Just for a change it's raining cats and dogs.' He specified that 'the rain is the fifth of our enemies and, perhaps, the most massacring of all'. On 8 December: 'This morning it is not raining, but the horizon is grey. Our artillery is operating, but without committing itself too much.' In the following paragraph: 'The rain of the past few days has lowered the level of Bersaglieresque "morale". We are all soaked to the skin, and have only a blanket and a coat: we are without our rucksacks and will not have them until we return to rest. Not a hem of blue: uniform sky, dull grey, like a friar's habit, and dripping.' The following day: 'Drizzle. However, it seems that the horizon wants to clear. The daily high calibre symphony begins. The Austrians fire little, using low calibre guns.' Below: 'A ray of sunshine has broken through the thick cloudy veil which had been hanging around for several days and mortifying us. The artillery takes advantage of it. One of our 280s opens up a ten-metre hole in the barbed wire of their trench. "They" pound us with shrapnel . . . The sky clears as do our spirits. The concert continues.' Throughout mid-December Mussolini wrote in this vein. But by 21 December he had resigned himself to the obvious: 'Today, the first day of winter according to astronomy, announced itself with a colourless sun. Towards the sea there is a wall of storm clouds.' A couple of sentences later it was all over: 'It now seems certain that the advance has been suspended.'

This was the point. The weather had been the barometer of Mussolini's ardour for the offensive. His chance of re-energizing his persona as charismatic warrior fluctuated accordingly, and once the hope of an Italian attack was dashed, the weather became what it was – bad, and a depressing corollary of inaction. On 30 December: 'Slothful and insidious weather, the stuff that cholera is made of . . . The whole encampment is white with lime, thrown without husbandry among the alcoves.' The last entry of the month began 'grey' and in the afternoon 'a pallid sun clears the horizon'. But this was not a prelude. That very evening Mussolini's regiment was on its way down to rest.

Disenchantment

How realistic were Mussolini's hopes for an offensive? And with what implications for understanding this and the remaining sections of the war diary? The military negotiations which took place between 15 and 16 November 1916 in Chantilly suggest that the period was one of regroupment on the part of the Entente powers as they sought to agree on the best way forward. But this was for 1917, not December 1916. The offensive accompanying Mussolini's weather observations in December 1916 was, therefore, of his own making. The Italian artillery fire that he so punctiliously monitored in December was obviously routine and defensive. Mussolini was in consequence deprived of the opportunity to engage in heroic acts even though he was now positioned in the crucial area of Cadorna's strategy. Situations in which his personal courage could be placed on public view had to be of his own making, and the inherent danger had to be made clear to what would otherwise have remained an unimpressed reader. In the 6 December entry, for example, Mussolini decided to observe the great artillery spectacle going on over-head: 'I, all alone, outside my den – at my own risk and danger – enjoy the aural and visual spectacle.' Apart from this, representations of himself are limited to responding to the accusation of shirking which reared its head again in the catholic weekly *Il Popolo di Siena* on 16 December. The latter anonymous article was particularly sharp in its satire and suggested that after eighteen months at the front Mussolini should have had at least a scratch, whereas so far he remained untouched. The article concluded that without any serious injuries Mussolini left himself open to the accusations of the catholic press, which in themselves 'do not leave glorious scars'. Mussolini became aware of this polemic in a postcard received from Bersagliere Silvio Filippi which he then transcribed into his war diary on 18 December. The fact that Filippi knew what to write suggests that behind the construction and defence of Mussolini's heroic persona lay elements of 'spontaneous' back-up: "'Finding myself on leave I do not forget to send you my most sincere greetings, together with those of my friends who were very surprised to hear that even you are in the trenches like any humble soldier.'"

Even before this Mussolini was using the war diary to challenge suspicions as to his previous and present whereabouts. On 12 December he wrote of a meeting with another corporal who informed him that 'I have always believed that you were at the front'. The same day three soldiers stopped in front of his dugout. He described them as 'a bit hesitant', a perplexity which probably reflected their embarrassment over revealing their suspicions. One of them broke the ice: "'Excuse the curiosity. Are you . . .?'" And before he could finish the question Mussolini replied "'Yes, I am.'" On 13 December another soldier exclaimed: "'I am so happy to see you again . . . I can now say that you too have been in this hell and that you haven't turned your back on your old comrades of [the class of] '84.'"

On 23 December Mussolini was visited by Amilcare De Ambris, a syndicalist friend, accompanied by Benedetto Fasciolo of the editorial team of *Il Popolo d'Italia* and at that stage a captain in the artillery. Mussolini described their arrival as a 'gesture of lively friendship'. But it was decidedly more than this. On leaving, Fasciolo declared: '"Here is where the war is."' He then wrote an article for *Il Popolo d'Italia* in which he depicted Mussolini as being much loved by all the soldiers, who in fact called him 'Benito'. Soldiers reportedly interviewed by Fasciolo reminded him that Mussolini '"without dodging, could have had a less uncomfortable life by going to write in the orderly room or in the major's office."' During the meeting with Mussolini, Fasciolo raised the question of Mussolini's alleged evasion of duty, and the other soldiers all began to laugh. When mess time arrived, Mussolini received his meat, broth and bread, and in a self-sacrificial gesture gave the meat to another soldier. When the fruit arrived, he made sure that everyone got an equal share. As they prepared to go, Fasciolo and De Ambris felt 'a pull at our hearts; a painful apprehension for [Mussolini] who is always in danger' (Fasciolo, 31 December 1916).

Yet in challenging the innuendoes of the catholic press about the authenticity of his war service, Mussolini was concerned to retain his links with popular catholic piety as a vital ingredient of front line experience. Reconciliation with the Church had already begun to form part of Mussolini's war diary on 15 November 1915, when he, an atheist, attended a service at Caporetto. On that occasion he transcribed a hymn's patriotic chorus: '"Oh mother, bless Italian virtue; Let our squads triumph in the holy name of Jesus."' On 20 February he rather kindly referred to an Alpini chaplain as 'a fine cut of a man with a rather meek way about him'. By 1 March he was on speaking terms with Father Michele and on 6 May the latter appeared once again in Mussolini's tent leaving some 'excellent Brazilian cigarettes' and a copy of a religious treatise on the moral reasons for Italy's war. This distinguished Mussolini from the orthodox anti-clericalism of his closest collaborators at *Il Popolo d'Italia*. De Falco accused *L'Avvenire* of 'doing favours for highly catholic Austria by informing her of our military movements'. He explained that the clergy attacked Mussolini because 'he is the man they fear because one day he will want to settle accounts with them too'. In fact, for De Falco, 'the priests and those who live off their salaries are natural fertilizer swarming with worms' (De Falco, 22 November 1916). Mussolini was more circumspect. He simply remarked, in an undated letter published in *Il Popolo d'Italia* on 27 December, that the fact that he was at the front 'isn't pleasing for the priests who – while knowing well that I have done thirteen and more months in the trenches – have nevertheless tried to label me a shirker' (OO, VIII: 309). In the 26 December war diary entry Mussolini was once again in the company of Father Michele: 'I hinted at the polemics raised by my winter leave and asked him if he would be prepared to testify on my behalf. "Very much so", he replied. "I would tell the truth, and that is that from the first day till now I have always seen you in the front line." Other officers were present.' Indeed, far from veering towards head-on collision with the Catholic Church, the December 1916 section of the war diary witnesses a major pro-clergy shift on Mussolini's part. We shall come back to this presently. First, we need to examine the more general context in which that shift occurred, namely Mussolini's response to the proposals to open up peace negotiations made public by German Chancellor Bethmann Hollweg in the Reichstag on 12 December.

The German proposals were doomed from the outset. On 7 November the American electorate had given Woodrow Wilson a second term in office. Twelve days later Wilson issued a note to the warring powers suggesting that peace should be sought. Britain responded by installing Lloyd George as Prime Minister, chosen by both main political parties as the one man who could pursue the war with new vigour. On 30 December the Entente turned down Germany's proposals, since peace on the basis of the status quo would have made Germany the effective victor. Whatever the scepticism of politicians, news of a possible peace had significant repercussions in the Italian trenches. In a 2 January 1917 letter to army corps commanders and to the Information Services of the High Command, Minister for War Morrone affirmed that:

> From the military Censorship Department of Como it has been noted that a high quantity of the soldiers' correspondence from that city reflects the repercussions of the well-known German peace proposal. Some speak of it as a certainty deriving from the recent military successes obtained by the Central Powers; others, latching onto rumours spread by systematic adversaries of our war, write of strikes and agitations which are supposed to have occurred in various cities of the Kingdom, and they interpret the possible deployment of armed garrisons as preventive measures against possible tumults or threats of revolt.

Morrone ordered commanders 'not to hesitate, where necessary, in using appropriate measures to energetically repress any single inopportune manifestation whenever it happens to occur' (ACS, PCM, b. 19, fasc. 4, s.fasc. 8, ins. 50).

Mussolini's war diary gives an interesting insight into the effects of the peace proposals on the Carso and how, in his view, they were to be dealt with. The news was brought to the soldiers by a mule driver on 15 December, but Mussolini already knew: 'I thought it must have to do with B. Hollweg's communications.' This means that, once again, he had been keeping his broader knowledge of the war to himself. This secrecy contradicts the flippancy with which he then dismissed the reaction among the soldiers: 'While knowing that I read the newspapers nobody has asked me anything. This indifference is symptomatic. Peace has been spoken about too often for such scepticism not to exist in the spirit of the men. "I'll believe nothing", said one of them, "until I see white flags on the trenches."' But something was definitely amiss. The following day, 16 December, Mussolini noted: 'This morning, in the dugouts, peace is being discussed. However, the predominant note is scepticism, as with the initial reception of the news.' So, peace *was* being discussed. Moreover, soldiers already looked for concrete signs of its realization: 'Someone has noted that this morning the artillery is silent.' Mussolini quickly scotched this: 'On our front, yes, but below, towards the sea, guns moan sullenly.' The following day again: 'In the dugouts the *German peace* is spoken about little' (Mussolini's emphasis). On 18 December: 'Some discussion of the German peace. The presumed condition that Italy should give the liberated lands back to Austria provokes general indignation. I bet that if there was a referendum you would not find ten soldiers ready to accept this condition. "After so much blood and so many sacrifices."'

As a matter of fact no such proposals had been made or would be made by Austria-Hungary. This was made clear by Sonnino in his speech to the chamber of deputies on 18 December, published in the papers the following day. Also, on 27 December 1916 the press published the text of Austria-Hungary's reply to Wilson, which called for negotiations but made no statement about territory. Back in Mussolini's war diary, news brought by two sappers on 19 December pointed to an unidentified and unexplained French victory which caused 'great joy among everybody'. For this very reason, 'peace is spoken about less than yesterday'. The 'victory' in question was undoubtedly the one issuing from the French offensive at Verdun which by 18 December had brought the line back to where it had been before Falkenhayn's offensive in February. Below, in the same war diary entry, Mussolini linked the peace rumours to his misinformation about Austro-Hungarian territorial demands and then linked both to Italy's fallen: 'Dialogue caught in the darkness: "Give back the lands we have conquered? This will never be!" "Our dead would cry vendetta!" "And not only the dead; also the living!" Tomorrow is the anniversary of the hanging of Oberdan.' Despite Mussolini's attempt to downplay the event, the seriousness of the crisis generated by the German peace proposals is clear from the way it clarified the role of the dead in the war diary: they marked the 'legitimacy' of territorial acquisition.

The German peace proposals also disturbed Mussolini personally. On 20 December: 'Talk of peace is still the order of the day', though he specified that '"nobody", I repeat *nobody*, wants to know of a "German" peace.' This sentence is highly contradictory, not only because it overturns previous assertions concerning the decline in talk of peace, but because the first 'nobody' is in inverted commas and hence suggests that at least somebody was prepared to accept peace on any terms, while the second *nobody* is in italics, hinting that absolutely nobody was talking of the 'German' peace (note the inverted commas around the word 'German'). This resort to emphases and inverted commas suggests a lack of comfort with the argument. It is only in an entry of 24 December that Mussolini becomes more credible in downplaying the effects of the peace proposals: 'Talk of "peace" is on the wane. Everyone understands and intuits that that time has not yet come.' In fact, we hear no more about it, except, that is, for the reappearance of the nationalistic clergy in the entries of 30 and 31 December.

The weight lent to the Church in these two entries suggests that it is the key to offsetting the effects of talk of peace without having to resort to repressive measures, such as those called for by Morrone. Again, Mussolini was not all of a sudden becoming a religious convert. He specified on 30 December: 'I do not comment, I transcribe' and 'I copy . . . I document.' But he documented in detail. Father Michele had been distributing Italian tricolour badges and a sheet of paper. Mussolini accepted both and transcribed the consecration contained on the latter. It argued that the French victory on the Marne occurred when General Castelnau invoked the Sacred Heart of Jesus and that by doing the same Italy could likewise achieve victory, '"a double victory: one over our political enemies, the other over ourselves for self-purification and self-elevation."' During the end-of-year mass held the following day, an unknown priest received the highest of praise from Mussolini:

> A simple-speaking orator, with a shrill voice and, most important of all, an Italian in the most ardent sense of the term. I liked his reference to the German peace which would be 'the peace of the victor who then places his foot on the chest of the vanquished', while our peace must 'consecrate the justice and liberty of peoples' and he finished with these words: 'Italy first of all and above all.' . . . I want here to register the first truly burning patriotic speech which I've heard in 16 months of war.

But Mussolini did not just rely on the Church or on the soldiers' own intuition to offset the effects of the German peace proposals. He was also prepared to pinpoint other real causes of low morale among the men. On 6 December he wrote: 'Mess arrives in the evening. It's our only distribution of food in 24 hours. The ration is reduced. But the appetite is the same.' This was not the end of it. On 13 December he expressed his discontent about flea treatment: 'I feel the first treading of fleas. There are anti-flea kits. Yeah. But you'd need one every fifteen days. The "kit's" efficiency is limited. After fifteen days the fleas walk tranquilly on the very "kit" that should have exterminated them . . . One flea more, one flea less . . .'. The following day he was complaining about the badly organized reliefs: 'The changeovers are too frequent. This explains the negligence of the soldiers when it comes to improving trenches. Since one is not staying long, there is no need to overtire oneself.' An examination of the official regiment diary shows that changeovers occurred every three days (AUSSME, entries for December 1916). On 18 December the colonel was doing the rounds: '"How are things?" "Fine", we reply. "Are you cold?" "Not really. But a flask of wine every now and then wouldn't go astray . . ." The colonel moves away.' On Christmas Day: 'Lean

Christmas. Of the gifts sent by the Committee, my company got a half a dozen sponge cakes (*panettone*) and the same amount of bottles.' This was hardly going to be a feast for anything up to 250 men. Mussolini finished on a sarcastic note: 'Mess was extremely special: stewed salted cod with potatoes. Special indeed!'

His irony is understandable. From December 1916 onwards stewed salted cod with potatoes had come to represent scarcity. Salted cod now replaced meat twice a week. Meat, in turn, had been reduced from 375 to 250 grams and bread from 750 to 600 grams. In fact, while the ration remained at 3,000 calories daily (not necessarily an inadequate quantity, especially if men were not involved in strenuous physical activity) it was nevertheless reduced from 4,000 calories (Melograni, 1969: 291), a not insignificant decline (especially in the meat ration) which will no doubt have been keenly felt. On 29 December Mussolini observed that 'the appearance of my fellow soldiers after a stretch in the trenches of the Carso begins to be pitiful'. This is not surprising. Besides the decreased calorific intake there was also insufficient clothing during what was a bitterly cold winter in Italy and all of Europe in 1916–17. And cholera was spreading in Mussolini's regiment (AUSSME, entry of 31 December 1916).

Mussolini's diary had therefore come a long way since the Shangri-La of 1915, though this is not to deny important elements of continuity. One link with the 1915 section is the sacredness of the geographical location. 'There is the Isonzo', he wrote on 1 December. 'Wide, deep blue, profoundly clear.' Not just the water, but the soil. On 14 December he wrote: 'My hands now have the mark of the highest nobility: they are dirty with the reddish earth of the Carso.' Another element of continuity is Mussolini's identification in December 1916 with officers. For example: 'The lieutenant who commands my company invites me to share the evening mess with the officers. With him are several junior lieutenants, one of whom has the command of my platoon' (5 December); 'The captain has given me the task of bringing a greeting to the colonel. The colonel has gone to the advanced trenches and I await his return. To the captain's good wishes I add my own' (24 December).

Mussolini also continued to portray his own charismatic persona as something projected onto politically passive soldiers. In a 27 December letter-article published in *Il Popolo d'Italia* he claimed that 'despite discomforts and dangers, I have the privilege of assisting in the formation of a *trenchocracy*, a new and better élite which will govern the Italy of tomorrow' (OO, VIII: 270–72; Mussolini's italics). From the evidence in this section it is clear, as in previous sections, that this new *trenchocracy* was to be identified solely with the middle-class officers. In December 1916 there are no examples of his charisma at work, and worker and peasants appear only fleetingly and are not the subject of any elaborate discourses. The only reference to workers is the 18 December entry in which one such soldier was said to have rejected the German peace proposal. On 1 December Mussolini wrote of how, on his return to the trenches in late November, he had been greeted by a peasant soldier: 'I remember how he wanted to carry my rucksack from Quel Taront to Minigos. I will never forget this act of affectionate kindness on the part of this humble . . . peasant.' This comment reveals a continuity with all parts of the war diary in that it represents profound paternalism towards the labouring classes. Indeed, on 12 December Mussolini wrote of a visit of the brigadier general who 'comes often among us and speaks man to man with the Bersaglieri'. For Mussolini, it was good to speak to 'these humble people' and 'to try often to come down towards these simple and primitive souls, who, despite everything, still make up a splendid human material'. Apart from the adjectives (humble, simple, primitive) the phrasal verb 'come down' is all revealing: workers and peasants were not part of the 'trenchocracy'.

An important element of rupture with previous sections of the diary is the disappearance of the fraternal brotherhood bound together by the deep emotions deriving from the shared danger of death in the liminal phase of the rite of passage. Although Mussolini still identified with officer paternalism towards the working classes, there are no accounts in December 1916 of the valorous episodes which so aestheticized the earlier community. Yet another rupture with the past is the use of the war diary as a means for more inner reflection (while continuing to write for publication). This occurred on Christmas Day 1916. There is no other passage in the war diary of this style and content and it is worth quoting and analyzing it at length:

Today is Christmas Day. Christmas Day. 25 December. The third Christmas at war. The date means nothing to me. I have received some illustrated postcards with the usual children and the inevitable Christmas trees. In order for me to find once more an echo of the poetry of this return, I must re-evoke my distant childhood. Today my heart has become as dry as these rocky dolines [grooves in Karst topography sometimes caused by the collapse of underground wells and caves]. Modern civilization has 'mechanized' us. The war has brought the process of 'mechanization' of European society to the point of exasperation. Twenty-five years ago I was a pugnacious and violent boy. The heads of some of my peers still bear the marks of my stone-throwing. A nomad by instinct, I went from morning to evening along the river and robbed nests and fruit. I used to go to mass. The Christmas of those days is still alive in my memory. There were very few people who did not go to church. My father and some others. The trees and hawthorn bushes along the road towards San Cassiano were rigid and silvered by the frost. It was cold. The first masses were for the early-rising old women. When we saw their heads peaking over the plain we knew it was our turn. I remember: I would follow my mother. In the church there were many lights and in the middle of the alter—in a small flowered cradle—lay the Baby born during the night. All of that was picturesque and played on my imagination. Only the smell of the incense disturbed me and at times caused me an unbearable nausea. At last a sound of the organ closed the ceremony. The crowd moved out. Along the road, a satisfied chatting. At midday steam rose from the traditional and delicious Romagna ringed ravioli on the tables. How many years or how many centuries have passed since then? A burst of cannon fire calls me back to reality. It's Christmas at war.

At the rhetorical level, this passage reveals traits of Mussolini's general method: earlier we saw that, in his view, soldiers were not interested in peace and were not talking about it, despite his own obsession with the issue and the fact that in reality the soldiers were discussing it. Here, Christmas is said to mean nothing to Mussolini and he then dedicates a whole passage to a detailed reflection on it. But the point is not Mussolini's distant past, since arguably the passage deals primarily with Christmas present. It is of interest that Mussolini had commented that same day on the scarcity of Italian sponge cakes (*panettone*) and bottles of wine, while he had not looked favourably on the stewed salted cod and potatoes distributed as Christmas lunch. In his reminiscences on Christmas past, his mind turned to the steam rising from the ring-shaped ravioli (*cappelletti*) for which his home region is still famous. Mussolini could not express his personal heroic qualities in the present war of position, but he was an effective warrior as a child and his nomadic wanderings were not limited by entrenched stasis. It is also noteworthy that his mother and father briefly entered the picture here, a fact which underlines the absence in the entire war diary of any thoughts concerning his wife and children. His parents appeared in the context of a discourse on church attendance. His father did not go, but we are not told why. Mussolini the child went, but perhaps only to please his mother. Not that the service had no positive effects on his child's imagination, as it did, though these were ruined by the disturbing perfume of religious incense. It is noteworthy in this regard that the December 1916 war diary as published in *Il Popolo d'Italia* in February 1917 contains a phrase or two absent from the 1923 edition. Following the line 'Italy first of all and above all' in the above-quoted speech by the nationalistic priest, the 1923 edition continues: 'I would have liked to shout "Bravo"!' The 1917 version states, however, 'I – a heretic – would have liked to shout "Bravo"!' Moreover, before the 1923 sentence 'I want here to register the first truly burning patriotic speech which I've heard in 16 months of war' the original version in 1917 has 'Once the mass began, I moved away, but . . .' and then continues with 'I want here to register' etc. Yet Mussolini had already shown himself to be open to popular religiosity in 1915 and since then his relationship with the clergy had improved beyond all doubt. In 1923, as head of government, he was beginning to resolve the anti-clerical/pro-clerical ambiguities of the war diary in favour of full reconciliation with the Church. In the original version, however, the ambiguities remain and are evidenced in that amazing 1916 journey to an idyllic Christmas past. In that passage Mussolini did not hide this state of mind, since he noted that his heart had dried up and that he, like Europe in general, had become 'mechanized'. Not only, therefore, had the previously quoted

7 April 1916 apotheosis of morale over machines been contradicted by the emphasis of machines over morale, but the idealism of the warrior community, constructed through the diary on the Isonzo in 1915, had become thorough disenchantment on the Carso by Christmas 1916.

Exit from Combat: Wounded Hero?

All things considered 1916 had not been a good year for Mussolini the heroic warrior. Yet he began 1917 on a positive note. On 1 January he wrote that '1916 died while I was marching on the road from Doberdò. I greeted 1917 on the march. That augurs well', while on 19 January he remarked: 'I cross the Isonzo once again. Great deep blue river. Italy was born on the Tiber and reborn on the Isonzo.' But unlike in 1915, Mussolini was heading for the rear, and the hope for an offensive had been illusory; in September 1915 he was fresh and enthusiastic, in 1917 he was tired, hungry and in many respects angry; he was also, as we shall see, gravely ill. Nor was the imminent rest going to remedy much for Mussolini and his fellow soldiers: the first ten days were spent in Palazzotto 'in a muddy desert' in 'huts and fold-up beds'. This was for anti-cholera injections, disinfection and an examination of excrement. The real 'rest' period began on 10 January when the soldiers moved to Santo Stefano near Aquileia. From Mussolini's war diary and the official regiment diary it is evident that most of this purported rest period was spent learning the use of grenade launchers. The official diary also informs that the time was spent practising frontal attacks in successive waves, an exercise which would hardly have taken the men's minds off the war. Mussolini recounted how he visited the museum in Aquileia. This was certainly allowed. However, since 19 November 1916 measures had been taken to curtail what was considered unsoldierly behaviour during rest periods. Men were now subject to Cadorna's circular of that date which prohibited various forms of entertainment. Not only was theatrical amusement prohibited in the war zone but even visits to bars and public places were limited, since soldiers' behaviour (and presumed misbehaviour and slovenliness) would have been on public view. One form of entertainment allowed was the use of prostitutes, though even here there was injustice: the officers benefited from the greatest comforts while the men were left in seedy, lurid and at times makeshift brothels (Melograni, 1969: 224–6).

After the 19 January entry, Mussolini's diary was all bad news. On 21 January: 'Bora [wind] of Trieste. Cold. Insignificant day. What great weather for dreadful "morale". Murmuring.' The entry of 27–28 January is short but crucial: 'Snow, cold, infinite boredom.' Following this Mussolini summed up his impressions with devastating brevity: 'Orders, counter-orders, disorder.' The month finished with the 30 January entry: 'The soldiers who come back from leave have for some time had terrible "morale". They murmur under their breaths about the *chaos* in Italy'

(Mussolini's italics). Mussolini assigned responsibility for the chaos to the talk of peace, especially by women. Already on 30 December he had opined in his diary (removed from the 1923 version) that 'the psychology of the woman barely touches the war and is absolutely incapable of penetrating its intimate tragic substance. For the woman, the man returned home from war presents the same "exotic" attraction as the man home from California and nothing more.' This misogynous discourse was not fortuitous. Between 1 December 1916 and 15 April 1917 it is thought that around 500 demonstrations took place in Italy involving many thousands of women. Some protested regularly every Monday (allowance day) for the return of their husbands and sons (Melograni, 1969: 300). In a letter to his sister on 18 February 1917, Mussolini returned to this subject with vehemence. As usual, he denied that the protests were having any influence in the trenches: 'As regards the women's demonstrations, only an echo of them has reached us here.' But he nevertheless called for harsh repression: 'I fully agree with the severe sentences. You understand that a few unconscious or fanatical women – ignobly influenced by the red priests – cannot be allowed to sabotage Italy and the *holy cause* of the Quadruple and to play the game of the Kaiser and his criminal comrades. A few examples, and they'll stop' (Mancini Mussolini, 1957: 67–8; italics in the original).

Before finishing in February 1917 Mussolini's war diary recovered slightly, most likely because on 1 February he was given command of a grenade launcher section. On 14 February he commented on a fallen soldier and how the dead consecrated and revitalized the conquered territory:

> A dead soldier wrapped in tent canvas passes. Few soldiers follow him. A priest makes a few gestures. The passers-by take off their headwear and move on. Last night the Austrians threw some bombs into our trench. At the foot of these hills are the cemeteries which consecrate them. Ours increases in size . . . The brief funeral did not interrupt the traffic and the movement of other men. My melancholy thoughts turn to that unknown soldier of Italy who goes underground while with its warmth the sky announces spring.

And on 22 February Mussolini killed (or probably killed) enemy soldiers for the first time. That day he wrote: 'This morning, at dawn, I gave the Germans their morning call, with an Excelsior bomb type B which landed right in their trench. The red point of a lighted cigarette went out and probably also the smoker.' But no sooner had he placed this notch on his pistol than on the afternoon of 23 February 1917 he was, or so it has traditionally been claimed, involved in an accident. A friendly grenade launcher exploded and Mussolini was hit by flying metal splinters. He was taken to the dressing station at Doberdò, then to the field hospital in Ronchi and away from the battlefield forever.

Until some recent publications by the author, nobody had ever seriously doubted the proposition that Mussolini was injured at the front and that this accounted for his convalescent leave of one year which was extended in August 1918 by another six months. Professional analysis of Mussolini's medical records (contained in ACS, SPDCR, FP/R 'Mussolini Benito', s.fasc. 5, ins. D) suggests, however, that he was not at all seriously injured. A handful of small pellet-type objects were removed from his body, and from his right thigh in particular; however, his hospitalization in Milan from 2 April to 11 August 1917 was for neurosyphilis in the form of *tabes dorsalis*, while the main treatment in late March at the field hospital, hence even before the transfer to Milan, was for the effects of a gumma (a kind of small, soft, rubbery tumour characteristic of advanced syphilis), which had caused inflammation of tissue in the marrow of Mussolini's right shin bone. In the Red Cross hospital in Milan, Mussolini was looked after by Dr Ambrogio Binda, a close friend of the Mussolini family, who disguised the main symptoms of Mussolini's syphilis by inventing an otherwise non-existent injury thus offering a viable explanation for the patient's inability to walk (which was actually due to syphilitic nerve lesions of the spinal bone marrow). But there were limits to Binda's loyalty: in his final report dated 24 July he recommended only two months' convalescent leave. This document was subsequently modified by a hand that was not Binda's, the sixty-day leave being struck out in favour of an unconvincingly (and illegally) inserted 'one year'. The transcribed copy of the same document was not written by Binda, but was altered by him so that the original sixty days was crossed out and 'one year' inserted. Examination of these two documents by handwriting experts suggests that Binda wrote his original report and falsified the copy in a way that betrays his reluctance to be involved in the affair. Powers greater than Binda were obviously at work. Bissolati was once again the key figure most likely behind the cover-up, just as in November 1916. *Il Secolo*, a newspaper close to him, was omnipresent in the entire affair. The King may also have been consulted on the issue, and had quite likely been scrutinizing Mussolini for some time, given that he visited Mussolini's bedside, remembered seeing the patient in hospital in 1915 and returned to say goodbye after doing his rounds. In short, this was no ordinary wounded soldier. The State authorities had clearly altered their perception of the danger represented by Mussolini the 'socialist revolutionary'. On 20 September 1915 Mussolini's colonel had sought to isolate him from the other soldiers by offering him an administrative job, while Zuppelli and Salandra had been reluctant to make him an officer in 1915–16, as we have seen. Also, in another diary entry, this time on 20 February 1916, that is in the days leading up to his 1 March 1916 promotion, Mussolini was once again sized up by a concerned colonel who wanted to know if he was still the same troublemaker that had caused him, as a member of the forces of law and order, so much aggravation in Milan. "'Old times!'" Mussolini replied, and the promotion was granted ten days later. Now, in 1917, under the Boselli government, with Bissolati as a junior minister and with Mussolini having clearly established his pro-State credentials, the institutions were prepared to defend his mythopoeically constructed charismatic persona against the socially and politically destructive implications of syphilis, to cover all this in a shroud of war heroism and to sponsor his return to the home front to combat the enemy within (O'Brien 2002a; 2003).

Mussolini wrote little in the first couple of months after his presumed accident. On 16 April he sent a good wishes telegram to the Congress of Bissolati's Partito Socialista Riformista (OO, VIII: 311), and on 18 April again wrote to his sister (Mancini Mussolini, 1957: 71). But progressively over the following six months, as war became revolution, he increased his journalistic output. The pen completely replaced the 'bayonet'.

–6–

War and Revolution
March–October 1917

Fascism must not only not oppose the agricultural masses, but must help them remove
their centuries-old and sacred hunger for the land.

Mussolini, *Il fascismo nel 1921*, 7 January 1921

When, in 1917, a few Italians were sticking it out in the trenches, the men of anti-
fascism were endeavouring to stab them in the back with the revolt of Turin.

Mussolini, Speech to the Senate, 2 April 1925

And if there had been a government which had imposed a severe discipline within,
which had dispersed with a whip the evil genius of the draft dodgers, and had severely
punished the defeatists and traitors with the necessary lead in the back, today the
history of the Italian war would have only luminous pages.

Mussolini, Speech in Milan, 25 October 1932

Nation, War and Revolution, May–June 1917

Down to February 1917 the war had created a sharp polarity for Mussolini
between the nation and its enemies. The international politics of the conflict had
been simplified further following the Italian declaration of war on Germany in
August 1916. But Mussolini's worldview became considerably more complex in
March 1917 when the Russian Revolution destabilized the Entente, reinforced the
currents of anti-war dissent in Italy, and posed the question of how the faltering
Italian military effort might best be galvanized anew to redeem the soldiers' sacrifice and achieve the imperial goals for which Mussolini had so ardently advocated
Italy's entry into the war. Revolution, in short, gave a new dynamic to the war and
its impact on Italian politics, and it was this that preoccupied Mussolini as he fully
reassumed the role of political journalist that he had partly placed in abeyance
when he became a soldier. Although he had episodically acted as a political agi-
tator during his eighteen months as a soldier, and had consciously constructed a
war diary for political ends, much of his attention had been occupied by the creation of the persona of an exemplary warrior and the incarnation of the élite of the
trenches. Now he was not only free to pursue his role as the leading journalist and

editorial inspiration of *Il Popolo d'Italia*, he was also licensed by powerful figures to do so. It is nevertheless noteworthy that from June 1917 onwards Mussolini went into semi-anonymity, signing his articles with the sole letter *M*. From behind this half mask he did not abandon the moral and political capital represented by the soldiers' sacrifice in the punishing war of stalemate. However, as a home front activist of considerable importance he had to find new ways of addressing and using it. *Il Popolo d'Italia* again provided the principal vehicle for this endeavour, and with the war diary placed in a drawer until 1923 the newspaper articles once again become our primary source.

In Russia between 7 and 11 March a wave of strikes and demonstrations hit Petrograd. Entire regiments mutinied and passed over to the side of the strikers. At the end of the five days thousands of workers and soldiers (most of whom were peasants) marched on the Parliament (Duma). On 12 March the Petrograd Soviet (council) of Workers' Deputies was formed. It demanded an end to the Tsarist regime and the convocation of a Constituent Assembly. With no significant military force behind him, Nicholas II abdicated on 14 March in favour of his brother Michael, and two days later Michael was forced to follow in his brother's footsteps. Workers wanted the eight-hour day and control over production; the peasantry, encouraged and supported by the soldiers, wanted the land; finally, workers, soldiers and peasants, men and women, wanted an end to the war. Political representatives of the Soviet did not, however, take power. Convinced that the revolution had to pass through a 'bourgeois' phase before socialism could become a reality, the 'orthodox Marxist' Mensheviks conceded the reins of the State to representatives of the order whose principal figure had just abdicated.

A Provisional Government was formed on 14 March with a nobleman, Prince George Lvov, as Prime Minister and Paul Miliukov, a key figure in the formulation of foreign policy under the Tsar, as Minister for Foreign Affairs. This did not augur well for peace moves and, indeed, pointed towards continuation of the war along previous imperialist lines. Contradictions were therefore rife between the Provisional Government and the Soviets of workers, soldiers and peasants which were propping it up. The Petrograd Soviet's 'Order no. 1', issued on 14 March, did away with badges of rank in the army and invoked the creation of political committees in every army unit. On 27 March it called on all peoples to end the war without annexations, without indemnities and in the framework of the rights of peoples to self-determination (Trotsky, 1967, I: Chs 7 and 9; Lincoln, 1994: Ch. 11). All of this spelled danger for the Entente and Italy, since it meant that Russia might pull out of the war and free up many of the approximately eighty-three German and forty-eight Austro-Hungarian divisions from the eastern front. Ostensibly compensating for this possibility was the fact that America declared war on Germany on 6 April. But American men and material would be slow in getting to Europe. In the meantime, the morale of the French Army received a major blow following the quick collapse of Nivelle's 16 April offensive on the Aisne against the Chemin des Dames. In May and June mutinies broke out involving tens of thousands of men, mostly from the area of the attack (Pedroncini, 1967).

It was not immediately apparent to opinion in the Entente countries that revolution would weaken the Russian war effort rather than strengthening it. The precedent of the French Revolution suggested that it might unleash the energies of a national-democratic mobilization against an enemy now deemed to be a counter-revolutionary menace. This was the view, for example, of Irakli Tseretelli, a Menshevik, who argued in the Soviet for a reconciliation of the struggle for peace and an unwillingness to weaken the army's resolve to defend the revolution. Not even this was good enough for Miliukov, who viewed it as the use of socialist terminology to mask a German-inspired plan to undermine the war effort (Lincoln, 1994: 360). From both these perspectives, Lenin's and the Bolsheviks' attempt to harness the pervasive sentiment for bread, peace and land could only be interpreted negatively. It was seen as directed against the revolution, inimical to the Entente, a subversive attempt to overthrow existing social relations, and, from all these angles, a domestic version of the foreign enemy.

Giovanna Procacci has traced in some detail the Italian interventionists' unfolding misinterpretation of the 'February Revolution' (February according to the Russian calendar of the day. All dates mentioned here in relation to the revolution are, however, as per the Western calendar). At first they saw in it a confirmation of their own perceived role in pushing Italy into the war in 1915, that is as a victory of the 'revolutionary' pro-war elements over the anti-national and peace-mongering 'enemy within'. They believed that in Russia one pro-war wing of the ruling class had taken power from another. But at the end of March, with diplomatic channels reopened and censorship eased, it became evident that the Russian masses and the Petrograd Soviet had been decisive in the overthrow of the Tsar. Procacci has shown that the Italian interventionists simply reworked this news so that it conformed to their previous biases. They concluded that the possible 'degeneration' of the Russian Revolution into a separate peace could only be down to the Leninists having stirred up the masses against the war. By early June interventionist pro-war illusions regarding the revolution had disappeared: now it was merely proof of the disaster to which the 'enemy within' could lead if its work was left unchallenged (Procacci, Gv., 1999: 253–315).

Il Popolo d'Italia shared in the original illusion as to the revolution's character. Its 16 March headline announced the 'victorious revolution against the Germanophile reactionaries' and it assured any concerned readers that the promoters of the movement had been recruited from liberal elements. Together with other Italian newspapers, it negatively assessed Lenin's return to Russia. On 21 April it referred to him as 'Germanophile' and reported that on arrival in Russia he had been 'crushed' by the indignant shouts and whistles of workers and soldiers. Mussolini, too, was involved in this original misunderstanding and consequent clarification of what was happening in Russia. On 24 May, in his first serious journalistic outing since his 'injury', he viewed the revolution positively, claiming that without it Russia would have already arrived at a separate peace. He recognized that the masses were an active component in the revolution, and suggested that the current instability of the republican government was normal (OO, VIII: 277–9).

The instability to which he was referring was no doubt the one issuing from the crisis provoked by Miliukov's 1 May note which reaffirmed Russian ambitions for territorial expansion. When the Soviet got word of the content of this document, mass demonstrations were called and political heads began to roll. On 15 May news was leaked of the resignations of Miliukov and Minister for War Alexander Guchkov. In the meantime, on 10 May, Lvov invited members of the Petrograd Soviet to join the Provisional Government. The new cabinet was formed on 18 May and included Alexander Kerensky, a Social Revolutionary (historically speaking a peasant-based party which, however, was now primarily urban) who became Minister for War. It is not clear just how much Mussolini knew about this transformation, since his article referred to Russia as 'the republic of Miliukov', when by 15 May Miliukov had already gone. What is evident, however, is that Mussolini was identifying the revolution with what in fact was a counter-revolutionary figure. He claimed that Miliukov would 'save Russia and the republican idea'. Yet Miliukov was neither a republican nor a revolutionary, and in fact worked to use the war against the revolution. Seeing in the Tsar the symbolic guarantee of landed interests, he had been involved in post-revolution attempts to restore him to power. He was almost certainly behind the injured veterans' pro-war demonstration of 29 April, a counter-revolutionary initiative which sought to prepare the ground for the publication of the note of 1 May (Trotsky, 1967, I: 176–7, 318). In its turn, *Il Popolo d'Italia* had supported the 29 April demonstration, interpreting it as proof of the anti-Lenin and pro-war content of the revolution. And as if to show that neither his nor his newspaper's support for such an anti-popular figure as Miliukov was fortuitous, Mussolini argued that the popular demonstrations in Russia were 'follies of the people', that the masses would eventually 'come to their senses' and that 'if needs be' this would be with 'shootings' (OO, VIII: 277–9).

The rapid construction and deconstruction of war myths was further accentuated by a renewed Italian offensive in May, the Tenth Battle of the Isonzo. The offensive aimed at the Bainsizza plateau which, together with the plateau of Ternova, would need to be captured in order to cover the left wing of 3rd Army troops advancing through the Vippacco valley against the Trstely-Hermada bulwark. Following an artillery bombardment on 12 and 13 May, General Luigi Capello's

Zona di Gorizia (a special command formed on 10 March) went over the top on 14 May. The Kuk fell into Italian hands as did Mount Santo, though the latter was lost again that evening during a counter-attack. At a meeting with Capello on the evening of 15 May Cadorna became convinced of the possibility of capturing Mount Vodice. He thus allowed Capello to keep the heavy artillery which was supposed to be transferred to the Duke of Aosta's 3rd Army by 18 May. Capello's men in fact conquered Mount Vodice, though this seems to have been at the price of a lost opportunity: that same day, 18 May, the 3rd Army was faced with only one division of enemy soldiers. Aosta's offensive was first of all put off until 20 May (when the heavy artillery eventually arrived), and then for a further three days due to bad weather. This gave the Austro-Hungarians sufficient time to use internal lines to transfer troops from the Mount Kuk–Mount Santo line to the exposed area. The 3rd Army nevertheless captured the salient of Hudi Log, moved into the zone of Fornazza and penetrated over 4 km at Flondar. When the offensive was called off on 28 May there were 111,794 Italian and 75,700 Austro-Hungarian casualties (Rocca, 1985: 196–203; Pieropan, 1988: Ch. 37; Isnenghi and Rochat, 2000: 195–200; Schindler, 2001: 205–15).

The setback on the Isonzo front triggered renewed misgivings in political circles about the capacity of the Italian war effort, as currently managed, to achieve victory and to quell the anti-war sentiment that was becoming more pronounced. Already in March a parliamentary grouping of right-wing interventionists had given life to a *fascio* which aimed to put pressure on the government to take firmer measures against internal anti-war tendencies. 'Committees of internal defence' were formed in the major cities. The government weakness to which they referred was in relation to the popular agitations which had been taking place all over Italy since the beginning of the year. Most recently, between 30 April and 10 May thousands of women from the countryside had converged on Milan (4,000 in the centre, 8,000 in the hinterlands, at least according to official reports) in protest against the war, arms production and in favour of the return of their menfolk (De Felice, 1963). Orlando, Minister for the Interior, was convinced that coercion alone would not have contributed to the prosecution of victory and that it was necessary to respect fundamental civil liberties (Orlando, 1960: 47–55). Yet between December 1916 and April 1917, 880 people were reported to the authorities for spreading 'false and alarming news', 2,300 with participation in 'subversive demonstrations and demonstrations against the war', while another 3,901 were arrested for the same 'offence' (De Felice, 1963: 468).

But none of this satisfied interventionists. They awaited the anniversary of Italian intervention on 24 May and used this occasion to seek Cadorna's support for a campaign against Orlando's policies and against the 'internal enemy', proposals which Cadorna backed. Two days later the Milanese committee, with the support of Bissolati's *Il Secolo*, published a document which argued for the installation of a 'war government', hinting that such a government already existed and could be found at the High Command headquarters in Udine (Melograni, 1969: 311–23; Rocca, 1985: Ch. 11). In short, a storm was brewing over dictatorship. On 5 June, in the first of a series of letters to Boselli, Cadorna blamed the military setback on poor troop morale, defeatist propaganda and government lethargy. He was almost certainly favourable to a more authoritarian, perhaps military, form of government, as is evidenced in his otherwise unnecessary visit to Rome in early June, which was called off only because of the success of a localized Austrian counter-offensive at Flondar on 4 June. On 6 June Bissolati, together with his colleague Ivanoe Bonomi and the republican Ubaldo Comandini, used Sonnino's declaration of Albania as an Italian protectorate as a pretext to open up a government crisis. They then demanded that Orlando be replaced by a more energetic and less Giolittian figure. Cadorna backed up this manoeuvre by sending two further letters to Boselli on 6 and 8 June. In the ensuing political crisis the 'Committees of internal defence' pushed for a non-legal solution. But Bissolati feared that pushing things too far might provoke an Italian version of the Russian Revolution. By 12 June he and the other two ministers were back in government and a cabinet reshuffle by Boselli saw Cadorna met half way by the removal of Minister for War Morrone and his replacement with General Gaetano Giardino (Rocca, 1985: 218–22).

As during the government crisis in June 1916, Mussolini remained silent until the political dilemma was over, resurfacing only on 15 June to ridicule what he saw as the inadequacy of the cabinet facelift (OO, VIII: 280–82). The following day he argued that the anti-war agitations of early May had been of Austrian doing and that not the weak government 'but the bulletins of the Carso offensive' had 'suffocated' them, since once the offensive was underway the whole country had been 'run through with a purifying enthusiasm' (OO, VIII: 283–5). That same day *Il Popolo d'Italia*'s front page demanded the substitution of the government with a war committee. Mussolini's 17 June article focused on precisely this issue, though it is not altogether clear what he meant by this term. He specified that while a war government would have 'no scruples when it comes to going beyond what in normal times constitutes the inviolability of laws, of institutions, of prejudices, of men,' he did not support the idea of a dictatorship as such, since this did not coincide with what he termed 'our libertarian political conceptions' (OO, VIII: 286–8). He seems, in other words, to have accepted extra-legal and dictatorial measures but wanted these embedded in some type of legal framework. At any rate, the immediate task of this legal-illegal government was made clear two days later in an article which reiterated the need to crystallize the enemy into one and one only: Germany. This now included a call for the removal of rights of circulation for German subjects on Italian territory and, as also demanded in his 15 June article, the confiscation of their goods (OO, IX: 5–8).

Hence as Mussolini's writing gained pace in terms of quantity and regularity he at no point borrowed the idea from the Russian Revolution that social reform (such as the Soviets' demand for land distribution) should characterize a renewed Italian war effort. Concerned over weakening home front morale in Italy and the failure of renewed Italian offensive operations he merely demanded more authoritarian government. But in Mussolini's eyes, the focus of a campaign for national remobilization remained the front line soldier for whom, speaking now from outside rather than as one of them, he claimed unspecified recognition. He argued, in his 15 June article, that the wealth expropriated from German subjects on Italian soil should be put towards a fund for the families of Italy's fallen (OO, VIII: 280–82). In an article of 27 June he explained the rationale behind this move towards satisfying the material interests of the combatants:

> If words are to remain impressed in the spirits [of the soldiers] as a stimulant to the carrying out of [their] duty and are not to be lost together with the echoes of speeches, then after ideal arguments the arguments of the 'real' need to be touched upon. The mediocre politicking government has not known what to say and has not wanted to say to the soldiers what needs to be said. We need to get out of the repertoire of vague phrases and assume concrete, solemn commitments which can be actuated immediately. (OO, IX: 18–20)

He then went on to list these 'concrete commitments' which were identical to those of the 15 June article. This was a far cry from calling for the expropriation of Italian landowners' property and its distribution to the peasant soldiers and their families. Yet these proposals represent an important move away from the non-material mobilization based on personal charisma, scintillating gestures and the officers' recounting of heroic actions which had so marked his war diary. How, then, did this new dependence on more 'concrete' social issues develop in the context of the deepening crises in Russia and Italy and in relation to the Italian interventionists' proposed war government?

July Days

In mid-1917 offensive warfare seemed to link the fate of Italy with that of the Russian Revolution. In order to win favour with Russia's increasingly concerned allies and to remobilize pro-war sentiment at home, Minister for War Kerensky decided on a new offensive. This began on 1 July when General Alexei Brusilov unleashed thirty-one divisions along a fifty mile front in Eastern Galicia. At first the offensive was an apparent success: 10,000 German and Austrian defenders were taken prisoner and, further south, General Lavr Kornilov captured 7,000 Austrians (Gilbert, 1994: 343; Herwig, 1997: 334). Kerensky could not contain his excitement. He saw in the spirit of the fighting soldiers a confirmation of the remobilizing potential of the revolution and the need to defend it against the Germans and Austrians (Lincoln, 1994: 408–9). But Kerensky's excitement was as misplaced as his conviction that the Russian soldiers could be mobilized by his scintillating but programmatically vacuous and hence socially conservative speeches. On replacing Guchkov he had thought to rebuild the army 'with charisma as his only offering and words as his only instruments'. There was little of the revolutionary about this offensive, even though ordered by the man who claimed to have been 'sent by the revolution' (Lincoln, 1994: 370–71). The offensive had *perforce* to be played up as a success for reasons of an internal political nature and most especially to challenge the pretensions of the Soviet to controlling military affairs and redefining the character of the war. 'From the outset of preparations for the offensive', Trotsky argued, 'there began an automatic increase of the influence of the commanding staff, the organs of finance capital and [Miliukov's] Kadet party' (Trotsky, 1967, II: 118). In his view, moreover, the only way Russian soldiers could have been convinced that the offensive formed part of a revolutionary defensive war was with the *immediate* abolition of existing socio-economic relations on the land. Failing this, it was destined to assume 'the character of an adventure' (Trotsky, 1967, I: 356).

Indeed, when the Austro-German counter-offensive began in mid-July it easily drove back the Russians in the central sector, chasing a retreating army through Galicia and Bukovina and inflicting 40,000 losses (Herwig, 1997: 334–5). As a consequence of the army's deepening disintegration Kerensky took over from Lvov as Prime Minister on 21 July. He sacked Brusilov and replaced him with Kornilov. In the meantime, mass demonstrations had been held in Petrograd between 17 and 18 July and were quickly transformed into a semi-insurrection. Bolshevik leaders managed, however, to convince protesters that the time to seize power had not yet come. But following the movement's withdrawal there was an enormous backlash. The Bolshevik press was closed down, Lenin fled to Finland and other Bolshevik leaders and supporters were arrested and imprisoned. By virtue of what was termed a 'mysterious succession' of events, that is the coincidence of the dates of the July insurrection and the military collapse, the Bolsheviks, and Lenin in particular, were labelled as agents of a German plot (Trotsky, 1967, II: Chs 1–4).

How did Mussolini assess the Russian July offensive and its consequences? And what role did he ascribe to his increasingly 'concrete' form of national remobilization in Italy via the Russian surrogate? On 5 July, when news of Brusilov's 'achievements' had been received, Mussolini wrote: 'I kneel before this double victorious consecration, against the Tsar first, against the Kaiser now.' He saw Brusilov's triumph as a victory over Lenin and also claimed that the offensive proved that land reform in the here and now was utopian:

The Russian peasant, who had abandoned the trenches to go to the land, to take possession once and for all of the land, has understood, with the profound orientation of those spirits not poisoned by earthly and divine theologies, that a separate peace would be a betrayal and that universal peace is not possible without the defeat of Germany. A mysterious but persuasive voice seems to have said: if you don't beat off the German threat, the land will never be yours. (OO, IX: 26–8)

Revolutionary social reforms were not, therefore, to be identified with those 'concrete commitments' which could be 'actuated immediately' and to which he had referred in the 27 June article. Later on in July Mussolini supported Kerensky's dictatorship. This had been voted for almost unanimously in the Petrograd Soviet on 22 July and was to take the form of a government of public safety with unlimited powers (Trotsky, 1967, II: 120–21). Like Trotsky, but with approval rather than disapproval, Mussolini saw this as a Bonapartist resolution of the February Revolution that would keep Russia in the war. He argued that 'at a certain moment the French Revolution was [Lazare-Nicolas] Carnot [organiser of the French revolutionary army] and then Napoleon'. His point was that, similar to the transition from Carnot to Napoleon, 'Russia today is Kerensky.' Kerensky represented 'the synthesis which conciliates and annuls opposites'. But while this statement contrasts with Trotsky's definition of the Bonapartist role which he believed Kerensky was seeking to assume by using his position to adopt force against perpetrators of anti-ruling class 'anarchy' but not against reactionaries (Trotsky, 1967, II: 143), in the very same article Mussolini confirmed precisely Trotsky's definition. He opened the piece by quoting a news agency dispatch from Petrograd, which in turn quoted an appeal from the Petrograd Soviet, which had agreed to Kerensky's 22 July proposal, to install a dictatorship. The document in question stated that a government of public safety would be formed in full agreement with the Soviet, that it would assume the form of a '"revolutionary dictatorship"' and that it would take '"a series of measures aimed at defending and reinforcing the front, pushing back the enemy, *introducing democratic and social reforms* and re-establishing revolutionary order with an iron hand"' (our emphasis). Crucially, however, when recalling this declaration later on in the article Mussolini removed one of its cornerstones. He wrote: 'The task of the dictator is fundamentally two-fold: '"a series of measures aimed at defending and reinforcing the front, pushing back the enemy and re-establishing revolutionary order with an iron hand."' He did not even insert the suspension points for the reference to 'democratic and social reforms' which he had suppressed. The reason for the censorship was made apparent at the end of the article: despite having always theorized that out of the chaos and carnage of war would issue revolution, he actually equated revolution with unacceptable 'chaos':

Revolution cannot be chaos, it cannot be disorder, it cannot be the undoing of every activity, of every limit on social life, as some extremist idiots in some countries opine. Revolution has a sense and historic import only when it represents a superior order, a political economic and moral order of an elevated sphere; otherwise it is reaction, it is the Vendée. (OO, IX: 77–8)

One can search Mussolini's articles in vain for any articulation of the elements that would go to make up this presumed 'superior political, economic and moral order'. Indeed, when, on 29 July, he returned to the morale of the Italian Army in relation to the lessons to be drawn from Russia, he resorted once more to undefined formulae:

As regards the internal conditions of the Italy of tomorrow we add: a 'social' content needs to be given to the war! Go to the soldiers: but not with uncertain promises which for their inherent inconsistency cannot raise enthusiasms, but with 'facts' which demonstrate to the men that the whole Nation is with them, that the whole Nation is concentrated in the effort of preparing a new Italy for the army which will return victorious from the re-conquered frontiers. (OO, IX: 82–4)

Even when, in one of the last articles of this period, Mussolini mentioned the land, the statement was innocuous. With reference to post-war demobilization he wrote on 16 August: 'Once back from the trenches, the peasants, who make up the majority of our army, will find their houses still in one piece and not destroyed as in France and the other invaded Nations. The land will not be devastated, but ready for fecundating labour' (OO, IX: 116–19).

What really mattered to Mussolini during this period was not social reform but the inter-related issues of the internal enemy and territorial expansion. When he dealt specifically with the collapse of the Russian Army he focused on the influence of the 'traitor' Lenin. He declared the need to 'fight against and give no truce to the Lenins of all countries until the victory'. The Lenins of all countries naturally included *Avanti!*, the 'organ of Italian "socialbochery"' which had given its '"unconditional support"' to Lenin (OO, IX: 74–6). As regards territory, however, international events conspired to undermine Mussolini's view of Italian war aims. French and British missions to the United States in April and May 1917 had let Wilson know that a secret agreement had been made with Italy in 1915, and had also revealed key elements of its content. Following these missions, Sonnino was more than concerned that the contents of the Pact of London were slipping away across the Atlantic (Rossini, 1991: 473–91). This preoccupation was underpinned by the fact that in April 1917 America did not declare war on Austria-Hungary and in fact teased out a separate peace in secret negotiations (Valiani, 1966a: 387–92).

France was also prepared to countenance this latter prospect. Even before American intervention, the Emperor Karl's brother-in-law, Prince Sisto of Bourbon-Parma, had contacted the French government with a view to opening discussions based on the proposal to evacuate Belgium, return Alsace-Lorraine and allow Serbia an outlet to the sea. No territorial concessions to Italy were foreseen during these contacts (Valiani, 1966a: 395–6; Pieropan, 1988: 262; Vivarelli, 1991, I: 186). These negotiations came to nothing, but they showed that France was not hostile to the idea of a separate peace. As for Britain, on 8 June, in the wake of the French mutinies, Lloyd George proposed to suspend the imminent British offensive in Ypres and to seek instead to isolate Germany militarily by negotiating a separate peace with Austria-Hungary (Gilbert, 1994: 338). He lost, but this did not thwart British hopes of getting Austria-Hungary to draw separate peace conclusions. Indeed, on 30 July British Foreign Secretary Arthur James Balfour made a speech in the House of Commons which focused only on the righteousness of France's territorial claims to Alsace-Lorraine, subordinating all other (undefined) commitments, and hence respect of the terms of the Pact of London (unmentioned), to military considerations. A detailed account of this speech was reproduced in the Italian press (for example on the front page of *Il Corriere della Sera* on 2 August). In the meantime, the southern Slavs were also moving. On 20 July, Pasić and Trumbić had signed an accord in Corfu which to all intents and purposes declared the birth of Yugoslavia (Bannan and Edelenyi, 1970: 256–61). Finally, in a note dated 1 August Pope Benedict XV urged the governments of the belligerent nations to put an end to what he termed the 'useless massacre'. The note was made public on 16 August and published in the papers the following day.

These world meetings, documents and statements informed Mussolini's territorial writings during the tumultuous period of the July days in Russia. As regards Britain, on 10 July he wrote that 'hundreds of thousands of treatises have been freely distributed and it has already been seen that certain currents of public opinion, especially in England, have been influenced by the Yugoslav thesis' (OO, IX: 39–41). On 15 July he responded to French Freemasons who in *Les Temps* had declared that there were 'no doubts' about Italy's rights to the Trentino, whereas Mussolini was, of course, also interested in South Tyrol up to the Brenner Pass (OO, IX: 49–51). On 3 August he conceded that Balfour had been forced to keep to abstract declarations, but he argued that the British Foreign Secretary had spoken rather flatteringly of Austria-Hungary when referring to it as 'old and great' (OO, IX: 93–6). Four days later he suggested that the Entente powers were privy to the Pact of Corfu and had effectively sanctioned it (OO, IX: 104–7). Out of hospital since 11 August, Mussolini was flabbergasted by the Pope's territorial proposals which were limited to the evacuation of Belgium and the French provinces, and negotiations as regards Alsace-Lorraine and the Italian *irredentia*. Mussolini affirmed that 'the peace proposed by Benedict XV is an Austro-German peace' (OO, IX: 120–22).

In short, Mussolini's programme of territorial expansion could not stand the test of the changed international scene on the one hand, and his refusal to envisage internal social reform as an element of mobilization on the other. At the level of representations this was expressed by an intensification of both poles of his 'war culture', that is with an increasingly demonized cosmology of 'enemies' who were cropping up everywhere: German subjects were wandering freely on Italian soil and conspiring against the Italian Army; Leninists in Russia were in the pay of the Kaiser and by inference so, too, were the socialist 'boche' of *Avanti!*; British and French allies were falling foul of Austrian-instigated 'Yugoslav imperialism' and heading ineluctably towards a dishonourable betrayal of the 1915 territorial accord; finally, the Pope was doing timely favours for the Central Powers and effectively acting as their spokesman. Would not a major success on the Isonzo put paid to all of these internal and external 'Austrian' contrivances?

Internal Upheaval, August 1917

The relationship between military offensive and domestic protest that character-ized the month of July in Russia found a parallel in Italy in the following month. On 17 August Cadorna launched an assault on the Carso that had been planned since May, and which has become known as the Eleventh Battle of the Isonzo. The objective was the plateau of Ternova to be reached via the Bainsizza plateau. If successful, the Carso would fall as would the entire Julia front. But this east-south trajectory is not what transpired. On 2 June Capello, hero of the Battle of Gorizia and now commander of the 2nd Army, presented an updated draft which contained some apparently innocuous 'secondary' manoeuvres further north from Aiba and Doblar. These were approved by Cadorna. However, these objectives had an any-thing but subordinate ring to them. The offensive had moved so far north that it now included actions against the Mrzli and Monte Rosso; the latter formed part of Monte Nero. And since the Duke of Aosta had also received approval to extend the 3rd Army's task from one of support to a full-scale offensive ranging from the Stol-Trstely to the Hermada, virtually the whole of the Isonzo front from north to south was now included in the attack.

The 2nd Army opened artillery fire from Tolmino to Mount San Gabriele at 16.00 on 17 August and the 3rd Army began on the Carso the following day. At dawn on 19 August Italian troops went over the top. It was Capello's northern ini-tiative which collapsed first. Also futile were the offensives against Mount Santo and those effected on the Carso. Some success was achieved with the XXIV army corps on Bainsizza under the command of General Enrico Caviglia. This penetra-tion, which benefited from the element of surprise, continued on 20 August. But it very quickly met with lack of water and reserves. Even so, on 21 August the advance proceeded and Auzza and the Vrh basin fell into Italian hands, as did the Kuk (not the one captured in the Tenth Battle of the Isonzo) later on that same day. Having taken stock of the situation, Cadorna ordered activity to be suspended on the Carso and for materials and men to be transferred to the Bainsizza. The Jelenik fell to Italian troops who were now moving towards the Chiapovano valley. Fieldmarshal Svetozar Boroević von Bojna, commander of Austro-Hungarian forces on the Isonzo, wanted to retreat to a new line from the Lom di Tolmino to Mount San Gabriele via the eastern margin of the Chiapavano valley and the northern margin of Ternova. Yet things were not as bad as they at first sight appeared to be. By 23 August the Italian push had waned due to lack of food and water and to the inability of Italian troops to move artillery forward on tortuous terrain. Aosta's inactivity on the Carso also meant that Boroević could now safely transfer his reserves to the Bainsizza. His men began to withdraw in an orderly manner beginning 24 August. Italian troops then moved into the 10 km gap left by the retreat. One of the enemy strongholds left vacant during the retreat was Mount Santo which the Italians duly occupied. On 26 August Cadorna decided that since the 2nd Army's attack had waned, attention should be focused on the Carso. That same day Italian troops in the forward positions noted stiffening resistance from the Lom to Mount San Gabriele. By 29 August the Austro-Hungarians knew that a rout had been avoided and that the Bainsizza plateau, despite Italian penetration, remained an important point of connection between the high and low Isonzo.

The Eleventh Battle of the Isonzo was the most bloody of the entire Italian campaign. Approximately 19,000 men died, while the majority of the over 35,000 MIAs were also counted as dead. Just over 89,000 men were injured, of whom about 10 per cent later died of their wounds. The Austro-Hungarians lost 85,000 men in battle and 28,000 through illness. Figures for Italian illnesses are not known. Penetration on the Bainsizza and the occupation of Mount Santo made no strategic difference. The bridgehead at Tolmino and the bulwarks of Mount San Gabriele and Mount Hermada were still well and truly in Austro-Hungarian hands. Despite further operations in September the Italian offensive was over and victory had not been achieved (Pieropan, 1968: Chs 42 and 43; Rocca, 1985: 239–44; Isnenghi and Rochat, 2000: 202–5; Schindler, 2001: Ch. 11).

Mussolini looked to Cadorna's latest offensive even more than he had to Brusilov's in order to restore national cohesion and a sense of direction to the war. He suggested that 'the Italians no longer look towards the Vatican from where there came a false word, but towards the Carso, solemn and tragic, from where, with the thunder of thousands and thousands of guns, the certainty of our victory reaches us' (OO, IX: 128–9). But the Papal note was nothing compared to the wave of popular hostility to the war that engulfed Turin at the time. Starting off as a women's protest against the shortage of bread on 22 August the agitation quickly spread to other sectors of the Turin working class. Paolo Spriano has shown that Turin workers, male and female, were under the enormous influence of events in Russia. This was confirmed during the visit of a Russian reformist delegation which aimed to promote the continuance of the war. On arriving in Turin on 5

August the visitors were greeted with the unexpected cry of 'Long live Lenin!' On returning to the city on 13 August, following their tour of other major centres, the delegation was met with a 40,000 strong crowd which shouted: 'Long live the Russian Revolution. Long live Lenin!' (Spriano, 1960: 225–8). Thus long before the bread crisis Turin workers were geared up for a fight against the war. Demands for bread merely provided a catalyst for a much deeper anti-war and revolutionary sentiment. Indeed, when bread was promised to protesters on 22 August it was rejected and the protest gathered pace into a full-scale anti-war general strike with street mobilizations, barricades and consequent State repression (Spriano, 1960: Chs 9 and 10 and esp. p. 236). By the time all was calm again on 26 August, around 50 protesters were dead and another 200 injured. About 1,000 were under investigation while 300 or so were sent to the front. Around ten law-enforcement agents were also killed (Spriano, 1960: 255–6).

Faced with the starkest challenge to national cohesion of the war so far, Mussolini grasped at the broken reed of Cadorna's offensive: 'It is sad, infinitely sad, that in Italy, while the army, the salt of the nation, fights and wins, in the back lines the parasites attempt to render vain the sacrifice of blood.' Against the unmentioned insurrection Mussolini counterposed the capture of Mount Santo. Like the press in general, he falsely presented the occupation of that mountain as the outcome of an Italian assault: his point was that 'faced with this superb proof [of Italian genius], defeatists are in a state of desperation. The victory of Italy is their ignominious end. They promised to celebrate their saturnalia on the corpse of the Nation. The Austrian defeat is their defeat. They try to impede it. It is complicity with the enemy' (OO, IX: 138–40). On 28 August Mussolini returned in more detail to the causes of the Turin protest, though he focused on the bread shortage rather than on the anti-war sentiment which really lay behind the protest. He observed that there was no shortage of grain in Italy and that the lack of bread was down to bureaucratic inefficiency (OO, IX: 143–5). This was true, at least to a point. Bread and flour distribution was often carried out using 1911 census figures. Uncoordinated organization allowed misunderstandings between civilian and military authorities and emergency situations were created where they need not have occurred (Procacci, Gv., 1990/91: 163; Dentoni, 1995: 31–51). At any rate, Mussolini claimed that inevitable deficiencies should not be allowed to assume 'the aura of gestures of complicity with the sabotaging manoeuvres of the internal enemies of Italy' (OO, IX: 143–5). He had therefore drawn a picture of Italy in August that differed from that of Russia in July. In substance, he was claiming that a successful offensive had redeemed an internal upheaval. But that he was less convinced of this than he would have his readers believe is witnessed by his response to the resulting pressure of both the offensive and the Turin insurrection on national cohesion and soldier morale. On 30 August he stated that the millions of lire confiscated from German subjects should still go to the soldiers' families, but with one important addition: 'Land to the peasants!' (OO, IX: 149–51).

New Fascist Intervention, September–October 1917

The road to this slogan had been a long and winding one. But how seriously did he take the proposal for land reform? A chance to show where he now stood was given as the Russian and Italian crises deepened. Between the end of the Eleventh Battle of the Isonzo and the beginning of the Austro-German Isonzo offensive on 24 October Mussolini published fifty-one articles, made one short speech (published in *Il Popolo d'Italia*) and sent a telegram (also published in *Il Popolo d'Italia*) to the mother of Filippo Corridoni on the anniversary of the syndicalist's death. The content of these pieces reveals a radical shift from his principal concerns in July and August. Only two articles out of this substantial block of material (3.8 per cent) addressed territorial disputes with the Yugoslavs (OO, IX: 178–80, 240–22). The Eleventh Battle of the Isonzo received no specific treatment, but was touched upon in various pieces (OO, IX: 188–9, 197). What, then, replaced the previously vital theme of the victorious offensive and territorial gain? Quite simply an obsession with domestic matters which accounted for 48 of the 53 published pieces, or a staggering 91 per cent, the majority of which were directed against the government, the parliament and Orlando's refusal to suppress civil liberties (OO, IX: 157–8, 159–61, 162–3, 164–7, 168–70, 171–3, 174–7, 181–3, 184–5, 186–7, 188–9, 193–6, 197, 198–9, 200–1, 202–3, 207–8, 209–14, 215, 216–17, 218–20, 221–3, 224, 225–6, 227–28, 229–30, 231–3, 234–6, 237–9, 243–5, 246–8, 249–52, 253–4, 255–7, 258–60, 261–3, 264–6, 267–9, 270–1, 272–4, 275, 276–8, 279–81, 282–4, 285–8, 289–92, 293–5, 296–8).

The fact is that the events of 22–26 August in Turin continued to plague Mussolini. Like the references to the Eleventh Battle of the Isonzo, one has to comb over fifty pieces for references to the insurrection. But those events colour his writing, as revealed by one question asked in an article of 17 October: 'Since the episode of Turin has there really and substantially been a change of direction in our internal policy?' (OO, IX: 267–9). From the first article of this series he was arguing that 'facts such as those of Turin require that those responsible, high up and low down, be identified' (OO, IX: 157–8). In attacking Orlando, Mussolini insinuated a direct link between Giolittism, the PSI, Turin, and a possible Italian defeat similar to the Russian one. On 8 September he remarked that 'it is precisely in Turin that the Socialist Party declares "with all its heart" that it is in solidarity with Lenin, whose decidedly reactionary and Germanic work is one of the main causes of the Russian defeat on the Riga front' (OO, IX: 168–70. Riga had in fact fallen into German hands on 3 September). On 10 September: 'From the grain point of view, the responsibility for the so-called facts of Turin falls in part on

Orlando and, from the political point of view, totally on him. All this with the aggravating factor of the extraordinary chronological coincidence between these facts and our offensive, a coincidence which gives things a slightly, I say only slightly, Leninist aspect' (OO, IX: 174–7).

What, then, did he propose as an alternative to the government's internal policy? The call for land reform appears only once, on 14 October. Even then, the article was not dedicated to the land question as such but to 'productivity' in general. Mussolini did not mention anything about how and when the land was to be taken away from its present owners. Indeed, the article finished by remarking that things were still 'premature' and that it was 'difficult to establish today how these great transformations are to come about'. He argued that if the government raised this issue immediately, it would 'give the combatants the firm persuasion that the State is orienting itself towards these principles' and that this in turn would 'bring to the front among the soldiers, and inside their families, an unbreakable block of energies which will be the best and absolute guarantee of our victory' (OO, IX: 258–60). In short, by raising the slogan 'Land to the peasants!' the government would increase morale and hence the possibility of victory without having to commit itself to anything concrete (since it was, after all, only 'orienting itself towards these principles').

Mussolini's ongoing refusal to embrace the cause of social reform is shown, amongst other things, by his attitude to events in Russia. Between 26 and 27 August a government-organized State Conference in Moscow attempted to show how unified the various sectors of Russian society were. The Bolsheviks, however, whose key leaders were still in hiding (Lenin) or in prison (Trotsky), had somehow managed to organize a massive counter-demonstration in the shape of a 400,000 strong strike, while Kornilov was preparing a military putsch. Kerensky originally supported Kornilov's idea, leading Trotsky to comment ironically that Kerensky was both the bearer of supreme State power and at the same time a criminal conspirator against it (Trotsky, 1967, II: 212). However, Kerensky only adopted this rather contradictory position so long as he believed that the putsch was designed to wipe out the Bolsheviks and destroy the political effectiveness of the Soviet. When he realized that the abolition of the Provisional Government was also part of Kornilov's plans he switched to oppose the putsch, even asking the Bolsheviks to use their influence in the army to convince the soldiers to fight Kornilov. Kornilov's putsch collapsed on 10 September having met with rapidly organized countermeasures in which the increasing influence and military organization of the Bolsheviks were evident (Trotsky, 1967, II: Chs 8–9; Lincoln, 1994: 412–25). Mussolini's treatment of these events relied on vague information which he nevertheless converted into clear conclusions. He argued that the February Revolution had not seen a clash of conservative and revolutionary forces, which only emerged in the present struggle. He informed readers that 'Kornilov is not a counter-revolutionary' and that 'we should be grateful to [him] for having posed the either-or'. The Soviet, on the other hand, was defined as 'irresponsible', and who won between Kerensky and Kornilov was therefore of no consequence, since what mattered was that either would 'pose a brutal end to the irresponsible annoying demagogy of the thousands of rallies and committees in Petrograd' (OO, IX: 190–92).

Mussolini's views on the Russian crisis were equally applicable to Italy. More than once he declared that 'we do not want reaction', but he then specified that this was 'in the political sense'. Beyond the 'big words of liberty and reaction' on 17 October Mussolini sought a compromise concept. He argued that 'on the eve of the third winter of war a word can and must be launched to the Italian people from the benches of the ministers, and it's this: *Discipline!*' (OO, IX: 267–9; Mussolini's emphasis). But six days earlier he had specified that 'wherever this discipline is not accepted freely and consciously it must be imposed, with violence if necessary, and even adopting that ... *dictatorship* that the Romans of the first republic resorted to in the critical hours of their history" (OO, IX: 249–52. Mussolini's emphasis). In the same period, he again called upon the social force which he deemed capable of salvaging Italy's increasingly threatened mission in the present and, more importantly, the future – the interventionists. In an article of 18 September he wrote: 'And now a question to the interventionists of all schools and ideas: will we allow Italy to be the next nation, after Russia, to be dishonoured by German Leninism? It is time to intensify the activity of our organizations to find ourselves ready for the day on which the [Italian socialists] try to transform their "highly respectable" opinions, which marvellously coincide with those of Boroevič, into facts' (OO, IX: 168–70). On 1 October he returned to this alternative vision of wartime authority: 'If the government doesn't take the necessary measures, then it is a suicidal government and, what is worse, it is a government which leads the Nation to suicide. The interventionists must therefore prepare themselves to confront the increase in social-neutralist "energy"' (OO, IX: 231–3). Seeking a symbolic expression of this alternative basis for national remobilization, Mussolini returned to the legitimizing moment of Italian entry into the war. Evoking the power of those 'memorable' days of May 1915, he wrote in September 1917:

Sometimes we still seem to hear in the air the echo of songs and the rumbling of multitudes in movement ... We stop and ask ourselves – riddled with that 'doubt' that is the hallmark of recognition of the intellectual aristocracies: has interventionism outlived its day? Is there still subject matter, opportunity, ability, necessity of intervention? Yes. Interventionism still has reason to exist for foreign policy, to keep watch so that Italy's admirable effort is recognized and not only exploited. Interventionism is above all needed for internal policy. Here interventionism assumes a politico-moral character.

He claimed that in 1915 interventionists had intervened to save the day from neutralism. Now 'we will intervene again' and, as before, 'we will sabotage the saboteurs' (OO, IX: 218–20).

Archive documentation shows that the *fasci interventisti* had been of a like mind in 1917. The Prefect of Ferrara informed the Ministry of the Interior on 25 May 1917 that in a meeting held two days previously, called to commemorate Italian intervention, the *fascio di difesa nazionale* voted in favour of adopting a concluding statement which felt 'the patriotic duty to energetically recall the attention of the governing authorities to the work of saboteurs of our Enterprise' and invoked 'energetic and timely measures against subjects of enemy states which still live undisturbed in Italy and in such conditions as to freely work against our Nation'. They further demanded that the government 'install an inflexible internal policy and inexorably strike anyone who conspires in any way against the supreme interests of the Nation'. Only in this way could the government 'count on the unconditional support of those parties which love their Country' (ACS, A5G, b. 94, fasc. 211, s. fasc. 7). In Rome, the Prefect reported on 6 June that the day before, 'in the offices of . . . *Il Popolo d'Italia*, various fascists met, among whom, apart from [Francesco] Paoloni [Rome correspondent of *Il Popolo d'Italia*], were the lawyers Pascazio and Guerazzi and the [*Il Popolo d'Italia*] journalist [Gaetano] Polverelli'. In another report from the capital dated 29 June 1917 we read that the Rome group was arguing that 'if the King and the Government are unable to fully carry out their duties against the external enemies and against the internal enemies of the Nation, then it will be left up to us to offer the solution to the problem, and with us there will be perhaps the most beautiful forces of the nation, that is military chiefs, high magistrates, the press and a large part of the bureaucracy' (both reports in ACS, A5G, b. 41, fasc. 77). Mussolini was less inclined to openly declare such dependence on the entrenched core of the State. In an article of 9 October he described interventionists using futurist-type adjectives such as 'young', 'without prejudice', 'elastic' and 'aggressive'. This left them 'in a privileged position when it comes to fighting what is old'. There was 'nobody who can block, limit or inhibit us'. And since they had 'no positions to lose or conquer' they could 'fight for the love of art'. This was 'a public of élites'; it was 'the public of the cities. The public that seeks, wants, walks' (OO, IX: 246–8). In alliance with industrialists, agrarians, army chiefs, magistrates and the State bureaucracy, this, in a word, was a fascist public in the making.

–7–

Victory Imagined
October 1917–November 1918

October 1918. Lightning advance beyond the Piave. Catastrophe of the enemy army.
Bulletin of 4 November . . . But is the war over in Italy? Not yet. We need to begin to
fight again . . . to defend the rights and above all the spirit of the Victory.

> Mussolini, Speech in Parliament, 19 March 1928

The Victory was luminously Italian. Combatants! Already with the battle of June, and
by the admission of the enemy himself, the resistance of the Habsburg Empire was
crushed; and if it is true that the Allies sent some Divisions, it is equally true that in
May 1915 we gave the Allies an entire army.

> Mussolini, Speech in Rome, 4 November 1928.

Mussolini and Defensive War

Following the Eleventh Battle of the Isonzo, Austro-Hungarian commanders
became convinced that, as men were running short and could not be readily
replaced, another Italian offensive in autumn 1917 or spring 1918 could not be
contained. On 26 August the Emperor Karl asked Kaiser Wilhelm to replace
Austrian troops on the eastern front and allow a strategic counter-attack against
Italy between Plezzo and Tolmino, the latter being the only part of the river Isonzo
not under Italian control. The Germans approved, but with the stipulation that they
were to be involved. They added seven special divisions to the eight Austrian divisions, all of which would form the 14th Austro-German Army (General Otto von
Below). Rather than aim at mountain peaks, the key attack was to proceed through
the Isonzo valley via Caporetto. This would cut off Italian troops on the
Mrzli–Mount Nero chain. Mounts Matajur, Maggiore, Kolovrat and Jeza would
likewise be encircled. As a consequence, Mount Globocak would fall, forcing
Italian troops stationed on the Bainsizza plateau and in the Carnia to retreat to a
new line between Gorizia, Udine and Pordenone. Ideally, too, Italy's 3rd Army
would have to withdraw from its advanced positions on the Carso. In short, the
battle plan pointed towards the occupation of the triangle formed by the river
Isonzo as it flows from Plezzo to Tolmino via the straits of Saga. Even if the offensive had only achieved these limited aims it would have been an enormous success.

By mid-October Italian troops had been pushed to the point of exhaustion. But this did not deter General Alberto Cavaciocchi, commander of the IV army corps covering Plezzo, from making morale-boosting speeches about the tiredness of the Germans. Capello, who was receiving treatment for nephritis, was completely out of touch with what was happening. Although not convinced that an attack was likely, he planned to confront one with an immediate counter-offensive and boasted about how many German prisoners he would take if the enemy dared try it on. So offensive-minded were Italian commanders, indeed, that Pietro Badoglio, commander of the XXVII corps stationed in the sector of Tolmino, had his troops in advanced offensive positions without reserves. Italy had forty-three divisions on the Isonzo, but only four were in the sector under threat. Three of these, which made up the IV army corps, were guarding the upper sector of the Plezzo–Saga–Tolmino triangle, whereas the trenches at Tolmino were defended only by the 19th division of the XXVII army corps, whose other three divisions were across the water on the Bainsizza plateau. There were no fortified defensive lines behind this stretch of front. For his part, Cadorna, who had just returned from holiday, remained profoundly sceptical about the invasion. Neither did Cavaciocchi and Badoglio alter his optimism: as late as 22 and 23 October they were still supplying their superior with positive assessments of the overall situation.

It was to be a rude awakening. Following heavy artillery bombardment beginning from Tolmino at dawn on 24 October, by 16.00 on the same day the 12th Silesian division was already at Caporetto. The advance from the Plezzo basin was likewise rapid, aided by the deployment of gas. That evening, the whole of the Isonzo triangle, including the mountains overlooking the plain, was under Austro-German control. Yet at 09.15 on 24 October Cadorna informed Capello not to use up too much ammunition, since this would be needed for a spring offensive. Told at eleven o'clock that Plezzo had fallen, Cadorna was not overly concerned. He considered the attack at Tolmino to be 'a bluff', and envisaged the transferral of artillery from the 2nd Army to the 3rd to defend against the real attack which he deemed likely to come on the Carso. In the meantime, following the enemy bombardment of 24 October, Badoglio was cut off from his corps. It is thought that once communication lines were cut his over-centralization of control over guns meant that his subordinates were left without orders, and that this explains the ensuing silence of over 500 pieces of Italian artillery. While there was resistance from some Italian units, these were isolated and, where not completely overrun, soon forced to surrender.

In a few days the entire Italian front collapsed. On the night between 26 and 27 October Cadorna ordered a general retreat beyond the river Tagliamento. From the Cadore to the Carso via the Carnia, 750 out of Italy's 850 battalions were forced to abandon positions conquered in almost two and a half years of fighting.

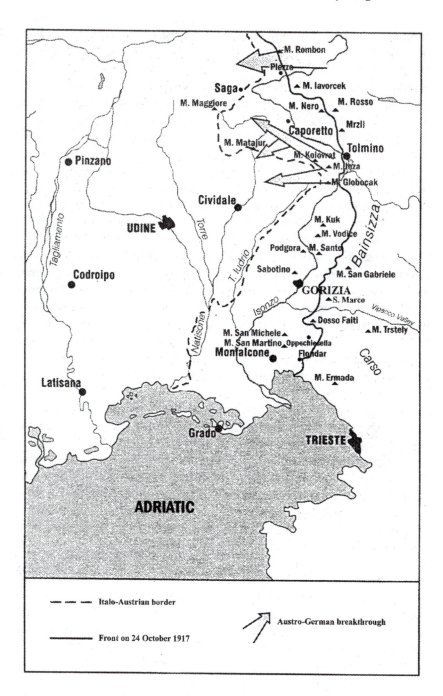

Figure 7.1 Austro-German offensive on Isonzo-Carso front October 1917
Source: adapted from Isenghi and Rochat (2000), page 375.

Hundreds of thousands of men, many disarmed and without commanders, made their way towards the designated river. The 2nd Army was the most badly hit. When, to its front line divisions of 670,000 men, we add an unspecified number of hospitalized soldiers and units working at the rear in areas such as logistics, air-fields and railways, a million routed men is not an unreasonable guesstimate. Moreover, since Italian Army divisions were made up of alternating brigades of infantry and fixed regiments of artillery, there was an enormous loss of guns and ammunition.

Two armies, however, escaped the brunt of the rout. Having lost about 20 per cent of their forces and heavy artillery, about 300,000 men of the 3rd Army on the Carso managed to retreat in reasonably good order as did 230,000 in the Cadore (the 90,000 men in the Carnia were almost all taken prisoner). On 4 November Cadorna issued the order to retreat to the river Piave beginning the following day. The last units were across the water by 10 November, while the 4th Army had com-pleted its withdrawal to Mount Grappa by 13 November. It would not be Cadorna, however, who would direct the defence operations on the Piave. On 8 November he was sacked and replaced the following day by Armando Diaz. In the meantime, five divisions of British and six of French troops were being transferred to Italy to be deployed as reserves. Once the immediate danger on the Piave had been allayed, two divisions of French troops were positioned between the Grappa and the Piave, while three divisions of British soldiers took up posts halfway along the river in front of the Montello.

Diaz was put to the test immediately. In an effort to break through onto the Veneto plain and encircle troops defending the Piave, already on 10 November the enemy attacked on the Altopiano dei Sette Comuni, and on 14 November moved against defending forces on Mount Grappa. Following offensives between 13 and 17 and between 22 and 24 November, most of the Altopiano was occupied by the Austro-Hungarians, though they did not manage to get beyond the southern margin of the plateau. Fighting on the Grappa came to a halt on 30 December due to exhaustion and to the transfer of the German troops to the western front. As regards the Piave, invading forces were held up by the river, which was swollen with autumn rain. All things considered, then, in what has come to be known as 'Caporetto' the Italian Army had suffered an immense disaster. However, the class of 1899 was available from 15 November and 300,000 of the disbanded men were reorganized into two new Armies (the 2nd and the 5th). A new front had been established (see Fig. 7.2) and, however tenuously, Italy was still in the war (Cadorna, 1921, II: Chs 10–13; Melograni, 1969: Ch. 6; Rocca, 1985: Chs 13–14; Pieropan, 1988: Chs 46–53; Labanca, 1997; Isnenghi and Rochat, 2000: 367–85, 428–42; Morselli, 2001; Schindler, 2001: Ch. 12).

In an act of callous self-exoneration, on 25 October Cadorna informed the Minister for War that 'about 10 regiments surrendered *en masse* without fighting'.

On 27 October he issued his notorious bulletin in which he accused units of the 2nd Army of having 'retreated in a cowardly manner without fighting' and of having 'ignominiously surrendered to the enemy' (Rocca, 1985: 287 and 292–93). National dissemination of Cadorna's 27 October statement was blocked by the outgoing government, and the notorious phrase rewritten as: 'The violence of the attack and the deficient resistance of some units of the 2nd Army.' But the army information service had already broadcast Cadorna's bulletin internationally. This gave the Austro-Hungarians the opportunity to implement a three-point plan hatched a week or so before Caporetto: defeat Italy on the battlefield, occupy its territory and saturate it with anti-government and anti-High Command propaganda (Cornwall, 2000: 80–81). The following leaflet, for example, was dropped from the air by the Austro-Hungarians on 29 October 1917:

> In such a critical moment for your nation, your Commander-in-Chief, who, together with Sonnino, is one of the most guilty authors of this useless war, resorts to a strange expedient to explain the undoing. He has the nerve to accuse your army, the flower of your youth, of cowardice, that same army which has so many times thrown itself forward in useless and desperate attacks! This is the payment for your valour! You have spilt your blood in so much fighting and the enemy itself has never denied its esteem for you as valorous adversaries. And your General dishonours you, he insults you to cover himself! (Quoted in Melograni, 1969: 398, n. 131)

In the week or so after 24 October Mussolini differed sharply from Cadorna over the causes of the defeat. He responded to the vexed issue of responsibility for Caporetto on 2 November. He did not refer to the wording of Cadorna's bulletin, limiting himself, rather, to the updated government version (which still mentioned inadequate resistance by some soldiers). Mussolini accepted the official explanation, though not without qualification: 'Very well: there may have been a moment of weakness and shame . . . But, mark you, this has happened to all armies, to all peoples and in all times . . . Our soldier will return to being what he was. His temperament has not changed . . . The valour of the Italian soldier is consecrated in eleven battles of the Isonzo; it is consecrated in the long line of cemeteries which from Saga to Monfalcone marks the passage of our sacrifice' (OO, X: 14–16). The following day he remarked that 'the capsizing does not lie in the loss of Udine, it lies in the bulletin which spoke of the deficient resistance of some units' (OO, X: 20–22). Mussolini's point, made clearer in his article of 8 November, was that there was more to that passivity than the cowardice which the bulletins were oversimplistically and accusingly claiming. He demanded that the government 'say how it came to pass that some units offered "deficient resistance" . . . The government cannot leave the country in the anxiety provoked by Cadorna's bulletin' (OO, X: 33–5). On 12 November he argued that factors other than the deficient resistance of some units, such as the dense fog (which had allowed enemy penetration without being seen) and the enemy's use of gas, had contributed to the defeat (OO, X: 45–7). Two days later he insisted that the government provide a chronological account of events during the week between 24 October and 1 November, 'not for purposes of "recrimination", but to use as a lesson'. He demanded 'a bit of truth for the country' and 'a bit of justice for the soldiers!' (OO, X: 50–51).

Mussolini's calls for justice went beyond his rejection of Cadorna's accusations. He supported measures taken by the government and the High Command to rectify the causes of the soldiers' discontent. For example, under Diaz daily calorific intake rose from 3,067 to 3,580 (Melograni, 1969: 460; Mangone, 1987: 92). When the first improvements were announced in December, Mussolini was ecstatic: 'In the name of God! Finally someone is beginning to understand what is needed, together with propaganda, to keep soldier morale high' (OO, X: 152–3). Under Diaz, rest periods and entertainment were more democratically organized; a new leave of ten days was added to the fifteen-day winter leave of the Cadorna regime; special leave periods were also granted to increasing numbers of soldiers who had to work the fields. And with two decrees of December 1917 Francesco Saverio Nitti, Minister for the Treasury, inaugurated free insurance policies of 500 and 1,000 lire for soldiers and NCOs respectively (Melograni, 1969: 460–61). There were no more summary executions (*decimazioni*), official executions for desertion were half the pre-Caporetto rate, and the highly feared 'torpedoings' (*siluramenti*), that is the sacking of officers scapegoated for Cadorna's miscalculations, were half the monthly figure under Cadorna. Finally, it is worth noting that from Caporetto to the armistice the death rate of Italian soldiers was drastically reduced by three-quarters (Mangone, 1987: 93).

To what degree did this more humane treatment of the soldiers find resonance in the political reasons for which Italy was fighting the war and the way this was expressed in military strategy? At the inter-allied conference in Versailles from 30 January to 2 February 1918 no offensive plans were hatched, just the occasional local counter-offensive. This was in keeping with pessimistic French and British forecasts that hostilities would end in spring 1919 at the earliest. This suited Diaz, who, in a phase of reconstruction of the Italian Army, was only too willing to limit his ambitions to improvements in position (Mangone, 1987: Ch. 3). Mussolini supported this defensive stance, linking it to a specific, and decidedly modified, understanding of Italian war aims. On 31 October he argued in favour of a non-egotistic politico-military strategy. He was pleased that the British and French press were now announcing the imminence of a unified command, since the 'fate of one ally is indissolubly linked to the fate of all' (OO, X: 8–10). With obvious reference to the arrival of French and British reinforcements, he noted on 3 November that 'today there is only one Entente Army . . . A number of elements which we cannot make public confirm our staunch faith. We will say only that the contribution of the Allies is grandiose' (OO, X: 20–22). He returned to this issue on 17 November, arguing that even 'the man in the street' had been 'insisting that the Entente become an alliance, that national idiosyncrasies finish, that national "sacred egoisms" conflate into a "sacred egoism" common to all threatened peoples' (OO, X: 58–60). In early December he claimed that 'our task is to resist in order to allow America to enter fully into combat. It is the weight of the New World which will crush Germany' (OO, X: 114–16), and he insisted that American intervention copper-fastened the democratic nature of Italy's war (OO, X: 127–9).

Mussolini's proposals became more deeply embedded in a democratic war policy in the first half of 1918. The pro-nationalities current in Italy, under the tutelage of *Il Corriere della Sera*, began to more vigorously pursue a policy of Italian fraternization with the Balkan peoples. A conference of nationalities oppressed by the Austro-Hungarian Empire was held in Rome between 8 and 10 April 1918. On 7 April Mussolini wrote that the Slavs 'now turn to Italy as their redeemer', adding that 'in these days we feel the omnipotence of the spirit of Mazzini. A politics which takes its inspiration from the prophet of the rights of peoples cannot fail' (OO, X: 433–5). The ensuing Pact of Rome was signed by Italy, Yugoslavia, Rumania, Poland and Czechoslovakia. It called for the defeat and dismemberment of Austria-Hungary (Amendola, 1919: 5–44). While it was never adopted by Sonnino, it had the approval of the new Prime Minister, Orlando, who had taken office in late October–early November 1917. On 11 April the government sanctioned the formation of a Czechoslovak legion which left for the front towards the end of May. Moreover, in various communiqués and conversations between April and June Orlando accepted that the Pact of London was now outdated and agreed to the division of Istria (Evans Line) as the basis of a future accord with the Yugoslavs (Vivarelli, 1991, I: 211–12).

The Pact of Rome emerged during a change in American foreign policy with respect to Austria-Hungary. The latter had originally responded quite positively to the tenth point of Wilson's fourteen-point plan for peace, since it recognized the right of the peoples of the empire only to 'the freest opportunity of autonomous development' and not to independent states. Similarly, in his speech to the Trades Union Congress on 5 January 1918 Lloyd George recognized independence for Poland, but only the right of autonomy to the subject peoples of the Austro-Hungarian Empire (Lloyd George, 1938, II: 1492–3). But following the Clemenceau–Czernin affair, in which it was revealed by the French Prime Minister that the Austrian Minister for Foreign Affairs had lied about Emperor Karl's recognition in March 1917 of the legitimacy of French territorial claims to Alsace-Lorraine, Robert Lansing, the American Secretary of State, realized that a separate peace with Austria-Hungary was unlikely. On 11 May he expressed approval of the Rome congress, and on 29 May announced American sympathy for the Yugoslav cause. On 5 June a joint declaration of France, England and Italy recognized Polish rights to independence and echoed American approval for Czechoslovak and Yugoslav objectives (Valiani, 1966a: 331 and n. 90, 365).

Writing on 7 June Mussolini argued that the 5 June joint declaration would never have been issued but for the political effects of the Pact of Rome and he also insisted that Czechoslovakia's right to an independent state should be immediately recognized (OO, XI: 113–15). But things took a further turn in the following weeks. On 24 June Lansing wrote to the Serb ambassador in America to inform him that the US now fully recognized Slav national rights (Lederer, 1966: 43). The Pact of Rome had therefore entered Wilson's New Diplomacy, and the Pact of London had been definitively superseded. As regards Italy's territorial claims, in the ninth item of his fourteen-point speech Wilson limited these to what he termed a 'readjustment' of Italian borders on the basis of 'clearly recognizable lines of nationality'. Caporetto therefore appears to have wrought a profound transformation in Mussolini, who now endorsed a radical reinterpretation of Italy's war from one of conquest and secret treaties to one for national defence and international liberation.

The depth of this mutation can be examined in the context of the Austro-Hungarian offensive of June 1918. On the one side stood the newly regenerated and democratic forces of Italy defending their invaded territory; on the other the Austro-Hungarian oppressor of peoples striving to save itself through one last sweeping offensive manoeuvre. The final plan foresaw attacks on the Altopiano dei Sette Comuni (Operation Radetzky), the Piave (Operation Albrecht) and the Montello, the latter serving as a pivot between the former two. All this was to be preceded by Operation Lawine (Avalanche), a diversionary attack beginning much further east from the Passo del Tonale. Radetzky and Albrecht were to be unleashed on the night between 14 and 15 June, while Lawine was to begin three days beforehand. As for the Italians, while troop morale was still causing concern for the High Command as late as April 1918, by May intelligence reported an improvement. All of the approximately 3,150 pieces of artillery lost in the October 1917 retreat had been replaced, revealing much about the changed balance of forces. In the whole of 1918 the crisis-ridden Austro-Hungarian Empire produced only 2,064 pieces of artillery. Italy's total artillery in June 1918 was 6,546 pieces which, although deployed in a generally defensive framework, was ready to be used for immediate counter-attack and even pre-emptive strikes. Crucially, two important lessons had been learnt from Caporetto. First, divisions were now made up of four regiments (twelve battalions) of infantry and one of artillery, all of which had to move as an indivisible unit. Secondly, almost a third of all forces were in reserve and all were facing the Piave to the east while ready to move to the west on a reasonably good system of roads and railways.

The Italian Army stood the test. Pinned down by Italian shell fire 'Operation Lawine' did not get beyond its starting point. On the Altopiano dei Sette Comuni, where there was the heaviest concentration of Austrian forces (174 battalions), the artillery of Italy's 6th Army met the enemy barrage blow for blow until 09.00 on 15 June when the Austro-Hungarian troops went over the top. The advance reached the limits of the resistance line but was pushed back with the aid of French and British troops. Austrian advances on the west of Mount Grappa did not endure. Italian assault troops were in action by the evening of 15 June, recapturing the previously lost terrain. On the Montello, Italian defence was weaker and the Austrian advance was able to link up with the offensive taking place to the left on the Piave. The latter initially went well for the Austrians. They managed to cross the river and set up two bridgeheads which soon became one. But the river began to rise, blocking the transportation of men and equipment to the far side. Moreover, the failure of 'Lawine' and 'Radetzky' meant that the Italian reserves could focus on the defence of the Piave. On 19 June the Montello was re-conquered, and although the Austrians resisted tenaciously on the Piave they retreated to the other side from 21 June onwards. The last bridgehead on the lower Piave was attacked by the Italians on 1 July. Five days later the Austrians were fully back on the other side of the river. The lines were exactly as they were before the offensive, the only difference being that there were 85,620 Italian, French and British, and 118,042 Austro-Hungarian casualties (Rostan, 1974: 200–217; Pieropan, 1988: Chs 62–68; Cervone, 1994: Ch. 3; Massignani, 1998: 42; Isnenghi and Rochat, 2000: 445 and 455–8; Schindler, 2001: 281–7).

On the day 'Radetzky' and 'Albrecht' were launched Mussolini could be found writing of the success of his paper's initiative to found a committee for the granting of scholarships to Serbian students to study in Italy. He argued that projects of the sort, which he had in fact begun in May (OO, XI: 91–2), would guarantee that 'the tangible solidarity between the Balkan peoples and ours will become indissoluble' (OO, XI: 126–7). The following day, a reasonably short and optimistic article argued that the Austro-Hungarian offensive would not pass. Mussolini's faith came from the fact that, as he saw it, the nation had 'finally come to the aid of the army' and that 'there has been a transformation in the mentality of our soldier' (OO, XI: 128–9). He insisted that the Italian government's new pro-Slav policy had contributed to the changed atmosphere at the front, but he was convinced that this was nothing compared to what that policy would produce in the future (OO, XI: 135–8). On 25 June he finished an article by quoting the anti-Austrian refrain of the *Inno di Garibaldi* composed in 1859: '*"Va' fuori d'Italia, va' fuori o stranier!"*', suggesting that, as in the verses of the song, Italy's war aims were limited to the defence of its own territory and the homes of its own people (OO, XI: 155–7). On 1 July Mussolini sang the praises of the Czechoslovak legion which had 'wet our Homeland's soil with its blood'. He added that their valour and that of the Czechoslovak citizens within the Austro-Hungarian Empire had contributed to the retreat of the Austrians. He concluded by insisting that it was high time Bohemia and Yugoslavia were recognized as independent states (OO, XI: 166–8). In a speech of 14 July, commemorating the fall of the Bastille, he announced that the war was 'to be inserted logically and historically in the French Revolutionary process' (OO, XI: 200–206). Mussolini, it seems, was a changed man.

Mussolini, Sonnino and Offensive War

Yet Mussolini's response during these crucial months was more complex than that of a Mazzinian democrat rallying to the defence of national territory against foreign invasion. In reality, he continued to adhere to an enlarged version of Italy's expansionist war aims, as indicated by his unaltered support for Sonnino. During the terminal crisis of the Boselli government Mussolini insisted on 27 October that 'Sonnino must stay. He represents the ideal continuation of our foreign policy.' We read that 'the substitution of Sonnino would amount to a leap into the abyss . . . a triumph for the external enemies' (OO, IX: 301–3). When Sonnino was reconfirmed at the end of the month Mussolini wrote that this represented 'a guarantee for us' and 'a bitter disappointment for our enemies' (OO, X: 11–13). On 27 November 1917 the Bolshevik government published the secret treaties which had bound Tsarist and then post-February revolutionary Russia to its allies. Over a month later Mussolini, who till then had said nothing about the published treaties, defended the Pact of London. A French socialist parliamentarian, Aimé Moutet, had recently challenged Italy's territorial pretensions beyond Trento and Trieste, arguing that the Pact of London represented the basis for future wars. Mussolini dealt case by case with Italy's territorial claims, justifying them all (OO, X: 179–81). An exception to this was Fiume, though this is most likely because Italian acquisition of that city was not contained in the Pact of London, and could not, therefore, have been contested by Moutet.

Moutet was just the beginning. On 7 January 1918 Mussolini misinterpreted the content of Lloyd George's 5 January speech to the Trades Union Congress, seeing in its terminology (that Italians had a right to be reunited with those of the same race and language) a de facto confirmation of Italy's claims to the 'Italian' territories of the Pact of London. For Mussolini, the five cities which had to 'return to Italy' were 'Trento, Gorizia, Trieste, Fiume, Zara' (OO, X: 204–6). On 8 January he corrected his assessment of the previous day, reminding readers that Britain had entered the war on the basis of the sanctity of treaties, particularly the 1839 accord which guaranteed the neutrality of Belgium. With such loyal allies, he argued, 'how can one doubt that . . . the peace of tomorrow will be the one we want?' (OO, X: 207–9). The hint, clearly, was that the peace would be based on Britain's loyalty to the treaty with which Italy entered the war as Britain's ally in 1915. On 13 January Mussolini stated that in both Lloyd George's and Wilson's speeches

Austria-Hungary 'has had a lot of good things said about it. Too good perhaps' (OO, X: 223–6). That same day he revealed the extent of his concern over Italy's declining position in the world by coming out of semi-anonymity. Since 15 June 1917 he had been signing his articles with the sole letter *M*, as we have seen. But the gravity of the situation after Caporetto compelled him to intervene with the full force of his political persona, and thus use his full surname. He argued that it was necessary for the American and British leaders to clarify what they meant so that the 'bad feeling which disturbs the [Italian] national conscience is rapidly eliminated'. He went into a philological analysis of the ninth point of Wilson's speech which, as we have seen, had referred to a 'readjustment' of Italy's borders along lines of nationalities. The Italian translation had come out as *sistemazione* which Mussolini then compared to the French translation, *réajustement*. He noted a significant difference between the two terms: the Italian one implying a 'sorting out' of Italy's territorial ambitions, the French one reducing Italy's 'fundamental problem of life or death' to 'a secondary, almost incidental question'. In challenging Lloyd George's assertion that the Italian-speaking populations of the Balkans had a right to be reunited with those of the same race and language, Mussolini argued that the British Prime Minister did not say where those populations were to be found, and hence did not clarify Italy's territorial claims. For Mussolini, then, Italy's borders were to expand 'from the mountains to the Adriatic' to incorporate those populations (OO, X: 227–9). Wherever there were Italians there was Italy.

How could Mussolini reconcile this position with his support a few months later for the pro-nationalities Pact of Rome? In an article of 30 March 1918 he inveighed against the nationalist imperialists for continuously putting democracy on trial as a concept alien to war, whereas there was no need, in his view, to presume such an antithesis, since 'the policies of Lloyd George are imperialist and democratic' (OO, X: 415–18). Renzo De Felice saw this article as ongoing proof of Mussolini's still democratic conception of the war, but his quotation from the piece removes all references to imperialism (De Felice, 1965: 399). The practical application of Mussolini's concept was evident in articles of 22 and 24 January 1918 in which he pointed out that if a policy of fraternization with the Balkan peoples was not pursued, Italy would have to prepare itself for 'great or small [territorial] renunciations' (OO, X: 261–3, 267–9). More explicit again was an article of 15 February: 'The Pact of London cannot be realized without a defeated Austria; and Austria cannot be disastrously beaten without a synchrony between military action and the political struggle of the nationalities oppressed within' (OO, X: 327–9: see also 276–9, 321–5, 332–5, 339–41; XI: 88–90). This, it should be noted, was also the strategy of the Pact of Rome. Giovanni Amendola, a member of the Italian delegation, noted that 'not only was the Pact of London not undervalued or suppressed, but we actually managed to convey the concept of its usefulness for all nationalities in as much as it committed the Entente to fighting to the end against Austria-Hungary' (Amendola, 1919: 21). While it was never an official accord, the Pact of Rome's ambiguous strategy was reflected in government policy. At the same time as Orlando was giving his blessing to the agreement, Sonnino was informing the American government that the Pact of London was unchanged (Vivarelli, 1991, I: 213). On 8 September 1918 Bissolati convinced the Italian cabinet to recognize the Yugoslav national movement. This was made public in Italy on 25 September and with the full approval of Mussolini (OO, XI: 373–7). It should be noted, however, that while the cabinet acknowledged the Yugoslav national movement it did not recognize Yugoslavia or a Yugoslav programme. No Yugoslav legion was formed in Italy despite the fact that 20,000 Yugoslav prisoners had volunteered to serve at the Italian front (Valiani, 1966a: 369–70).

How, though, did Mussolini and the government's foreign policy stand in relation to the defensive war being conducted at the military level? On 3 April Ferdinand Foch received the command of allied strategic operations and in that same month, and again in July, he requested Italian offensives on the Altopiano dei Sette Comuni. These were both rejected by Diaz, who was convinced that the French saw the Italian war theatre as merely complementary to their own (Cervone, 1994: 159–60). Yet while this coincided with Mussolini's calls for defensive war after Caporetto, already in an article of 3 January 1918 Mussolini could be seen using a *tactic* of defence for the ultimate aim of victory, which could only be achieved by an offensive military *strategy*. He warned the nation thus: 'Don't believe for one minute that from now on our task in the world war is that of only stopping the *boche* from climbing down from the Altopiano or crossing the Piave. Convince yourself, rather, that we need . . . to pass in the shortest time possible from the defensive to the offensive in order to liberate our provinces *before the end of the war*, since it is essential that we take, through arms, this precious Italian territory from the hands of our enemies' (OO, X: 194–6; Mussolini's emphasis). The proximity of this statement to Moutet's intervention in the French Parliament cannot be coincidental. Nor can it be fortuitous that on 15 January Mussolini claimed that Britain and America's changing behaviour towards Italy was 'due to our defeat at Caporetto' and that Italy needed 'to begin the war again, with desperate obstinacy' (OO, X: 236–9). On 20 February we read: 'It is said that to call for a maximum anti-Habsburg programme from the banks of the Piave is utopian. But we reply that it is precisely because we are on the Piave that the maximum programme is imposed on us. Either the Pact of London . . . or a peace signed on the Piave. This latter policy is, however, inadmissible, for the honour and future of Italy' (OO, X: 339–41).

Despite the importance he ascribed to this issue, Mussolini left it aside, dedicating almost all articles between 23 February and 23 March to domestic matters (which will be discussed in the following chapter), the massive German offensive on the western front which began on 21 March (OO, X: 398–9, 402–4, 405–6, 407–9, 410–11, 412–14, 419–21, 422–3), the Congress of Rome (OO, X: 433–5, 436–9, 440–41), and the Clemenceau–Czernin affair (OO, X: 424–7; OO, XI: 5–7). But, following the unexpectedly successful second German offensive in Flanders beginning 9 April, he returned to the theme of the offensive on 18 April, arguing that by continuing in what he called the 'passive strategy' the most the allies could hope for was 'not to lose' (OO, XI: 10–13). After a third surprise attack on 27 April had brought the Germans to the Marne, he briefly returned to the subject on 6 May, noting that the same critique of the 'passive strategy' and the continuous 'waiting for "punches in the stomach"' had been expounded in the French journal *La Revue des Deux Mondes* (OO, XI: 43), an article which he translated and reproduced in *Il Popolo d'Italia*. On 3 June he raised the subject with even more vigour, this time pointing to military theory to back his argument. He wrote that 'the purely and simply defensive strategy is an imbecilic absurdity' and that 'the texts, the sacred texts, the extremely sacred official and unofficial texts of military schools [say] that only the offensive gives victory' (OO, XI: 105–7). It is therefore noteworthy that during the Austro-Hungarian June offensive Mussolini was only concerned with the defensive as a tactic, never as a strategy. On 16 June he stated that 'if our troops manage to block the enemy's impetus in the front lines, as has happened to this point, [Caporetto] will be cancelled, and as it was for eleven times previously, victory will return to being Italian' (OO, XI: 128–9). This could not occur solely by blocking the enemy's forward thrust, and the following day he argued (incorrectly) that the Italian defence against the Austro-Hungarian June offensive had been marked by its transformation, within twenty-four hours, into a counter-offensive (OO, XI: 130–31). Clearly all this put Mussolini out of tune with the defensively minded High Command around Diaz. Or did it?

A number of factors militate against drawing one-sided conclusions on this issue. Diaz, like the British and French, was sure the war would not end until the following spring at the earliest. Moreover, after Caporetto he had had to reconstruct not just the morale of the army but its logistics. Then, following the Austro-Hungarian June offensive, he was over 85,000 men down and was fearful of a transfer of German troops to the Italian front. Finally, a failed Italian attack would have given the Austro-Hungarian Army a significant boost (Rostan, 1974: 220–21). But the possible long-term political repercussions of such an approach were expressed by the Italian ambassador to France, Bonin Langare, in an 8 September letter to Orlando. Clearly feeling the pressure of a French press campaign against Italian inaction, he wrote: 'On the one hand our allies ask us to undertake an offensive to which the most competent judge, our High Command, feels unable to consent; on the other the renunciation of an offensive threatens to lead us insensitively to a military isolation which could also have the long term effect of a type of political isolation' (quoted in Cervone, 1994: 161). Indeed, while

Diaz' stance was supported completely by Nitti, and somewhat less by Orlando, it was rejected totally by Sonnino who was concerned that Italian passivity would endanger the Pact of London during the peace negotiations (Cervone, 1994: 154–6).

In France, the tide definitively turned in the Entente's favour after their June–August counter-attack, and on 3 September Foch ordered unceasing offensives along the whole of the western front. The Germans began retreating from the St Mihiel Salient on 8 September and in the following days were shaken by an enormous attack which saw American troops in action (Gilbert, 1994: Chs 24 and 25). On 12 September Mussolini urged those readers impatient for Italian action to 'keep calm', assuring them that 'Diaz' hour will also come'. But he could likewise not help noticing that the success of Foch's counter-offensive on the western front 'highlights our three-month long inaction' (OO, XI: 351–3). Further allied successes were achieved in the Balkans and Palestine in mid- to late September. By 8 October the Hindenburg Line had been broken and twelve Belgian divisions, accompanied by one French and one British army corps, recaptured Dixmude and from there moved to the Lys. Fearing, not without reason, that the war would end with the Italian Army still on the Piave, Diaz began to move.

Victory from the Water to the Wild, October–November 1918

On 29 September Colonel Ugo Cavallero presented his four-point plan for an Italian offensive. Speed, surprise and the minimum forces for maximum results, all of which constituted the fourth point, led to the decision to focus on the Veneto plain. Cavallero's plan foresaw an attack along twenty kilometres from the Montello salient to the islets of Papadopoli, with the main thrust being Ponte della Priula–Conegliano–Vittorio Veneto so as to divide the adversary's 6th Army from its 5th. This plan was immediately modified by General Enrico Caviglia, commander of the 8th Army, the main agent of the attack on the Piave, who wanted to cross the river at more points so as to reduce risk. He also extended the attack further north to Vidor and moreover suggested, and received approval for, diversionary attacks by the 4th Army (General Giardino) on Mount Grappa. Diaz accepted the general thrust of this plan, though in his update of 13 October he added that the 4th Army on the Grappa was to be ready to receive orders to reach the Primolano–Arten line. He created two small armies, the 10th and the 12th. The former, under the command of Count Frederick Rudolph Lambert of Cavan, a British General, was to be inserted on the right of Caviglia's 8th Army, while the latter, under the command of General Jean-César Graziani, a Frenchman, was to be inserted on Caviglia's left.

On the very day that Diaz presented his plan Germany announced that it was ready to accept an armistice on the basis of Wilson's fourteen points. On 16 October

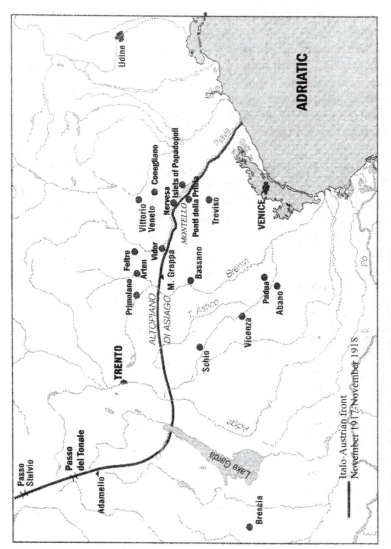

Figure 7.2 The final year November 1917 – November 1918
Source: adapted from Isnenghi and Rochat (2000), page 439.

the end of the Dual Monarchy was officially recognized by the Emperor Karl. Clearly, the Italian offensive had to get underway, and quickly. Yet the Piave was flowing too strongly (2–3 metres per second) for an attack to begin in the planned direction. All attention was therefore turned to Mount Grappa. In the new plan dated 21 October Diaz' immediate objective was now the Primolano–Arten–Feltre line (4th and 12th Armies under the command of the former). Everything had to be ready for the evening of 23 October. But this meant that there were now two plans: one for the Grappa, the other for the Piave. It also meant that there was little time to adequately prepare what was now a full-scale offensive on the Grappa. On 20 October Wilson declared that his fourteenth point (the autonomy of peoples in Austria-Hungary) had been overtaken by events and that it was now up to those peoples themselves to decide their future. Non-German-speaking units on the Italian front began to dissolve, as the right to self-determination had now super-seded talk of federation. Two days later a Croat brigade on the Grappa refused to go into the line, while the day after that, on the Altopiano dei Sette Comuni, two Hungarian divisions rebelled, declaring that they wanted to return home to defend their country against Serbia. By the morning of 24 October Hungary was inde-pendent. There was effectively no Austrian or Hungarian government, and, as Rajecz Stephan von Buriàn had resigned, no Foreign Minister.

When the Italian offensive finally began on the Grappa on 24 October the polit-ical circumstances to which it responded meant that Italy paid dearly both in human and political terms. On the plain it heavily outnumbered the adversary: between Vidor and the islets of Papadopoli about twenty divisions were facing nine, while 3,570 pieces of artillery were up against 835. On the Grappa, however, it was an altogether different story, since eleven divisions and 1,385 pieces of artillery faced eight front line divisions and three reserve divisions, plus 1,460 pieces of artillery. With rain and fog having exacerbated already badly aimed artillery fire, Italian troops on the Grappa went over the top at 07.15 on 24 October. The names of the Asolone, the Pertica, the Prassolan, the Col della Berretta, the Col del Cuc, the Valderoa and the summits of the Solaroli are associated with heavy fighting that led to nothing. By 26 October it was evident that if victory was to be achieved it could only be on the Piave. Cavan's men in fact gained control of the islets of Papadopoli that day, though more serious manoeuvres were blocked by the fast-moving river. Meanwhile, the Austro-Hungarian Empire continued to disintegrate. Reserve troops were beginning to rebel, particularly Hungarians and especially the marching formations. On 28 October the peoples of the Empire learnt that the alliance with Germany had been broken, that a separate peace had been proposed to Wilson, and that Czechoslovak and Yugoslav independence had been recognised. The 26th reserve division (Czech) refused to carry out the order to attack Cavan, and in the 6th Army, stationed further north, more and more front line troops rebelled.

On the evening of 29 October the whole of Caviglia's 8th Army could finally cross the river at Nervesa and at the Ponti della Priula. But there was to be no major battle. Orders from the Austro-Hungarian General Staff to counter-attack against the British failed due to low troop numbers (only eight battalions) and refusal. Only on the Grappa was there any resistance. Boroević advised the Austrian High Command to inform the Italians that he intended removing his troops from the Veneto. However, at this stage there was no effective army whose retreat could be organized. When the Italian Bisagno and Sassari brigades entered Conegliano the strategic objective of the offensive had been reached: the Austro-Hungarian 6th and 5th Armies had been separated on the plain. In the back lines the enemy formations dissolved and at Pola its navy declared non-belligerency. The Austrians called a halt to hostilities at 03.30 on 3 November, and the armistice was signed at 15.00 that same day, to become operative twenty-four hours later. This latter stipulation gave the Italians the time to round up retreating Austro-Hungarian soldiers. In the meantime, Trieste was occupied by sea without resistance (Mangone, 1987: Ch. 7 and Appendix pp. 191–8 for the complete texts of Cavallero's and Diaz' plans dated 2 September and 12 October 1918 respectively; Cervone, 1994: Chs 4–5; Isnenghi and Rochat, 2000: 460–62; Schindler, 2001: 297–311).

All this meant that there were no enemy forces to confront the 8th Army once it had crossed the river. Where, then, was the military 'victory', so vital for the consecration of Italian territorial 'rights' as per the Pact of London, to be found? Certainly not on the Grappa where the Italians had been fought to a standstill. What the Grappa offensive did offer, however, was a serious fight which, if linked to the crossing of the Piave, would lend greater credibility to the 'victory' on the plain. Yet to achieve this link it would need to be demonstrated that the Grappa offensive was subordinated to the one on the Piave. This explains the desperate 29 October telegram from Orlando to Diaz.

I believe it opportune that the cycle of our actual offensive be brought to 24 October. It seems to me that the link can be easily accounted for in terms of the need for strong pressure on the enemy in the mountain zone as a necessary preparation for the action on the Piave. The reason for which it has so far been unmentioned can be easily attributed to motives of strategic discretion, that is so as not to let the enemy know of the real nature of our intentions. This concept can be explained in supplementary communications of the Command, organizing their diffusion not only among Italian correspondents but above all foreign ones. I do not need to explain the importance of this backdating of our offensive in relation to the increasing news of an imminent armistice. (Quoted in Melograni, 1969: 505)

According to Caviglia's re-elaboration of Cavallero's original plan this was in fact the case, as the offensives on the Grappa were deemed purely diversionary. But by the time the 8th army had crossed the Piave it was clear that the offensive on the

Grappa was no longer secondary. As Pier Paolo Cervone (1994: 179–80) points out, a problem with characterizing the Grappa offensive as subordinate is that 67 per cent of all Italian, French and British casualties, that is 25,000 out of 37,461, were on that mountain.

Before coming back to Mussolini, it is worth briefly examining Diaz' 4 November victory bulletin, which dated the battle from 24 October onwards, hence linking the Grappa battle with the more general 'victory'. Interestingly, Diaz stressed neither the Grappa nor the Piave, preferring to highlight the 'highly daring lightning advance of the XXIX army corps on Trento, blocking the retreat routes of the enemy armies in the Trentino'. Victory is here associated with the rounding up of retreating, non-combative enemy troops, and the 'collapse of the enemy front' is then said to have been 'determined' in the west by the 7th Army and in the east by the 1st, 6th and 4th Armies. In other words, the 'highly daring lightning advance' moved westward towards the Trentino, not eastward towards Conegliano and Vittorio Veneto. The truth is that the 1st Army, of which the XXIX corps was a unit, suffered only 292 dead and the 7th Army only forty. The 6th lost more (567) but only began operations on the Altopiano on 1 November. None of this bore comparison with the losses of the 4th Army on the Grappa. The emphasis on the 'highly daring lightning advance' in the Trentino and the manner in which it 'determined the collapse of the enemy front' did have the benefit, however, of inventing a victorious military offensive and removing the 'victory' from the area where British and French troops were involved. Indeed, it should be noted that in the final battle the most significant progress was made by the 10th Army under Cavan, who arguably commanded the crossing of the Piave. Granted, both the 12th and 10th Armies are mentioned in the bulletin alongside the 8th Army of Caviglia. 'From the Brenta to the Torre', it states, 'they continue to push back the fleeing enemy'. But when all the forces of the British, French, Czechoslovak and American contingents are totalled (three divisions, two divisions, one division and one regiment respectively), they are greatly overshadowed by the fifty-one Italian divisions mentioned in the same line. Victory, in Diaz' bulletin, is an essentially Italian, royal and military affair, the last of these being especially evident in the fact that the government, the population and the navy are not cited (Isenghi, 1989: 62–6; Isenghi and Rochat, 2000: 462–4, esp. n. 71). The King and the Duke of Aosta are the only two people mentioned. The former is said to have guided the army to victory when at no stage in the war had he commanded the armed forces. As regards Aosta, he had a relatively negligible role in the final battle and appears in the bulletin to affirm that the 3rd Army was 'returning to the positions previously conquered, and which it had never lost'. This was an allusion to the Duke's blamelessness in relation to Caporetto, since, as we have seen, the 3rd Army retreated without having been defeated on the Carso. At the time of the Caporetto rout Diaz himself was commander of the XXIII army corps, which formed part of the 3rd Army. Diaz' bulletin is therefore a potion of rhetoric and exaggeration: apart from the 'highly daring lightning advance', he grossly augmented the number of enemy divisions (declaring seventy-three when there were only fifty-seven) by including transferred or dissolved divisions, and counting as divisions some brigades stationed between the Stelvio and Lake Garda (Cervone, 1994: 232). All this combined with a massive geographical shift from the river to the mountains in order to establish a military 'victory' where there was none.

In what way can Mussolini's writings of this period aid our understanding of the character of Italy's 'victory' in November 1918 and its subsequent codification in the Diaz bulletin? As the final battle began Mussolini was unaware of any attack having begun on the Grappa. His 24 October piece, which called on Italy to 'Give back Caporetto' to the Austro-Hungarians one year to the day after the defeat, was undoubtedly written on 23 October and hence was oblivious of any offensive (OO, XI: 436–8). But even articles published on 25, 26 and 27 October knew nothing of the fighting on the Grappa. All were dedicated, rather, to Germany's requests to America for peace and Wilson's diplomatic but negative response to them. What is clear from these articles, however, is that Mussolini was for the rejection of a diplomatic armistice and for the resolution of the conflict on the battlefield (OO, XI: 439–41, 442–3, 444–6). Even when he discussed the Italian offensive on 29 October he did not mention the Grappa, focusing all attention on the crossing of the Piave. Other major concerns were, however, also aired. First, there is the date of the beginning of the offensive, which Mussolini tied in with the dramatic events of the previous year: 'On 24 October 1917 it was the enemies who from Plezzo to Tolmino broke through our lines and reached the inviolate and inviolable Piave; on 24 October 1918 it is the Italians who move to the attack, placing their feet once again on the soil contaminated by the barbarian and hunting away the invader.' Secondly, like Diaz, whose victory bulletin spoke of the Austro-Hungarian Army as 'one of the strongest armies in the world', Mussolini was keen to establish the strength of the enemy faced by the Italians once they had finally crossed the water. He wrote: 'The Austro-Hungarian army still represents perhaps the only efficient force among all those upon which the Danubian empire rests.' Unaware of (and most likely unconcerned about) the facts, he stated also that 'the merit of our troops is increased by the fact that they find themselves faced with an enemy that is not disbanding'. Finally, he thanked the High Command 'for having taken note of the moral discomfort which, little by little, with the exchange of various "notes" [between Wilson and the Central Powers], was making itself felt among conscious and hopeful public opinion which "rightly" feared that a possible armistice would take us by surprise on the Piave, with the enemy on our soil' (OO, XI: 447–8).

On 31 October he dealt with Austria-Hungary's requests to Wilson for an armistice. He asked why the Emperor had turned to the United States 'instead of to Diaz or Franchet d'Esperey'. His answer was that they did so 'to avoid confessing their *military* defeat to the world . . . Our enemies intend to defraud us of our military *victory*' (OO, XI: 449–51; Mussolini's emphases). The following day, Mussolini's article mentioned the offensive on the Grappa but in such a way as to separate it from what was happening on the east bank of the Piave. He noted that the Austro-Hungarian war bulletins spoke of Austro-Hungarian victory on the Grappa given that the Italians had failed to make a breakthrough on that mountain, but that their tone changed once the Italians had managed to cross the river. In other words, Mussolini's perception of the Grappa offensive was not that of a preparatory manoeuvre to facilitate the Piave offensive, but of another action whose effective failure was secondary in any case to the victory on the Piave. He was, however, keen to establish that even on the Piave the Austro-Hungarians were continuing to put up a hard fight:

> The Austro-Hungarians have not 'fraternized'. They have fired off thousands of cannons and unleashed thousands of machine guns. After bitter fighting they have been overcome. Our advance is not but the consequence of our success achieved with living force; that is with living blood, at extremely high risk and with a daring and superb tenacity. The military rout may determine the collapse in morale of the whole Austro-Hungarian army, but till now the phenomenon is of a military character. (OO, XI: 452–3)

The territorial corollary of this 'military victory' was not long in coming. On 1 November Mussolini wrote that 'it is with the sword that Italy will enter Trento, Gorizia, Trieste, Pola, Fiume and Zara. It is with blood that Italy marks her borders on the Alps and again baptizes as *nostrum* the no longer "bitter" Adriatic' (OO, XI: 454). On 3 November he argued that 'the consequences of this event, even from the point of view of our relations with the Slav world which will share borders with us, are incalculable' (OO, XI: 455–7). On 7 November Mussolini's insistence on Italy's territorial rights as a consequence of 'victory' brought him into contact with that all-important geographical shift effected in the Diaz bulletin. From the British press he had found a number of quotations from Austro-Hungarian bulletins between 26 and 28 October. In order to establish that the enemy had fought to the bitter end, and hence that Italy's 'victory' was of a military character, we find Mussolini journeying through the Grappa, not the plain: 'The one of 26 October reads: "To the east of the Brenta the desperate struggle continued until the early hours of the morning. The sector of combat was again Mounts Asolone and Pertica, which fell several times into enemy hands but which were reconquered by our counter-attacks . . . The conduct of our fine soldiers was beyond all praise."' Mussolini went on: 'Another enemy bulletin of 28 says: "In the mountains and to the east of the Brenta (Grappa front) the battle raged with equal intensity all day." Having narrated the phases of the struggle around Col Aprile, the Asolone, the Pertica and the Spinoncia, the Austrian communiqué of 28 October declares: "The conduct of our troops was absolutely equal to that of the previous battles.'" Mussolini claimed that this proved 'the character of the battle which was taken up and won by the Italian army'. At the very end of the article the reader was alerted to the fact that 'the world is watching us and so are the combatants of the Piave!' (OO, XI: 464–5). But this is the only time the river is mentioned in this piece.

When it came to consecrating territorial claims with the Italian dead, Mussolini would later find more evidence in the mountains and on the plateaus than on the water. On 1 February 1919 he responded to a *Manifesto* of Serb intellectuals circulated at the Paris conference, which gave Serbia credit for the defeat of Austria due to the rebellion of the Viennese Caesar regiments. Against this Mussolini quoted the Austro-Hungarian war bulletins which showed the tenacity and sacrifice of the Italian troops between 24 and 31 October as decisive at the so-called Battle of Vittorio Veneto. His point was that the Serb regiments only 'rebelled' once they had been defeated by the Italians at the cost of 30,000 Italian dead. He concluded his article: 'Dead, magnificent dead of the Grappa, of Montello, of the Pertica, of the Solarolo, of the Asolone, of the Col Rosso, and all you dead of 40 months of war do you not hear? The peoples who have seen their freedom flower from your blood today insult you. Today they throw the stones of their profound profanation on your graves. Today they try to dirty your flags and your glory' (OO, XII: 187–92). It is important to note here that in order to highlight Italy's high casualty rates Mussolini pointed almost exclusively to the Grappa (Pertica, Solarolo, Asolone), the Altopiano dei Sette Comuni (Col del Rosso) and the west bank of the Piave (Montello, no doubt in reference to the June 1918 defence of the Piave). The east bank of the Piave, where the 'victory' purportedly took place, is again unmentioned.

It is therefore evident that in 1918 Mussolini still understood the war as offensive in both political and military terms. In order to safeguard the territorial ambitions contained in the Pact of London and beyond it had to culminate in an Italian military victory which would undo the Caporetto defeat. Yet as we have seen, there was also a domestic social dimension to the San Sepolcro programme. How was this dealt with by Mussolini in the last year of the war? Interestingly, Mussolini paraphrased a section of the Diaz bulletin, replacing the defeated external enemy with the enemy within. The Diaz bulletin reads: 'The remnants of what was one of the strongest armies in the world climb back in disorder and without hope through those valleys which they had descended with such proud surety.' On 6 November Mussolini wrote that 'the enemies of Italy are in full rout. The remnants of what was official Italian socialism climb back without hope through the valleys that they had descended with such proud surety with the stupid and criminal illusion of "Caporettozing" the magnificent people of the new Italy' (OO, XI: 461–3). It is to the implications of Mussolini's treatment of the internal enemy after Caporetto that we now turn in the final chapter.

–8–

Envisioning Fascism
October 1917–November 1918

The agrarian problem is different from region to region and is of a grandiose complexity. Be careful of certain ready-made phrases!

Mussolini, *Il fascismo nel 1921*, 7 January 1921

So that hierarchs are not dead categories it is necessary for them to flow into a synthesis, make everything converge towards a single aim and have their own soul inserted into the collective soul. This means that the State must express itself in the most elect part of a given society and must be the guide of the lower classes.

Mussolini, *Stato, anti-Stato e Fascismo*, June 1922

If politics is the art of governing men, that is of orienting, utilizing, educating their passions, their egoism and their interests as part of more general aims which almost always transcend the individual life because projected into the future, if this is politics then there is no doubt that the fundamental element of this art is man.

Mussolini, *Preludio al Principe di Machiavelli*, 1924

In the silent coordination of all forces, under the guide of one man only, lies the perennial secret of every victory.

Mussolini, *Elogio ai gregari*, February 1925

Italy Divided

In a vote of confidence taken on 25 October 1917 the Boselli government was defeated by 314 votes to 96. Strictly speaking, however, the Orlando government which took office at the end of the month was not the political progeny of Caporetto. The Boselli cabinet was already in its death throes amidst the heated atmosphere of Parliament, which had reopened on 16 October. The debate was still going on when the Austro-German invasion began, but, like the rest of the country, including the military command, neither the government nor the Parliament knew anything of the military situation. As for the origins of the Orlando cabinet, in some respects it was the expression of an attempt at national pacification following a spring and summer of popular anti-war activity on the one hand, and coup plotting on the other. So pressurized were the interventionists, and so reanimated were the socialists and Giolittians after their neutralist thesis had to all intents and purposes been proved right, that Bissolati's nerves cracked. On 18 October he came out with his notorious phrase against the socialists: 'To defend the backs of the army I'd even shoot you.' For this utterance he risked being thrown out of government, and was only saved by, amongst other things, the intervention of the King (Procacci, Gv., 1999: 305ff).

While, therefore, the Orlando government was formulated during the height of the Caporetto crisis, it was very much born of the Turin insurrection, which had in fact dominated the parliamentary debate. The new cabinet's very inception thus reflected a deep division between workers and the State over the character of the war, a difference which could not be assuaged by a government committed to remobilizing national resources in order to continue that same conflict. Recent research has corrected the erroneous view that the workers' protest movement was purely economic in motivation (Procacci, Gv., 1999: 147–205). As regards the peasants, it is noteworthy that even Arrigo Serpieri's paternalistic and socially conservative 1930 assessment of the rural classes at war does not conceal peasant disaffection, the word 'hate' coming out strongly in Serpieri's reconstruction of the peasants' wartime attitude towards employers, landlords and the State (Serpieri, 1930: 54–61). Paradoxically, calls for 'Land to the peasants', which had been raised after the February Revolution by Aurelio Drago, a parliamentarian close to Bissolati, did nothing to attenuate the growing bitterness. Drago's proposals were undoubtedly demagogic (Papa, 1969: 20–25), but, as Serpieri argues, whether sincere or insincere the 'Land to the peasants' slogan penetrated the consciences of peasant soldiers and was further radicalized by the expectation of imminent peace that was widespread in 1917 (Serpieri, 1930: 83–91).

The Orlando government's project of national reconciliation thus had a utopian ring to it, given that the cabinet came into being at the moment when the divisions in Italian society were reaching a new peak, not abating. Caporetto undid whatever unlikely chance Orlando had of engineering a sacred union. In a country such as Italy, where the manner in which the war was conducted created more lacerating social and political traumas than in other countries, divisions could only deepen following the invasion (Procacci, Gv., 1999: 43–145). The 'hate' that peasants felt for bourgeois landlords and property owners intensified, for example, during the October–November retreat from the invaded provinces of the Veneto. For various reasons, including proximity or otherwise to town centres, politically informed citizen misinformation about the gravity of the invasion, and the varying degrees of affective ties to the land, the majority of the approximately 300,000 inhabitants who escaped across the Piave was made up of local politicians, the middle classes and the agrarian landlords, while the 900,000 or so who remained behind were predominantly peasants (Corni, 1992: 7, 10–12). The latter were convinced that their masters had escaped the suffering that they were undergoing during the occupation, and were enraged in their equal conviction that the escapees would return after the war to reclaim the property they had abandoned (Serpieri, 1930: 91–3). What emerged during and after Caporetto was a mass popular transition from satisfaction with peace alone to a conviction that things could never be the same again, and that change was both necessary and inevitable. The defeat of the Italian Army therefore contributed to an intensification of pre-existing eschatological visions of the future to be ushered in after the armistice. This future might be in the form of a new socialist order, especially since the October Revolution in Russia had shown that the taking of power by workers and peasants was a real possibility. Alternatively, more retrogressive options were proposed by catholic fundamentalists who envisioned a peace based on the certainties offered by the more archaic values of order. Or again, pro-Wilson democratic interventionists presaged a world based on peace between the nations, class reconciliation and a renewal of the liberal institutions (Procacci, Gv., 1999: 369ff).

There was, however, another eschatological vision on offer. As hundreds of thousands of Italian men made their way towards the rear, and as the Bolsheviks took power in Russia, the Italian ruling class, and large sections of the middle classes, trembled. Not only might they be the object of mass wrath and revolution, but military defeat could mean a separate peace, and hence, as they saw it, national ignominy and shame. Thus right at the moment when anti-war sentiment was accelerating, pro-war currents accentuated their push for national remobilization to continue the war on to victory. And if revolutionaries had Lenin, if catholics had weeping statues, and if democrats had Wilson, the pro-war current, radicalized by the military defeat and by the national and international contexts in which it was set, also had its symbol for political and cultural mobilization – the enemy within (Labanca, 1997: 73–5). The lion was not going to lie down by the lamb.

Around the middle of December a *fascio di difesa parlamentare* was formed by 150 deputies and ninety senators. It was headed by nationalist imperialist figures such as Matteo Pantaleoni and the former priest Giovanni Preziosi, whose newspaper, *La Vita italiana*, became the *fascio*'s organ (De Felice, 1962: 503). The *fascio* emerged as a response to the 12 December vote which agreed to hold parliamentary sittings in secret sessions. The *fascio* deemed this to reflect the resurfacing power of neutralists who could now feel safe to speak their anti-war minds behind closed doors (Melograni, 1969: 426). Despite being a minority in the Parliament the *fascio* was a boisterous, aggressive and, it would appear, effective formation which created an intimidating atmosphere designed to unnerve socialist speakers and pressurize the government. On 16 December socialist deputy Filippo Turati urged his companion Anna Kuliscioff not to worry about his and his colleagues' 'skins', but at the same time he noted that 'the [anti-socialist] conspiracy, even though well known and exposed [as unfounded] every day by us, is worsening rather than abating'. A few days later he put his name down to speak, but then had second thoughts, since 'after six or seven hours of this environment no good feeling can last for long; and, if I should now speak, I'd be the most miserable of orators'. He revealed on 21 December that the danger went beyond being shouted down in parliament: 'We are now surrounded and followed all day and night by an escort of plain-clothes policemen.' Following his speech of 22 December he remarked that 'the whole right wing is on top of you like a herd of demons, each sentence is interrupted by cries and shouts . . . [all of which] takes away your voice, your energy . . . the possibility of following any type of logic and of remembering where it was you left off' (Turati–Kuliscioff, 1977, IV, Tome 2: 791, 803, 811, 812).

The psychological pressure was also felt by the ostensibly conciliating Orlando. In his speech of 22 December, published in the press the following day, he announced that he was not prepared to enter into discussions regarding the responsibilities for the military rout. He deplored generalized attacks on Swiss subjects and on the catholic clergy, but was rather less opposed to generalizations when it came to the PSI. He argued that 'authoritative socialists have affirmed that the cause of the defeat was the party itself'. When socialists protested, he retorted that this showed how they 'cannot be considered members of a political party, just affiliates of a criminal association'. It was during Orlando's premiership, indeed, that repressive measures were taken against PSI leaders: Lazzari and vice-secretary Nicola Bombacci were arrested in mid-January 1918, and in February were given thirty-five and twenty-six month prison sentences respectively, not to mention heavy fines (Melograni, 1969: 444–5).

But of greater significance is the self-remobilization of right-wing forces which occurred in society in the same period. Giovanna Procacci has identified these as the lettered and professional middle classes who in the months after Caporetto rediscovered their social *raison d'être* in patriotic sentiment and actions. State functionaries, clerks and pensioners were joined by doctors, engineers, architects and lawyers in a generalized attempt to remedy the effects of a deeply felt responsibility (due to a previous neglect and apathy) for what had happened on the high Isonzo. At one level this took the form of seeking succour in membership of the many private associations and patriotic bodies which sprang up all over Italy after Caporetto. Messages of solidarity and loyalty were accompanied by concrete acts of aid to refugees and the war needy. But the nature of the Caporetto disaster influenced the character of this mobilization in another direction. A profound sense of impotence and anguish combined with group solidarity and identity to cement a sense of belonging which was defined not only in terms of those who formed part of the group, but over against those who did not. This psychological condition became manifest in collective myths which sought to explain the disaster of Caporetto in extraordinary and almost supernatural terms. In an irrational over-response based on a 'betrayal of reason' and a 'hysteria of hate', the newly mobilized middle classes vented the rage of their rediscovered pride on the 'internal enemies' whose acts of sabotage had, in their schema, led to Caporetto and to the subsequent threat to national identity and culture represented by the invader. So fanatically fired up were they that their activities included spying on neighbours and fellow travellers on buses and trains and reporting presumed treachery to the authorities (Procacci, Gv., 1999: 317–50). It was in this Italy, as polarized in society as it was in the realm of cultural representations, that Mussolini, a journalist veteran of the July days in Russia, the revolt in Turin, two enemy invasions and any number of failed military endeavours, offered his unique response.

Renewing the Culture of War

On 31 October 1917 Mussolini argued that if anything 'positive' had come out of Caporetto and the invasion of a sizeable portion of national territory it was that Italian socialism had been shown up as 'a localized state of mind of determined groups' which was not yet 'a general tendency of the masses'. Indeed, he felt that the invasion had begun to undermine support for the PSI. This was proven by the fact that workers now understood that 'the proletariat is in the Nation, not outside it' (OO, X: 8–10). On 4 November he returned to this theme, arguing that the defeatists' work 'of corruption and moral demolition, prosecuted tenaciously for thirty months' had not penetrated 'the heart of the masses' and had not managed 'to halt the generous yearnings of the proletarian soul' (OO, X: 23–5). He urged the government to inaugurate a 'war policy' and argued that refusal to do this out of fear of a socialist reaction was 'shortsighted', since 'the industrial proletariat has turned its back on the PSI' (OO, X: 73–4). Yet despite this presumed decline in the PSI's prestige among workers, Mussolini asserted that 'official Italian socialism . . . must be treated as a more dangerous enemy than the one pitched on the left bank of the Piave'. He asked if Orlando intended to tolerate the weakening of the nation's morale, and finished by declaring that 'we demand reaction. Perfectly [censorship]. We demand "reaction" against the few [censorship] to save the "liberty" of 36 million Italians' (OO, X: 80–82). On 24 December he referred to Claudio Treves as 'the parliamentarian of Caporetto' (OO, X: 164–5). This was because in a speech of 12 July 1917 Treves had declared: 'Next winter no more trenches' (Treves, 1983: 107). On Christmas Day Mussolini wrote that 'our army, which . . . has rediscovered its warlike spirit, must be protected in the rear from the underhanded and criminal blows of the Italian Lenins. Caporetto must not happen again' (OO, X: 166–8).

We shall return to the socialists and the working class presently. For the moment, it is worth noting that on 7 December Mussolini gave greater theoretical vent to his view on the internal enemy, which was not limited to socialists. He suggested that the people living on Italian soil were divisible into two categories: 'Italians and foreigners/enemies.' The enemies, however, could be 'Italians or Germans' all of whom 'circulate freely in our cities, wallowing in our momentary disasters, undermining our resistance with every type of manoeuvre, and sanguineously insulting us with their very presence' (OO, X: 121–3). In the days and weeks after Caporetto Mussolini spilt quite a bit of ink over enemy subjects on Italian soil. In so doing he resorted to a cultural and political remobilization of a kind not envisaged earlier in 1917 as part of his response to the February Revolution in Russia. On 22 December 1917 he wrote:

> So that Italy is Italy, so that Italians become Italians, so that, in short, it is possible to be ourselves, and not only in terms of laughable political indulgence but in terms of the more substantial aspects of economic and spiritual autonomy, we must impress an anti-German character on our war, a character of liberation from Germanism which, in its different forms – from the universities to the workshops, from the banks to the docks – had reduced us to one of its commodities. The anti-German 'military' war must be completed within. The arrest of enemy subjects, the confiscation of their goods are some of the forms of this war. (OO, X: 158–60)

He returned to this question on various occasions. On 2 November, for example, he argued that 'throughout the whole of Italy subjects of enemy states roam freely, spying and carrying out highly dangerous work of moral sabotage' (OO, X: 17). At the beginning of December he asked: 'Has or hasn't the government made a decision to move against enemy subjects? The increased surveillance which has been announced from the official agencies is insufficient. It is the presence of these gentlemen, the simple fact of their presence, as innocuous as you like (which is highly unlikely and in many cases to be excluded), which strikes and offends Italian citizens' (OO, X: 105–6).

The converse of the enemy subject is evidenced in the same article. It is to be identified with the Italian refugees from the invaded regions of Friuli and Veneto. On 28 November, indeed, Mussolini called on Italians to 'love the refugees'. The latter functioned to galvanize national fraternal sentiment: 'The enemy invasion must make [this warm air of love] more delicate and deep, it must tighten even more the link between the people from the Alps to Sicily, today united in common pain and in the common prospect of fighting and winning' (OO, X: 89–91). In the 2 December piece he asked: 'Isn't it inhuman to ask refugees from Friuli to sleep on straw in the depths of winter?' He proposed to 'requisition the apartments of Germans, strongly disinfect them and give them to the refugees of our invaded lands' (OO, X: 105–6). He inserted this particular enemy category into his call for a conflation of all areas of the national territory into a 'war zone'. What this implied was made clear on 8 December when he wrote:

The 'war zone' must be an oxygenated zone, where the atmosphere must not be polluted by the presence of Germans, be they male or female, large or small, adults or children. And because many of them wear the comfortable mask of Italian naturalization [censorship] put on at the eve of the war or later, it is necessary to 'review' these naturalizations and adopt radical provisions against these 'naturalized' people without distinctions of any sort, since 'naturalization' only makes them more dangerous still. In short, in Milan alone these phoney naturalized enemy subjects [censorship] exceed perhaps a thousand people. A good strong sweep of a brush is what is needed for this enemy ballast. And please do not begin, in the name of heavens, to cite exceptions, to listen to recommendations, even if coming from parliamentarians or senators, to adopt a new 'take it case by case' in order to establish the greater or lesser levels of enemy subject innocuousness. It is a singular principal canon of war that in all ways and in all forms the enemy must be damaged. The enemy subjects which remain here among us – with relative authorizations from German or Austrian authorities – are belligerents. They don't fight with guns, but they use other arms to help Germany. Forbearing, indulgence and humanity towards them is as stupid as it is criminal. We await daily the arrival of this high, true, deep and no longer deferrable operation of 'urban cleansing'. (OO, X: 124–6)

Mussolini's argument culminated in 1918 with a call to intern enemy nationals in concentration camps (OO, X: 191–3, 199–201, 210–11, 252–4; XI: 214–16, 217–19, 253–4, 306–8).

Two observations are appropriate here. First, in order to sustain his view on the supposedly new-found patriotism of the working class Mussolini had to put the best gloss on anti-worker repression. Workers certainly undersigned patriotic initiatives in the period after Caporetto, but these were organized by pro-war employers who in turn had the backing of the most severe legislation 'against defeatism'. The latter, the so-called Sacchi decree, had been issued on 4 October 1917 by the Boselli government. Anyone caught in the act of 'depressing the public spirit' by even the most innocuous of previously acceptable utterances was liable to prosecution (Melograni, 1969: 444). Hence on pain of months or even years of imprisonment, workers were blackmailed into signing declarations, contributing to the national loan, and not uttering even the most inoffensive of anti-national phrases. Despite these pro-war attestations, workers for the most part remained untouched by Italian patriotism. Their positive response to calls to aid refugees from the invaded regions should be seen as action informed by humanitarian values (Procacci, Gv., 1999: 338–9). Secondly, and as we have seen, in the days after the unleashing of the Austro-German offensive Mussolini, like everyone else on the home front, did not actually know what was going on and even demanded that the government provide an explanation. Yet despite his professed lack of knowledge, he identified Italian socialists and enemy nationals on Italian territory as the cause of the defeat. Hence notwithstanding his difference with

Cadorna over the alleged responsibility of the soldiers, he agreed with the latter who, like frustrated commanders in other countries, raised the spectre of a 'stab in the back'. In a telegram to Boselli on 27 October 1917, Cadorna had in fact affirmed that 'the army falls not under the blows of the external enemy, but of the internal enemy' (quoted in Melograni, 1969: 397–8).

Not surprisingly, therefore, Mussolini quickly aligned with other forces who had reached identical conclusions. On 18 December he wrote an article in praise of the *fascio parlamentare*. The framework in which this acclamation unfolded was once again that of a 'war culture' polarization which left no room for grey areas: 'In short', he wrote, 'there is a new fact which determines a new situation. "Parliamentary union" on the one side, "Fascio di difesa nazionale" on the other.' Mussolini saw the *fascio* as a response to the false 'semi-national, a-national or anti-national' unity of 'those who wish for, or prepare, a peace of betrayal and shame'. The government would now have to choose between 'the patriots' and 'the defeatists'. Orlando could not think of arbitrating between the two, since the die had finally been cast: 'He must base himself on the "fascists" and above all seek the . . . aid of the Nation . . . A bit of energy on the part of the "fascists"; a bit of energy on the part of the Government, and *overt* defeatism will be reduced to silence and innocuousness' (OO, X: 146–8; Mussolini's emphasis). Did Mussolini's construction of a polarized world of national and anti-national ins and outs represent a temporary attempt at cultural remobilization in response to the crisis of Caporetto with the sole aim of securing victory? Or was Caporetto a catalyst for testing out proposals for a continuous state of cultural mobilization, of permanent 'war culture', as a model and vision for the post-war future?

The Art of the Journalist

An article of 23 May 1918 points to the first possibility. In it Mussolini argued that 'we have never demanded dictatorship under the species of eternity, we have never invoked dictatorship as a permanent political regime, we have only ever invoked it as a necessary exceptional regime for the exceptional period which is the war' (OO, XI: 88–90). But as Procacci notes, the social projection of a world in which conspirators and plotters are on the rampage often contains within itself a counter-proposition for a new type of social order. It is in an imagined future society underpinned by 'a new hierarchy of values' and 'purified of corrupting agents' that the generators of the present myth rediscover the identity and security which they have lost in the here and now (Procacci, Gv., 1999: 367). Other of Mussolini's pieces suggest that his intensified 'war culture' in 1917 and 1918 formed the basis of one such palingenesis. As regards enemy subjects on Italian soil, for example, he insisted on 25 August 1918 that the State's commandeering of their property should not be a temporary affair and that it was unthinkable that 'once the war is over the Germans can come back again – assuming they left in the first place – and, in their factories, in their villas and in their companies, recommence the work interrupted in May 1915' (OO, XI: 306–8). This internal subject had as its external corollary the continued exclusion of Germany from a future international political formation. Indeed, one of the reasons for Mussolini's scepticism about the formation of the League of Nations was that in his view it could not possibly exist, since Germany and its allies would *perforce* have to be excluded (OO, XI: 175–8, 179–81, 182–6). But it should be noted that Mussolini's aversion to the League of Nations also reflected Italy's weak position in relation to its allies in the conflict over territorial issues. His article of 13 January 1918 insisted on Italy's rights to territorial expansion over against suggestions that the League would do away with the need for petty squabbling over who owned this or that sector of a frontier (OO, X: 227–9). The demonization of Germany and of German subjects on Italian soil was, therefore, bound up with a more general suspicion that the post-war international order would be marked by any number of objections to Italy's territorial ambitions on the part of an increasing number of rivals in the present.

On 29 October 1917 Mussolini called on all Italians to put aside their political discords and form a national pact to face the crisis: 'What matter our doctrinal differences? ... Today Italy is on the line, the Italy of today and tomorrow.' Here, despite the apparently non-prejudicial form (everybody was to leave aside their previously held beliefs), Mussolini called on all political persuasions to base themselves on the nation. Moreover, this proposed national alliance appears to have been informed by deep-rooted strategically nationalist considerations. On 2 November Mussolini presented the nation in biological terms, as an 'organism', as 'physical flesh' which had been 'torn' and upon which had been inflicted 'the most ferocious torture' (OO, X: 14–16). In a speech of 30 November he argued that 'man cannot ignore the Nation like a tree cannot ignore the soil that feeds it ... To deny the Nation means to deny one's mother, especially when the Nation is passing through a critical hour' (OO, X: 98–101). The nation also had a militarily social content both in the present and the future. In the here and now 'the Nation must be the army, just as the army is the Nation' (OO, IX: 307–9). On 9 November Mussolini demanded: '*the whole Nation must be militarized*' (OO, X: 36–8; Mussolini's emphasis). As regards the future, right in the days when the *fascio di difesa nazionale* was forming Mussolini had argued for a post-war society based on what he termed the 'trenchocracy' which, as he saw it, was being forged at the front. As we saw in Chapter 5, Mussolini had developed this concept in late 1916 and in his war diary had pinpointed the junior officers as the élites in question. Now, a year later, he suggested that this 'trenchocracy' would be altogether different from previous social phenomena given expression in a political label: 'The words republic, democracy, radicalism, liberalism, "socialism" itself, have no more sense: they may have one tomorrow, but it will be that given to them by the millions of "returnees". And it may be a completely different definition.' When exemplifying, however, he chose only to redefine socialism which 'might be an anti-Marxist and national socialism, for example. The millions of workers who will return to the furrows of the fields will, after being in the furrows of the trenches, realise the synthesis of the antithesis: class and nation' (OO, X: 140–42).

What, in terms of social organization, was meant by 'national socialism'? When dealing in 1918 with the post-war society Mussolini betrayed something of an obsession with the working class. He feared what he saw as its potentially destructive power and was concerned to redirect it onto the safe terrain of the nation. Moreover he furnished evidence for the submission of sectors of the industrial proletariat to this vision. On 23 April 1918 pro-war workers in Genoa were described as 'authentic workers' in as much as 'they plant themselves solidly on the national terrain' (OO, XI: 21–2). And on 12 May he showed that anti-Germanism could still provide a useful culturally mobilizing tool in the post-war period. He conflated the Italian working class' interests with those of Italian businessmen in an alliance of mutual interest against German capitalism. He praised those national syndicalist workers and formerly 'revolutionary socialists' who 'concern themselves . . . with the destiny of industries after the war', since it would be 'an unforgivable crime – above all from the working class' point of view – to strike to death the marvellous Italian industrial creation which, in time of peace, must frustrate every possible new attempt at penetration and German hegemony' (OO, XI: 54–6). But for Mussolini, not even pro-war workers ought to dabble in politics. Writing on 12 June he argued that the syndicalism he had in mind for the future was best expressed by the UIL precisely because of that organization's 'a-political nature'. While declaring its adhesion to the war, the UIL 'does not wave the interventionist flag', as interventionism 'is an essentially political phenomenon'. Rather, 'it is important that [workers] do what they are doing: their duty.' Discipline 'must be accepted' and where necessary, 'imposed' (OO, XI: 117–19). This 'duty' was best expressed when workers 'work in silence' (OO, XI: 128–9). In an article of 1 May he argued that if workers took over production, then 'after a week the national economy would be drained of its blood to the point of starvation, to the point of chaos'. This was because workers 'have neither the muscles nor the brains' to '*ensure the maximum individual and social wellbeing*' (OO, XI: 33–6; Mussolini's emphasis).

In an article of 1 August 1918 he announced the removal of the subtitle 'Socialist daily' from the front page of *Il Popolo d'Italia*, replacing it with 'Combatants' and producers' daily', whose meaning he explained as follows: 'To defend the producers means to combat the parasites: the parasites of blood, among which the socialists are the first, and the parasites on labour who can be bourgeois or socialists' (OO, XI: 241–3). He returned to these themes in other articles before the end of the war (OO, XI: 348–50, 354–5, 356–60, 366). To prove his point that disaster would be unleashed on the nation if the working class meddled in politics, Mussolini dedicated various articles to the Bolshevik Revolution. The thesis was a straightforward one: when not subjective agents of the Kaiser, the Russian revolutionaries were at best objective ones; working-class political independence and revolutionary politics could therefore only ever aid the enemy and lead to 'horror' and the necessary prostration in front of German threats, such as had occurred at Brest-Litovsk. 'International socialism', he claimed on 2 March 1918, 'is a German weapon. It is a German invention' (OO, X: 111–13). Again, he returned to the same theme on various occasions before the end of the war (OO, X: 148–51, 202–3, 336–8, 350–52, 358–60, 361–2, 372–4, 384–6, 392–4; XI: 8–9, 60–64, 71–3, 190–93, 247–9, 341–4, 395–6).

What type of government was to oversee this social system in which workers kept out of politics and got on with their work without wreaking havoc on the nation? In place of potential 'chaos', Mussolini envisaged a heavily structured social formation. In the 1 May article he wrote:

> One shouldn't speak of equality among men in the sense of removing class distinctions, but of establishing strong hierarchies and social discipline. As long as men are born with different 'talents', there will always be a hierarchy of abilities. This leads to a hierarchy of functions and the hierarchy of functions – listen! listen! – will logically, naturally, fatally provoke a hierarchy of powers with associated categories and subcategories. We're talking about *organizing the State* . . . . (Mussolini's emphasis)

Mussolini informed workers that 'you are not everything . . . There are others who cannot be left out of consideration' (OO, XI: 33–6). Were these others, like the workers, 'only a part of the economic game' in the 'enormously complex organisms' which were modern societies? For Mussolini, the answer was emphatically no. Rather, these 'others' were to be the organizers of the new State. First of all, however, this militarily disciplined 'hierarchy' of 'talents' required a leader. On 27 November Mussolini argued that the urgency of the present hour showed that something – or rather someone – completely different from the present form of government was indicated: 'In this moment the Italian people is a mass of precious minerals. It needs to be forged, cleaned, worked. A work of art is still possible. But a government is needed. A man. A man who, when it occurs, has the delicate touch of an artist, and the heavy fist of a warrior. Sensitive and volitional. A man who knows the people, loves the people, and can direct and fold it – with violence if necessary.' This man could head 'a war government which lives only for the war. A government which prefers truth to lies and brutality to euphemism. A flexible government which adjusts its actions to circumstances and environment. Propaganda for the ingenuous and the ignorant, lead for the traitors' (OO, X: 86–8).

Someone like who? A great industrialist perhaps? In an article of 21 January 1918 Mussolini certainly had the highest of praise for this category. With the

Lombardy bourgeoisie sizing up to make a huge financial contribution to the war Mussolini wrote: 'We are pleased that the industrial class, that is the class of the bosses – producers (and not only "exploiters", as was said in the old jargon of socialism) – is becoming aware of its strength, of its importance, of its historical task' (OO, X: 258–60). In the article of 1 August 1918 his programme for 'defending the producers' was said to amount to 'allowing the bourgeoisie to complete its historical function' (OO, XI: 241–3). In this very same period Mussolini seems to have solidified links with Ansaldo, an arms manufacturer in Genoa. Following Caporetto, Ansaldo obtained important advertising space in *Il Popolo d'Italia* (De Felice, 1965: 415). Mussolini visited Ansaldo on various other occasions in the spring and summer of 1918. The 'authentic workers' to which he referred in his article of 23 April 1918 were those of Ansaldo whose representatives supplied the flag for presentation to a gun battery, the weapons for which were supplied by Ansaldo itself. Mussolini was the speaker at the ceremony (OO, XI: 18–20). He flew to Genoa on 1 July, an experience that merited an article on 3 July in praise of Ansaldo which, he claimed, formed part of the 'new Italian race of producers, builders, creators' (OO, XI: 169–71). On 31 July he announced the closure of the Rome edition of *Il Popolo d'Italia* (which had opened in October 1917 as a reaction to the Papal note), specifying that it was a now superfluous dead weight (OO, XI: 239–40). According to Renzo De Felice, on the other hand, the proximity of this announcement to the 1 August article in which he openly rejected socialism in favour of a society of combatants and producers is better understood in terms of the unashamed identification with Ansaldo. On 1 August Mussolini was again in Genoa, this time to open a new editorial office of *Il Popolo d'Italia* (OO, XI: 508–10). Neither was Ansaldo his only source of advertising revenue. In an article of 26 July Mussolini boasted of the noteworthy increase in his newspaper's advertising income from 5,728 lire in January 1918 to 43,783 in March. In the first half of 1918 he earned a grand total of 166,944 lire thanks to advertisements from industrial, commercial and financial sectors of the bourgeoisie. He made these figures public in an article of 26 July 1918 (OO, XI: 223–5).

But this evidence suggests that Mussolini's admiration for the bourgeoisie was not unrequited. While he looked to the capitalists to fulfil their 'historical mission', important capitalists were looking to him. In Mussolini's vision of the future the bourgeoisie was certainly to keep its effective social and economic power, but it should be remembered that in the 27 November 1917 article he wrote of an 'artist', not an industrialist, as the required leader of a nation at war. Who did he mean by this? Perhaps the nationalist imperialist poet Gabriele D'Annunzio fitted the bill? Or better, the futurist Marinetti who had shown himself capable of moulding war, industry and nationalism into an art? As we saw in Chapter 1, futurism placed artists at the head of a new social organization in a continuous state of struggle and war. Mussolini, however, did not see things this way, or at least not fully. In a speech in Bologna on 19 May 1918 he identified a third figure, who, in the context of the war, had shown himself to be smarter and more far-sighted than either industrialist or poet:

> What this war means, in its historical import, in its development, has been intuited by two categories of persons, beyond, that is, the people: the poets and the industrialists. By the poets, who, with their exquisitely sensitive souls, grasp the still dark truths before the average person does; by the industrialists who understood that this was a war of machines. Between the two let us place the journalists; who are poets enough not to be industrialists and industrialists enough not to be poets. And the journalists have on many occasions preceded the government. I speak of the great journalists who had the outer ear always open in the direction of the vibrations emanating from the outer world. The journalist has at times foreseen what those in charge have unfortunately seen too late. (OO, XI: 79–87)

The shortlist of candidates was rapidly being reduced to one – Mussolini himself. He had obviously decided to redimension the persona of the charismatic war hero and to focus instead on that other persona, the home front journalist, that had accompanied him throughout the war. The war diary had collapsed, as had the warrior credentials of its creator, its artist, whose self-mythologizing portrayal of a charismatic hero at the centre of a warrior community had failed to live up to military stasis and neurosyphilis. Now he was ready to take his talents as an 'artist', reinvest them in the role of journalist which he had fully reassumed after February 1917, and launch himself as the leader of a future society whose common denominator would be war. What other pictures did the artist paint of the future society and his function in it?

An examination of Mussolini's position on the land question suggests that he was already practising his proposed 'flexible' 'art' just after Caporetto. On 16 November he sought to explain the rout in terms of the peasants' lack of identity with the nation. To counter this he argued that '*to weld the peasants to the nation, the land must be given to the peasants*' (OO, X: 55–7; Mussolini's italics). But apart from support on 20 November for the proposals put forward by parliamentarian Ettore Ciccotti for the opening of a pro-peasant credit institute (OO, X: 67–8) we read no more about the land question. The theme disappears from Mussolini's writings. In planning for the post-war demobilization, Mussolini argued on 14 May 1918 that two million agricultural workers would be returning to the fields, but the point of his observation was that farmhands would easily find work due to increased demand and shortage of labour (OO, XI: 57–9). When dealing with the question of soldiers' material interests on 5 August he limited his claims to a pay bonus when they were standing guard in the front line (OO, XI: 250–52). This suggests that the slogan 'Land to the peasants' only ever had the demagogic function of remobilizing peasant sentiment for the war, and that once the main military danger had passed

Mussolini 'artistically' adjusted his actions 'to circumstances and environment' by conveniently leaving the land question aside.

As regards the 'lead for the traitors' which the 'man' was to be ready to dole out, on 1 March 1918 Mussolini demanded that the government use the news that silk and cotton dealers had been secretly supplying the enemy in order to give an example of how far it was prepared to go when dealing with treason. 'How much blood cries for revenge! We invoke an example. A summary trial: execution' (OO, X: 355–7). On 17 May he rejected the findings of a military court which had sentenced a certain Cesare Santoro to twenty years' imprisonment for espionage. Santoro escaped the death sentence because his services had not been useful to the enemy. Mussolini latched onto a parliamentary question from the 'fascist' Angelo Abisso who described the sentence as 'bland'. Since deserters got the firing squad, 'why not do likewise with a traitor?', Mussolini asked, since desertion and betrayal 'amount to the same thing?' (OO, XI: 68–70).

Where, then, might the mass support base for this artist-journalist national leader be identified? Who were the 'others' that would organize the State while the working class got on silently with its work? On 10 November 1917 Mussolini made reference to a social stratum which identified fully with the war, knew what it was about and was ready to volunteer to fight it. He called for the formation of a volunteer army and claimed that he had received any number of supporters for this project:

> Adhesions are pouring in by the hundreds. They are young students of the classes not yet called up who offer themselves in groups; they are clerks who ask to renounce the privileges of their forms; they are professionals and bourgeois who declare themselves ready for all renunciations and sacrifices; they are old men who want to lavish their remaining energies on the cause of the Nation invaded and ravaged by the enemy. (OO, X: 39–40)

Or again, in the already mentioned article of 14 May 1918, Mussolini argued that the government commission which had been set up to deal with the post-war period after demobilization needed to 'take advantage of suggestions from below'. Not from workers and peasants, however, but 'from those who are in direct contact with the population, who know its needs and, even more, its psychology' (OO, XI: 57–9). Obviously an intermediary stratum between the ruling and lower classes. This is why it is important that in his 14 June article on workers' duty and discipline Mussolini argued that 'the manual worker must obey the architect' (OO, XI: 117–19). Similarly, in his 1 August piece he opined that among the 'producers' in a society of 'producers' pride of place was to be given to those whose labour 'doesn't make the forehead sweat and doesn't bring warts to the hands', but 'whose social utility is certainly superior to that which can be supplied by a day's work of a Libyan labourer' (OO, XI: 241–3).

Mussolini was no doubt pinpointing elements of the professional classes which Procacci has evidenced as lying behind the many national committees that surfaced in Italy after Caporetto (Procacci, Gv., 1999: 317–50). The affinity between their eschatological vision and Mussolini's 'war culture' is evident. Even before Caporetto Mussolini had identified these social subjects as the potential reorganizers of post-war Italian society with him as their head. It will be remembered in this regard that in his war diary he had ascribed a pivotal role to the middle- and lower-middle class lieutenants and captains as the cement of a warrior community. Then, as now, a socially and politically exclusive *trenchocracy* of junior officers recognized the centrality of Mussolini and his newspaper. We have seen that the *fasci* meetings in various Italian cities shared much in common with Mussolini's project. Other evidence supports the view that this ideological allegiance was now reproduced in the various committees which appeared all around the country after Caporetto. The Prefect of Florence reported to the Minister of the Interior on 10 December 1917 that a 'committee of assistance and civil resistance' of around thirty people had just been formed under the leadership of Michele Terzaghi, a lawyer. The following demands were made on the government: '1. Removal of enemy subjects and revision of naturalization; 2. Confiscation of their goods and property to build a fund for combatants and their families; 3. Energetic action to indicate to all of the people the absolute duty of resistance for undoubted victory, for the salvation of the Homeland, liberty and civilization' (ACS, A5G, b. 96, fasc. 212, s.fasc. 10, ins. 2). On 26 December the same Prefect noted that 'a vast association of interventionists' was being built 'in all the cities of the Kingdom, but with headquarters in Milan or Rome. Their declared aims were 'victory at all costs' which did 'not exclude, where deemed necessary, the assumption of an antagonistic approach to the constituted powers'. The Prefect of Milan reported on 11 February 1918 that the local *fascio* had set itself the task of 'combating defeatists and enemy subjects who to this day reside in the Kingdom'. He noted the presence of Ottavio Dinale, one of Mussolini's closest collaborators (ACS, A5G, b. 96, fasc. 212; b. 41, fasc. 77). The 'fascio of professionals for national defence' was in fact founded in Milan on 17 January 1918 by doctors, lawyers, engineers, architects, commissioners for oaths, vets, chemists, building foremen and land surveyors (Procacci, Gv., 1999: 323, n. 9). In response to widespread insecurity the middle-class committees demanded a hierarchical reorganization of society based on reassuring traditional values (Procacci, Gv., 1999: 324–5).

The task of disseminating this conservative and anti-socialist vision among the fighting men was once again ascribed, and self-ascribed, to the middle-class intelligentsia who went on to form the *Servizio P* (Propaganda Service) and the closely related trench journals. These two phenomena represent what has been described as a 'return of the intellectuals' to a position of protagonism after two and a half years of obscurity (Isnenghi and Rochat, 2000: 401). The middle-class individual educator had rediscovered his/her social identity at the service of the nation and in privileged relation to the anonymous mass. The *Servizio P* was primarily oral in nature. Officers were to go among the men and discreetly raise pro-war discussions whose content had already been planned around the *Servizio P* table. The nature of the operation left few records, so it is difficult to know what was said, how it was delivered and, most importantly, how it was received. For this reason, Gianluigi Gatti's ground-breaking study on the *Servizio P* dedicates virtually no space to the theme of propaganda production. At the present state of research only guesses can be hazarded as to the effectiveness of the service in relation to more concrete issues which directly concerned the men under the Diaz command (such as the end of futile offensives, better insurance payments and food). But Gatti gives the following circular of the 2nd Army in March 1918 as best summarizing the strategy of the *P* officers: 'Aims: To defeatist propaganda and to the natural apathy deriving from the prolongation of the war counterpose *obligatory, organized*, unitary, easy, convincing and practical propaganda, in such a way as to create "public opinion" in the units and, through this, raise the spirit of the country and acquire trustworthy data on the morale of the troops' (emphasis in the original). Gatti points to a profoundly opportunistic strategy which suggests that any ostensibly democratic themes that might have been discussed in the 'casual' conversations were only ever harnessed to the immediate task of fighting the war. On 3 August 1918, for example, a circular from the 8th Army on the Piave stated: 'Propaganda must be WAR ACTION, thus agile, plastic, without fixed schemes, without crystallizations and rhetoric. It must adapt to events, always "blending in" with new moral exigencies' (capitals in the original). The nationalist imperialist Alfredo Rocco, whom we met in Chapter 1 and who was a *Servizio P* officer in the 1st Army, is reported to have gone one step further, ordering his men to issue 'even false news and information'. But within this pliable and opportunistic method resided the dogmatic character of *whatever* concept was being conveyed. On 17 July 1918 the weekly bulletin of the XII army corps insisted: 'Do not allow the truth of what you are expounding to be discussed: be careful to distinguish between the ignorance which asks to be enlightened and the sophism which vibrates the viper's tongue' (Gatti, 2000: 91 and Ch. 6).

What, then, was this kernel of 'truth' that the odd 'viper' and 'sophist' sceptic was sometimes prepared to question? The papers of Giuseppe Lombardo Radice, a figure we met in Chapter 2 and who was central to the formulation of the 'points of conversation' to be raised by the officers of the *Servizio P*, are enlightening in this regard. Lombardo Radice listed about forty ideas, the first of which aimed to generate hatred for the enemy by presenting him as a user of spiked iron clubs, a murderer of women, children and injured men. Other subjects to be raised were the material improvements which had been granted to the soldiers, internal resistance, the negative consequences of a premature peace ('all those deaths in vain; workshops closed; invasion of German capital and workers; unemployment and hunger for Italian workers'), and the benefits of victory ('individual and collective well-being'). Lombardo Radice insisted on spreading the notion that this was a war of and for the proletariat, and that 'only a few dangerous imbeciles can speak of imperialism'. While focusing on the penury of the Italian labouring classes his propaganda points identified the cause of this in 'that bullying congregation of industrialists and salesmen which called itself *Mitteleuropa*' (Melograni, 1969: 471–2). Thus while ostensibly rejecting the 'imperialist' character of Italy's war, and while insisting that the *Servizio P* concentrate on transmitting the notion of an 'economic' and 'non-political' war, the 'truth' which was not to be questioned by the 'vipers' was precisely that this was a war through which the social and political power of the Italian bourgeoisie and agrarians was to be reproduced. The flexibility of *Servizio P* propaganda was informed by the strategy of presenting the geo-politics of inter-imperialist rivalry in such a way as to mobilize the patriotic sentiment of peasant soldiers against the *enemy* ruling classes.

Mussolini's handling of the slogan 'Land to the peasants' was not dissimilar to the general method of the *Servizio P*. He used it flexibly and as a 'war action' device and then, in keeping with the *Servizio P* maxim of not resorting to 'crystallizations', dropped it. Rumours about land to the peasants certainly circulated in the trenches, but these did not have an official character. Antonio Papa's analysis of the land question in Italy during the war points to demagogy and elision as endemic in the post-Caporetto days. His scrutiny of trench journals concludes that more common than promises of land to the peasants were discussions of life and work in the fields, and how land would be reclaimed and malaria defeated. Alternatively, against the 'ignorant peasants' who had brought on Russia's downfall, Italian peasants were praised for their discipline (Papa, 1969: 29–36). Indeed, it is in the trench journals that the essence of the *Servizio P*'s conservative function has been best illustrated. In January 1918, on Mount Grappa, there appeared *La trincea*; in February *L'Astico* was issued on the plateaus; in March the first large-scale product, *La tradotta*, made its debut among the ranks of the 3rd Army; *La Ghirba* came out in the same month, and would eventually reach a production run of up to 40,000 per issue. By the middle of June about fifty such publications were in circulation. Moreover, the High Command struck a deal with some standard newspapers which, in exchange for the publication of propagandistic articles, were rewarded with the purchasing at wholesale price of several thousand copies of their numbers which were then sold to the men at retail price by the High Command. Among these papers were *Il Corriere della Sera*, *Il Resto di Carlino*, *Il Secolo* and *L'Arena* of Verona (Melograni, 1969: 468–9). So, too, was *Il Popolo d'Italia*, which together with the national imperialist *L'Idea Nazionale* represented an important political source for the more official trench journals (Isenghi, 1977: 214).

It has been argued that the latter have reflected 'a process of . . . recomposition of the bourgeoisie . . . its image of itself, its ideological models and its hegemony' (Isnenghi, 1977: 55). It is not clear, indeed, that the propaganda of the trench journals was aimed primarily at the peasant and worker soldiers at all. Rather, it is likely that junior officers were re-educated by journalists and propagandists of their own class in and through a stereotyped, profoundly conservative and biased caricature of the 'people'. The same can arguably be said for the *Servizio P* strategy (Isnenghi, 1977: Pt 1, Ch. 8; Gatti, 2000: Chs 4 and 5). In this sense, both the trench journals and the *Servizio P* tested programmatic waters, in which reforms such as financial assistance were directed towards incorporating the masses into a well-functioning paternalistic and authoritarian State. Predominant in the trench journals are images of the woman, home fires, the family and the fields, King, Country and Church (Isnenghi, 1997: 96, Pt 2, Chs 1 and 3).

It is in terms of the Catholic Church that we can divine both another element of Mussolini's future social vision and his 'artistry' as a political journalist. On 18 May 1918 he stressed that he was 'not a priest-eater' and that he did not practise anti-clericalism (OO, XI: 74–5). While, as we have seen, there was to be no future for socialism if it was not 'national socialism', he was prepared to 'reconcile' with Benedict XV, despite the clash over the Papal peace note of August 1917. Mussolini never adduced the peace initiative as a possible factor in the collapse of the front in October–November 1917. In summarizing the events of 1917 on New Year's Eve, he mentioned the 'Papal manoeuvre', but merely noted that this had been followed by Italy's successful conquest of the Bainsizza (OO, X: 182–4): Caporetto was an altogether separate issue. On 6 April 1918 he criticized Benedict XV for his 'neutrality', after which the Pope reappeared in the already-quoted article of 18 May and not again until 17 September in a piece which, once again, had nothing to do with Caporetto (OO, X: 428–9). It is legitimate to suspect, therefore, that Mussolini's diplomacy and potential 'reconciliation' with the Catholic Church (see above, Chapter 5) fitted into his broader vision of the post-war society and the role of social control which that organization could exercise.

One of the most important themes in the trench journals, and one dear to the hearts and minds of the remobilized middle classes, was that of a hierarchical society organized for war which was a harbinger of the post-war social order. This, for Isnenghi, is 'the primary narrative vision' of the trench journals. But something else was required to sustain it: 'an irrepressible anti-neutralist rancour' which amounted to 'an obsession for the incumbent presence of defeatists in the rear lines and at the front', plus 'an only slightly veiled criticism of the weakness of the government', all combined with 'anti-Bolshevik fabulation' and 'precocious falling out with the parliamentary institution'. In short, a pantheon of 'disorder' presented to the soldiers as the real reason for the Caporetto defeat, a vast 'stab in the back' by elements of the home front, which would exonerate the soldiers of the accusations of treason that had fallen on them. And since the 'legal' forces were incapable of containing this wave of insidiousness, some trench journals proposed to legalize 'illegal' violence (Isnenghi, 1977: 214, 231ff).

In the days after the formation of the *fascio di difesa parlamentare* practical experiments were carried out in this 'legal' illegality. On 19 December 1917 Giuseppe Emanuele Modigliani, a socialist parliamentarian, was physically attacked by nationalists when heading to a Rome restaurant. Turati avoided the assault only because he had stayed behind to write to Kuliscioff (Turati and Kuliscioff, 1977, IV, Tome 2: 807). Following Caporetto, Modigliani's name appeared together with those of Turati and Treves on leaflets which were circu- lated at the front bearing the slogan 'we want peace'. On 1 November Turati claimed that this was a campaign of lies conducted by the High Command and aimed at scapegoating the socialists for the defeat (Turati and Kuliscioff, 1977, IV, Tome 2: 706). On 14 December, six days before he was attacked, Modigliani's name appeared in a deprecating article by Mussolini (OO, X: 137–9). Modigliani was not badly beaten (he was back in Parliament the following day). Perhaps this meant that the attack amounted to a warning. This, at least, was the opinion of Anna Kuliscioff, writing to Turati on 21 December. But the attack affected Kuliscioff in a way that it was probably meant to: namely she felt frightened and intimidated. She was convinced that it was tied into the 'fascist obstructionism' evident in the two-hour parliamentary speech by *fascio* member Gian Battista Pirolini, who had punctiliously documented the existence of an enemy spy ring. Pirolini, it should be noted, received Mussolini's support for his speech (OO, X: 158–60, 169–71, 175–8, 353–4). Kuliscioff theorized, however, that the attack had been carried out by overzealous Carbonari conspirators, diehard secret society nostalgics who in their day had fought for Italian unification but who had now 'found refuge on the right-wing mountain'. She believed that 'those sur- viving Carbonari are as hateful as they are funny', but what she did not consider funny was a point made by Turati in his speech of 20 December. On that occasion he had declared that if right wingers were thinking of re-evoking the atmosphere of intimidation of the days of May 1915, they would 'first have to pass over our dead bodies'. Kuliscioff wrote:

What perversion, what bestial impulses, what general degeneration! It makes me shiver just to think that in cold blood, without heat, without passion, without real fanaticism, one can carry out such ignoble and repugnant gestures. Neither do I like your threat about them having to pass over your dead bodies if they want to regurgitate the May days. To make threats of that sort you would need to be sure of having an army of organized proletarians behind you, which may or may not wake up if the Carbonari murder one of the socialists identified as a symbolic expression of defeatism. (Turati and Kuliscioff, 1977, IV, Tome 2: 808–9)

Kuliscioff's Carbonari theory was an interesting attempt at a conceptualization of what was happening. In hindsight, however, it is more accurate to speak of the ongoing genesis of fascism in the First World War.

Conclusion

If more or less mangled words suffice to hang a man, out with the pole and the noose! If fascism has been nothing but castor oil and truncheons, and not rather a superb passion of the best Italian youth, the guilt is mine! If fascism has been an association for delinquents, I am the leader of this association! If all the violence has been the result of a given historical, political and moral climate, very well I am responsible for this, because this historical, political and moral climate was created by me with propaganda that goes from intervention to today.

Mussolini, Speech in Parliament (inauguration
of the dictatorship), 3 January 1925

In his *L'Italia nella Prima Guerra Mondiale* Italian military historian Piero Pieri argued that the democratic interventionists were at the vanguard of the call for intervention during the period of Italian neutrality. By these he meant 'the republicans, radicals and Garibaldines; in other words, the representatives of the tradition of the old Action Party [of Mazzini and Garibaldi]'. All other interventionist tendencies then 'followed' this call. And while the nationalist imperialists made reference to the same Risorgimental and irredentist tradition during the interventionist 'debate', Pieri insisted that that democratic inheritance was 'safe in the hands of others!' (Pieri, 1968: 51–6).

Yet if this was so, why did post-war Italy finish in fascism? One obvious response is that it need not have. But for Italy to take the path of 'democracy' as a political expression and continuation of a Mazzinian democratic war, forces would have been required that could have presented a relative and viable programme. It seems, on the other hand, that Bissolati, the key figure of democratic interventionism, was left with little to offer but his resignation from a government in which he had in any case always been isolated. Whenever he had found support, this had not been from a mass democratic movement, but from the authoritarian and profoundly right-wing *Generalissimo*, Luigi Cadorna (Rocca, 1985: Ch. 10), and from Mussolini who admired him for his 'Jacobin' outbursts in October 1917 against the socialist enemy within (OO, IX: 275, 276–8, 279–81). It is interesting in this regard that Pieri never linked his patriotic rhetoric with an account of his own combat experience in the First World War. The same was true of Adolfo Omodeo, who cited the Garibaldine letters of any number of NCOs to back up his characterization of the war as 'The Fourth War of the Risorgimento', but who never linked this definition to an account of his own combat experience (Omodeo, 1934). According to Giorgio Rochat, this is explained by the fact that both Pieri and Omodeo feared what such an analysis might have uncovered (Rochat, 1976: 37). Not even a democratic interventionist who did leave an account of his combat experience manages to convey a democratic message. Emilio Lussu's 1938 novel, *Un anno sull'Altipiano*, bequeaths a vision of an isolated individual who is incapable of giving expression to revolt against the anti-democratic effects of the war's political character (Lussu, 2000).

Democratic interventionism could not offer a programmatic option either during or after the conflict because the conflict had nothing to do with democracy. Mass demands for radical and even revolutionary social and political change after the armistice came not from adherents of interventionism, but from workers and peasants, that is from those broad sectors of society deeply opposed to the war. The character of Italy's war as one of aggression is reflected in the continuous presence of Sonnino as Foreign Minister, in the military strategy of offensive warfare, and in the authoritarian domestic aims of the social, political and military élites. Yet if the democratic interventionists were incapable of transforming their imagined war into a political programme, other forces were seeking to draw programmatic conclusions precisely from the war's real nature.

At the Paris peace conference Italy's status as a relatively minor imperial power was underlined when her ambitions for hegemony in the Balkans were thwarted by the United States. This much at least was obvious to Alfredo Rocco in December 1918, as we saw in Chapter 1. But if, by preparing to recommence the war, the élites were to reap the fruits of their imperialist and anti-democratic endeavours of 1915–18, a new type of political authority was required, since the traditional forms of liberal government had shown themselves to be inadequate, and would soon prove to be incapable of reaffirming State authority in the war's aftermath. This, indeed, was Rocco and Corradini's point, and they wished to see the State oversee a reorganization of society in readiness to reaffirm Italy's claims to imperial supremacy. The power of the Italian Nationalist Association lay precisely in Corradini's perception of the need for clearly stated aims and programmatic clarity. Rocco, indeed, would later become the architect of the fascist totalitarian and authoritarian State. What was missing from this programme as the reorganization of society for war? Rocco would go on to design the fascist State, but he would not be the leader of it. That task fell to another man – Benito Mussolini. As we saw in Chapter 1, the Italian Nationalist Association dissolved into the Fascist National Party soon after the March on Rome, and before disappearing into political oblivion Corradini dedicated his 1925 volume of speeches to Mussolini. Somewhere along the line, another programmatic proposal, another form of political authority – Mussolini's – had won the day.

Paradoxically, before the Nationalist Association could be convinced of Mussolini's programme, he had to be convinced of theirs. We have shown that

Mussolini's transition to the nationalist-imperialist vision was completed on the outbreak of the war, which crystallized the far-right political and cultural tendencies towards which he had already inclined, albeit tentatively and inconclusively, before 1914. For this reason, it is difficult to imagine the emergence of fascism without the war, and Mussolini himself was of this view. In informing readers of the upcoming fascist meeting of 23 March 1919, he remarked on 18 March that fascism's task would be to bring to successful completion the 'revolution' whose 'first phase' had begun with Italian intervention in May 1915 (OO, XII: 309–11). On 18 April 1919 he wrote that the fascist attack on the socialist demonstration and the *Avanti!* offices was an expression of 'popular interventionism, the good old interventionism of 1915' (OO, XIII: 64–6). Or again, when it became clear that he was in favour of Italian realignment with Germany in 1919 to prepare a new war against Italy's former allies, he turned once again to 1915: on 24 May, the fourth anniversary of Italian intervention, he argued that that date 'remains the decisive date not only of the history of Italy but of the human species', and that it was this which rendered 'completely artificial' the entire policy of the victorious allies at Versailles (OO, XIII: 147–9).

That Italian intervention would create a rupture with Italy's past had been argued by Mussolini even before intervention itself. The personal and national renewal represented by the event was then given symbolic expression by Mussolini in his war diary, most especially in the baptismal ceremony on the Isonzo in 1915. Similarly, the pride of place afforded to Italy's fallen soldiers in the fascist programme of March 1919 was the programmatic crystallization of what Mussolini argued after 24 May 1915: like the sacred waters of the river Isonzo, they, too, represented a newly expanded Italy, as their blood staked an unquestionable right to the territory on which it had been spilt. They were moreover the heavenly projection of an ideal social situation on earth, representing, as they did, a class society based on war but devoid of class antagonism. With the war over, the dead were remobilized into service as a primary element in the call to take up arms against the 'plutocratic' nations who had defrauded Italy of its 'rights' based on its 'victory'. One of the dead remobilized was Mazzini, the figurehead of the ideal community bound together not by class interest but by sentiment and religious-based brotherhood. Of course, even this 'Mazzini' had been defined in the war, as incontrovertible proof of the 'democratic' nature of Italy's pretensions to territorial expansion. But this was a Mazzini reinterpreted through the grid of the Nietzschean Superman and the will to imperialist power, both of which he had come to represent for Mussolini and many others in the pre-war cultural ferment.

While fascism would go on to give a whole new meaning to Italian imperialist foreign policy which would vastly exceed the liberal strategy (Collotti, 2000), it is nevertheless the case that the imperialism of the San Sepolcro programme stemmed directly from Italian war aims at both the political and military levels, as we have seen, and in this sense nascent fascism represented continuity with the liberal State. Indeed, the fascist programme of March 1919 represented a proposal to realize the external and internal vision of a future which had already been imagined *within* the war, and, indeed, from its very outset. From a very early stage in his campaign for Italian intervention Mussolini was aligned with the national imperialists and the Salandran conservative élites on an interrelated programme of territorial expansion and anti-socialism. Herein lies the error of Renzo De Felice. Convinced that early fascism was a left-wing phenomenon, he could not but continue to characterize the pre-1919 Mussolini as a socialist. De Felice thus misinterpreted Mussolini's interventionist radicalism as an expression of a cleavage from the left, when it actually resulted from a radical shift towards the far right. While the present book has demonstrated that there is certainly some basis for arguing, *pace* De Felice, that Mussolini underwent a right-wing involution after Caporetto, we have shown that this was as an intensification of his 'war culture', itself an expression of a nationalist imperialist political strategy. The 'war culture' adopted by Mussolini even before Caporetto was locked into a vision of present and future society which sought to reaffirm conservative, paternalistic and anti-popular values in a strongly hierarchical, authoritarian and totalitarian political order dominated by the domestic and imperial interests of industrialists and agrarians.

But Mussolini also argued that something more than repression was required if broad sectors of the population were to be convinced of the necessity for the restructuring of the State in readiness for ongoing war. While sharing the strategic vision of the élites, Mussolini rejected their dismissal of mass sentiments and used his newspaper and his war diary to fashion a model for a new type of mobilization: in place of State repression and the inevitable resistance that this would give rise to, Mussolini proposed a form of charismatic authority through which sentiment could be mobilized on a politically and socially conservative basis. When the war finished Mussolini was armed with the programme of Corradini combined with a theory of mobilization that was a substitute for the State while also reconfirming the State's authority by virtue of the politically innocuous character of the mass mobilization effected.

However, the underlying premise of this mobilization was that on the call to arms the masses had to be deprived of socialist political leadership and organization. The 'enemy within' was essential to the 'war culture'. We have shown that it served as a negative cultural representation for the self-mobilization of the middle and lower middle classes which Mussolini identified as the moral, ethical and intellectual pivot of a future community based on war. Through his newspaper, his speeches and his war diary, Mussolini effected a mythification of himself as a warrior hero and political journalist who, by his very position in the scheme of things, was a potential political leader of a society in which the lower classes knew and passively accepted their place, where diehard oppositionists could expect to meet the physical force of armed militias, and where the middle and dominant classes had their thirst for order satisfied.

But fascism represented a far more definitive rupture with the liberal State in terms of the new form of political authority through which it proposed to reorganize society in order to better pursue the above imperialist strategy. Not only was Mussolini ready to resort to anti-socialist violence using not the police or the army but armed squads recruited from within society, but he was also, unlike both liberals and nationalist imperialists, attuned from an early stage in the First World War to the need to secure popular consent. To this end he projected himself as a charismatic figure and invoked a spectrum of cultural mobilization from 'Mazzini' to 'Victory' via the moment of 'Intervention' and the supreme sacrifice of the 'Fallen Soldier'. Thus the adoption of the Myth of the Great War as the founding event of fascism and the kernel of the regime's cosmos of cultural representations was not completely opportunistic. Mussolini clearly exaggerated somewhat when, in the quotation given at the beginning of this Conclusion, he ascribed to himself the sole responsibility for having created, through his writings and oratory activity, 'the historical, political and moral climate' for the genesis of fascism. Those conditions emerged, rather, in the Great War as an offshoot of its imperialist character combined with the liberal State's failure to politically and culturally mobilize the nation in order to pursue it without digging its own grave. They were further enhanced by the failure of the workers' revolution in the *biennio rosso* (1919–20) and, indeed, the conditions for fascism's rise to power itself as a mass movement could only come on the wave of that failed revolution (Trotsky, 1971: esp. 189–92). Fascism was, therefore, an anything but irresistible phenomenon (Behan, 2003). Yet it was certainly Mussolini, through his paper and his speeches, who, from 1914 onwards, gave the most coherent expression to the issues arising throughout the war and who could present his proposal in a programmatic form in the immediate post-war period. This amounted to nothing less than the invention of fascism, an at that time historically novel form of political authority with which he would govern Italy for twenty years and lead it into the next world conflagration.

Bibliography

Writings of Benito Mussolini

Opera Omnia, Susmel, E. and Susmel, D. (eds), 44 Vols, Florence, La Fenice, 1951–1980.
Il mio diario di guerra, Milan, PNF, 1923.

Archives

ACS
a) Segreteria Particolare del Duce, Carteggio Riservato, 1922–43.
b) Mostra della Rivoluzione Fascista, bb. 17–20.
c) Ministero degli Interni. Direzione Generale di Pubblica Sicurezza. Divisione Affari Generali Riservati, A5G, Prima Guerra Mondiale, and Stampa italiana, F1, 1890–1945.
d) Presidenza del Consiglio dei Ministri, Guerra Europea.

AUSSME
a) Diario 11° Bersaglieri, armadio 16, Sezione 111aB, numero 1763d.

Books and Articles

Ake, C. (1966/67), 'Charismatic Legitimation and Political Integration', *Comparative Studies in Society and History*, 1: 1–13.
Albertini, L. (1951), *Vent'anni di vita politica*, 2 Vols, Bologna, Zanichelli.
—— (1968), *Epistolario*, Barie, O. (ed.), 2 Vols, Milan, Mondadori.
Albrecht-Carrié, R. (1938), *Italy at the Paris Peace Conference*, New York, Columbia University Press.
Althusser, L. (1971), 'A Letter on Art in Reply to André Daspre', in Althusser, L., *Lenin and Philosophy and Other Essays*, London, New Left Books: 203–8.
Amendola, G. (1919), *Il Patto di Roma*, Rome, Quaderni della 'Voce'.
Anon, (28–29 December 1915), 'Benito Mussolini abbandona il fronte e torna al "Popolo d'Italia"', *Il Mattino*.

Anon, (16 December 1916), 'Dove'è il caporal fracassa?', *Il Popolo di Siena*.

Anon, (24 September 1917), 'La proposta socialista per un'inchiesta sui giornali', *Avanti!*

Anon, (1976), *Bersaglieri*, Milan, COGED.

Aronson, A. (1991), *Studies in Twentieth Century Diaries: The Concealed Self*, Lampeter, Edwin Mellen.

Arros, (30 December 1915), 'La favola', *Il Popolo d'Italia*.

Askew, W. C. (1959), 'The Austro-Italian Antagonism, 1896–1914', in Parker, L. and Askew, W. C. (eds), *Power, Public Opinion and Diplomacy*, Durham, NC, Duke University Press: 172–221.

Audoin-Rouzeau, S. and Becker, A. (1997), 'Violence et consentement: la "culture de guerre" du premier conflit mondial', in Rioux, J. P. and Sirinelli, J. F. (eds), *Pour une histoire culturelle*, Paris, Seuil: 251–71.

Balestra, G. (1993), 'Gli allievi della scuola militare di Modena (1895–1910)', *Ricerche Storiche*, XXII, 3: 569–606.

Bannan, A. J. and Edelenyi, A. (eds) (1970), *Documentary History of Eastern Europe*, New York, Twayne Publishers.

Battisti, C. (10 October 1914), 'Cesare Battisti e le dichiarazioni di Benito Mussolini', *Il Resto del Carlino*.

Becker, J-J., Becker, A., Audoin-Rouzeau, S., Krumeich, G., Winter, J. (1994), 'Pour une histoire culturelle comparée du premier conflit mondiale', in Becker, J-J., Becker, A., Audoin-Rouzeau, S., Krumeich, G., Winter, J. (eds), *Guerre et cultures 1914–1918*, Paris, Colin.

Behan, T. (2003), *The Resistible Rise of Benito Mussolini*, London, Bookmarks.

Beltramelli, A. (1923), *L'uomo nuovo*, Milan, Mondadori.

Bissolati, L. (1923), *La politica estera: Scritti e discorsi di Leonida Bissolati*, Milan, Treves.

Boro Petrovich, M. (1963), 'The Italo-Yugoslav Boundary Question 1914–15', in Dallin, A. et al., *Russian Diplomacy and Eastern Europe 1914–1917*, New York, King's Crown Press: 162–93.

Bosworth, R. (1979), *Italy, the Least of the Great Powers: Italian Foreign Policy Before the First World War*, Cambridge, Cambridge University Press.

—— (1983), *Italy and the Approach of the First World War*, London, Macmillan.

—— (2002), *Mussolini*, London, Arnold.

Brain, J. L. (1977), 'Sex, Incest and Death: Initiation Rites Reconsidered', *Current Anthropology*, 18, 2, June: 191–208.

Cadorna, L. (1915), *Attacco frontale e ammaestramento tattico*, Rome, Ufficio del Capo dello Stato Maggiore.

—— (1921), *La guerra alla fronte italiana fino all'arresto sulla linea del Piave e del Grappa (24 maggio 1915–9 novembre 1917)*, 2 Vols, Milan, Treves.

Cafagna, L. (1970), 'La formazione di una "base industriale" fra il 1896 ed il

1914', in Caracciolo, A. (ed.), *La formazione dell'Italia industriale*, Rome-Bari, Laterza: 135–61.

Caracciolo, A. (1996), 'Roma', in Isnenghi, M. (ed.), *I luoghi della memoria: Simboli e miti dell'Italia unita*, Rome-Bari, Laterza: 163–72.

Carducci, G. (1959), *Giambi ed epodi*, Palmieri, E. (ed.), Bologna, Zanichelli.

Cervone, P. P. (1994), *Vittorio Veneto: l'ultima battaglia*, Milan, Mursia.

Chabod, F. (1952), *Orientamenti per la storia d'Italia nel Risorgimento*, Rome-Bari, Laterza.

—— (1961), *L'idea di nazione*, Rome-Bari, Laterza.

—— (1997) [first published 1965], *Storia della politica estera italiana dal 1870 al 1896*, Rome-Bari, Laterza.

Clausewitz, C. von (1993) [first published 1832], *On War*, Howard, M. and Paret, P. (eds), London, David Campbell.

Cohen, D. L. (1972), 'The Concept of Charisma and the Analysis of Leadership', *Political Studies*, September: 299–305.

Colapietra, R. (1958), *Leonida Bissolati*, Milan, Feltrinelli.

Collotti, E. (2000), *Fascismo e politica di potenza: Politica estera 1922–1939*, Milan, La Nuova Italia.

Corner, P. (1975), *Fascism in Ferrara 1915–1925*, Oxford, Oxford University Press.

—— (2002), 'State and Society, 1901–1922', in Lyttelton, A. (ed.), *Liberal and Fascist Italy 1900–1945*, Oxford, Oxford University Press: 17–43.

—— and Procacci, Gv. (1997), 'The Italian Experience of "Total" Mobilization', in Horne, J. (ed.), *State, Society and Mobilization in Europe During the First World War*, Cambridge, Cambridge University Press: 223–40.

Corni, G. (1992), *Il Friuli Occidentale nell'anno dell'occupazione austro-germanica 1917–1918*, Pordenone, Edizioni Concordia Sette Pordenone.

Cornwall, M. (2000), *The Undermining of Austria-Hungary: The Battle for Hearts and Minds*, London, Macmillan.

Corradini, E. (1925), *Discorsi Politici (1902–1924)*, Florence, Vallecchi.

D'Annunzio, G. (1915), *Per la più grande Italia: Orazioni e messaggi*, Milan, Treves.

De Biase, C. (1964), 'Concezione nazionale e concezione democratica dell'intervento italiano nella prima guerra mondiale', *Rassegna storica del Risorgimento*, January–March: 79–88.

De Falco, G. (22 November 1916), 'L'ennesima canagliata de' preti', *Il Popolo d'Italia*.

De Felice, R. (1962), 'Giovanni Preziosi e le origini del fascismo (1917–1931)', *Rivista Storica del Socialismo*, 17: 493–555.

—— (1963), 'Ordine pubblico e orientamenti delle masse popolari italiane nella prima metà del 1917', *Rivista Storica del Socialismo*, 20, September–December: 467–504.

—— (1965), *Mussolini il rivoluzionario*, Turin, Einaudi.

—— (1966), *Mussolini il fascista: La conquista del potere, 1921–1925*, Turin, Einaudi.

—— (1968), *Mussolini il fascista: L'organizzazione dello Stato fascista*, Turin, Einaudi.

—— (1975), *Intervista sul fascismo*, Ledeen, M. A. (ed.), Rome-Bari, Laterza.

De Grand, A. J. (1971), 'The Italian Nationalist Association in the Period of Italian Neutrality', *The Journal of Modern History*, 43: 394–412.

—— (1978), *The Italian Nationalist Association and the Rise of Fascism in Italy*, Lincoln, NE, University of Nebraska Press.

Del Negro, P. (1979), *Esercito, Stato, Società: Saggi in storia militare*, Bologna, Cappelli.

—— (1988), 'La professione militare nel Piemonte costituzionale e nell'Italia liberale', in Caforio, G. and Del Negro, P. (eds), *Ufficiali e società: Interpretazioni e modelli*, Milan, Angeli: 211–30.

Dentoni, M. C. (1995), *Annona e consenso in Italia, 1914–1919*, Milan, Angeli.

Didier, B. (1976), *Le journal intime*, Paris, PUF.

Dorso, G. (1949), *Benito Mussolini alla conquista del potere*, Turin, Einaudi.

Eagleton, T. (1976), *Criticism and Ideology*, London, New Left Books.

—— (1986), *The Ideology of the Aesthetic*, Oxford, Blackwell.

—— (1991), *Ideology: An Introduction*, London, Verso.

Echevarria II, A. J. (2002), 'The "Cult of the Offensive" Revisited: Confronting Technological Change Before the Great War', *The Journal of Strategic Studies*, 25, 1, March: 199–214.

Eco, U. (1994), *The Italian Metamorphosis, 1943–1968*, New York, Guggenheim Museum.

Etherington, N. (1984), *Theories of imperialism: War, Conquest, Capital*, London, Croom Helm.

Farinelli, G., Paccagnini, E., Santambrogio, G., Villa, A. I. (1997), *Storia del giornalismo italiano: Dalle origini ai giorni nostri*, Turin, UTET.

Fasciolo, A. B. (31 December 1916), 'La visita ad un "imboscato" (Il caporal maggiore Mussolini nelle sue funzioni)', *Il Popolo d'Italia*.

Fava, A. (1982), 'Assistenza e propaganda nel regime di guerra (1915–1918)', in Isnenghi, M. (ed.), *Operai e contadini nella grande guerra*, Bologna Cappelli: 174–212.

—— (1997), 'War, "National Education" and the Italian Primary School, 1915–1918', in Horne, J. (ed.), *State, Society and Mobilization in Europe during the First World War*, Cambridge, Cambridge University Press: 53–69.

Forcella, E. and Monticone, A. (1998) [first published 1968], *Plotone di esecuzione: i processi della Prima Guerra Mondiale*, Rome-Bari, Laterza.

Fortes, M. (1969), *Kinship and the Social Order*, London, Routledge and Kegan Paul.

Franzinelli, M. (2003), *Squadristi: Protagonisti e tecniche della violenza fascista 1991–1922*, Milan, Mondadori.

Friedrich, C. J. (1961), 'Political Leadership and the Problem of Charismatic Power', *Journal of Politics*, 23: 3–24.

Gatti, G. L. (2000), *Gli ufficiali P nella Grande guerra: propaganda, assistenza, vigilanza*, Gorizia, Libreria Editrice Goriziana.

Geertz, C. (1975), *The Interpretation of Cultures*, London, Hutchinson and Co.

Gentile, E. (1975), *Le origini dell'ideologia fascista, 1918–1925*, Rome-Bari, Laterza.

—— (1986), 'Fascism in Italian Historiography: In Search of an Individual Historical Identity', *Journal of Modern History*, 21: 179–208.

—— (1990) [first published 1977], *L'Italia giolittiana*, Bologna, Il Mulino.

—— (1993), *Il culto del littorio: la sacralizzazione della politica nell'Italia fascista*, Rome-Bari, Laterza.

—— (1999) [first published 1982], *Il mito dello Stato nuovo: Dal nazionalismo radicale al fascismo*, Rome-Bari, Laterza.

—— (2002), 'Fascism in Power: the Totalitarian Experiment', in Lyttelton, A. (ed.), *Liberal and Fascist Italy*, Oxford, Oxford University Press: 139–74.

—— (2003a), *Renzo De Felice: Lo storico e il personaggio*, Rome-Bari, Laterza.

—— (2003b), 'Totalitarismo al potere', *Millenovecento*, 10, August: 10–24.

Gentile, G. (1975) [first published 1925], 'Manifesto degl'intellettuali italiani fascisti agli intellettuali di tutte le nazioni', in Gentile, E., *Le origini dell'ideologia fascista, 1918–1925*, Rome-Bari, Laterza: 459–66.

Gibelli, A. (1998), *L'Officina della Guerra: La Grande Guerra e le trasformazioni del mondo mentale*, Turin, Bollati Boringhieri.

—— (1999), *La Grande Guerra degli italiani*, Milan, Sansoni.

Gilbert, M. (1994), *First World War*, London, HarperCollins.

Giolitti, G. (1967) [first published 1922], *Memorie della mia vita*, Milan, Garzanti.

Gramsci, A. (1979), *Selections from the Prison Notebooks*, Hoare, Q. and Nowell Smith, G. (eds), London, Lawrence and Wishart.

Gregor, A. J. (1974), *Interpretations of Fascism*, Morristown NJ, General Learning Press.

—— (1979), *Young Mussolini and the Intellectual Origins of Fascism*, Berkeley, CA, University of California Press.

Henderson, J. (1984), 'L'iniziazione nella pratica analitica', in Scapparo, F. (ed.), *Volere la luna: La crescita attraverso l'avventura*, Milan, Unicopoli: 29–53.

Herwig, H. H. (1997), *The First World War: Germany and Austria-Hungary 1914–1918*, New York, St Martin's Press.

Hibbert, C. (1962), *Benito Mussolini: The Rise and Fall of Il Duce*, London, Penguin.

Hobsbawm, E. J. (1983), 'Mass Producing Traditions: Europe 1870–1914', in

Hobsbawm, E. J. and Ranger, T. (eds), *The Invention of Tradition*, Cambridge, Press Syndicate of the University of Cambridge: 263–307.

Horne J. (ed.) (1997), *State, Society and Mobilization in Europe During the First World War*, Cambridge, Cambridge University Press.

—— (1999), 'Smobilitazioni culturali dopo la grande guerra 1919–1939', *Italia Contemporanea*, 215, June: 331–9.

—— (2000), 'Corps, lieux et nation: la France et l'invasion de 1914', *Annales HSS*, 1, January–February: 73–9.

Howard, M. (1976), *War in European History*, Oxford, Oxford University Press.

—— (1992), 'Uomini di fronte al fuoco: la dottrina dell'offensiva nel 1914', in Paret, P. and Labanca, N. (eds), *Guerra e strategia nell'età contemporanea*, Genoa, Marietti: 215–30.

Keegan, J. (1999), *The First World War*, London, Pimlico.

Isnenghi, M. (1970), *Il Mito della Grande Guerra*, Bologna, Il Mulino.

—— (1977), *Giornali di trincea 1915–1918*, Turin, Einaudi.

—— (1982), 'Usi politici di Garibaldi: Dall'interventismo al fascismo', *Rivista di Storia Contemporanea*, Fasc. 4: 513–22.

—— (1985), 'Il diario di guerra di Benito Mussolini', *Quaderni di retorica e poetica*: 123–30.

—— (1989), *Le guerre degli italiani: Parole, immagini, ricordi, 1848–1945*, Milan, Mondadori.

—— and Rochat, G. (2000), *La Grande Guerra 1914–1918*, Milan, La Nuova Italia.

Kreis, S. (ed.), (2003), 'The History Guide', *www.historyguide.org/europe/duce.html* [accessed September 2003].

Labanca, N. (1997), *Caporetto: Storia di una disfatta*, Florence, Casterman.

Langella, P. (1988), 'L'accademia militare di Torino nell'età giolittiana', in Caforio, G. and Del Negro, P. (eds), *Ufficiali e società: Interpretazioni e modelli*, Milan, Angeli: 317–61.

Lazzari, C. (21 November 1914), 'Chi paga?', *Avanti!*

Lederer, I. J. (1966), *La Jugoslavia dalla conferenza della pace al Trattato di Rapallo*, Milano, Il Saggiatore.

Lenin, V. I. (1974) [first published 1917], *Imperialism, the Highest Stage of Capitalism*, New York, International Publishers.

Lepre, A. (1995), *Mussolini l'italiano: Il duce nel mito e nella realtà*, Milan, Mondadori.

Lincoln, W. B. (1994), *Passage Through Armageddon: The Russians in War and Revolution*, New York, Oxford University Press.

Lloyd George, D. (1938) [first published 1933–34], *War Memoirs of David Lloyd George*, 2 Vols, London, Ivor Nicholson and Watson.

Lombardo Radice, G. (4 October 1914), 'Quel che dice un capo del partito ufficiale', *Il Giornale d'Italia*.

Lussu, E. (2000) [first published 1938], *Un'anno sull'Altipiano*, Turin, Einaudi.

Maciulli, V. (1993a), '*La paga di Marte:* Assegni, spese e genere di vita degli ufficiali italiani prima della grande guerra', *Rivista di Storia Contemporanea*, 4: 569–95.

—— (1993b), 'Il sistema delle scuole militari in età liberale (1860–1914)', *Ricerche Storiche*, XXII, 3: 533–67.

Mack Smith, D. (1994), *Mazzini*, London, New Haven.

Malagodi, O. (1960), *Conversazioni della guerra 1914–1919*, Milan, Napoli.

Malatesta, M. (1977), *Il Resto del Carlino (potere politico e potere economico a Bologna dal 1885 al 1922)*, Milan, Guanda.

Mancini Mussolini, E. (1957), *Mio fratello Benito*, Ricci Crisolini, R. (ed.), Florence, La Fenice.

Mangone, A. (1987), *Diaz*, Milan, Frassinelli.

Marinetti, F. T. (1996), *Teoria e invenzione futurista*, De Maria, L. (ed.), Milan, Mondadori.

Massignani, A. (1998), 'Elementi di confronto con l'artigliera austro-ungarica', in Curmai, A. and Massignani, A. (eds), *L'artigliera italiana nella grande guerra*, Vicenza, Rossato: 41–50.

Mayer, A. J. (1968), *Politics and Diplomacy of Peacemaking: Containment and Counterrevolution at Versailles 1918–1919*, London, Weidenfeld and Nicholson.

Mazzini, G. (1961), *Antologia degli Scritti Politici di Giuseppe Mazzini*, Galasso, G. (ed.), Bologna, Il Mulino.

—— (1976), *Giuseppe Mazzini Scritti Politici*, Della Paruta, F. (ed.), Tome I, Turin, Einaudi.

McNeill, W. H. (1983), *The Pursuit of Power: Technology, Armed Force, and Society Since A.D. 1000*, Oxford, Blackwell.

Melograni, P. (1969), *Storia politica della Grande Guerra 1915–1918*, Milan, Mondadori.

Monelli, P. (1950), *Mussolini piccolo borghese*, Milan, Garzanti.

Morozzo della Rocca, R. (1980), *La fede e la guerra: Cappellani militari e preti-soldati*, Rome, Studium.

Morselli, M. (2001), *Caporetto 1917: Victory or Defeat?*, London, Frank Cass.

Mosse, G. L. (1987) [first published 1980], *Masses and Man: Fascist Perceptions of Reality*, Detroit, MI, Wayne State University Press.

—— (1990), *Fallen Soldiers: Reshaping the Memory of the World Wars*, Oxford, Oxford University Press.

Nemeth, L. (1998), 'Dolci corrispondenze. La Francia e i finanziamenti a "Il Popolo d'Italia" 1914–1917', *Italia Contemporanea*, 212, September: 605–15.

Nettl, J. P. (1967), *Political Mobilisation: A Sociological Analysis of Methods and Concepts*, London, Faber and Faber.

Oakeshott, M. (1972) [first published 1939], 'The Social and Political Doctrines of

Contemporary Europe', in Cohen, C. (ed.), *Communism, Fascism and Democracy: The Theoretical Foundations*, New York, Random House: 328–39.

O'Brien, P. (2002a), 'Al capezzale di Mussolini: Ferite e malattia 1917–1945', *Italia Contemporanea*, 226, March: 5–29.

—— (2002b), 'Mussolini ditattore senza programma?', *Italia Contemporanea*, 229, December: 733–6.

—— (2003), 'Wounded Hero? Mussolini's War Injuries of 1917: A Reappraisal', *Journal of Postgraduate Studies*, Dublin, Trinity College: 9–30.

—— (May 2004), Review of Gentile, E. (2003), *Renzo-De Felice. Lo Storico e il Personaggio*, Rome-Bari, Laterza. In *Modern Italy*, 9: 121–4.

Oliva, G. (1996), 'Il tricolore', in Isnenghi, M. (ed.), *I luoghi della memoria: Simboli e miti dell'Italia unita*, Rome-Bari, Laterza: 5–13

Omodeo, A. (1934), *Momenti della vita di guerra: Dai diari e dalle lettere dei caduti 1915–1918*, Rome-Bari, Laterza.

Oomen, T. K. (1967/68), 'Charisma, Social Structure and Social Change', *Comparative Studies in Society and History*, 1: 85–99.

Orlando, V. E. (1960), *Memorie, 1915–1919*, Mosca, R. (ed.), Milan, Rizzoli.

Pancrazi, P. (22 November 1914), 'Il più mediocre dei socialisti: Benito Mussolini', *Il dovere nazionale*.

Panunzio, S. (1914a), 'Il lato teorico e il lato pratico del socialismo, *Utopia*, 15–31 May.

—— (1914b), 'Il Socialismo e la guerra', *Utopia*, 15 August–1 September.

Papa, A. (1969), 'Guerra e terra 1915–1918', *Studi Storici*, January–March: 3–45.

Papini, G. (1903a), 'L'ideale imperialista', *Leonardo*, I, 1.

—— (1903b), 'Chi sono i socialisti?', *Leonardo*, I, 5.

—— (1904a), 'Il congresso del dissolvimento', *Il Regno*, I, 21.

—— (1904b), 'O la classe o la nazione', *Il Regno*, I, 37.

—— (1904c), 'Distinguo!', *Il Regno*, I, 53.

Passerini, L. (1991), *Mussolini immaginario: storia di una biografia*, Rome-Bari, Laterza.

Pedroncini, A. (1967), *Les mutinieries de 1917*, Paris, PUF.

Perfetti, F. (1986), 'La "conversione" all'interventismo di Mussolini nel suo carteggio con Sergio Panunzio', *Storia Contemporanea*, XVII, 1, February: 139–67.

Pieri, P. (1968) [first published 1965], *L'Italia nella Prima Guerra Mondiale*, Turin, Einaudi.

Pieropan, G. (1988), *1914–1918 Storia della Grande Guerra sul fonte italiano*, Milan, Mursia.

Pini G. and Susmel, D. (1953–58), *Mussolini l'uomo e l'opera*, 4 Vols, Florence, La Fenice.

Posani, R. (1968), *La Grande Guerra*, 2 Vols, Florence, Sadea.

Pozzi, G. B. (1921), *La prima occupazione operaia della fabbrica in Italia nelle battaglie di Dalmine*, Bergamo, Società tipografica editrice bergamasca.

Prezzolini, G. (1903), 'L'aristocrazia dei briganti', *Il Regno*, I, 3.

—— (1904a), 'La borghesia può risorgere?', *Il Regno*, I, 7.

—— (1904b) 'A chi giova la lotta di classe?', *Il Regno*, I, 18.

—— (1904c), 'Le due Italie', *Il Regno*, I, 26.

—— (1910a), 'Che fare?', *La Voce*, II, 28.

—— (1910b), 'Risposta di Prezzolini', *La Voce*, II, 32.

—— (1910c), 'Nel VII anniversario della nascita del "Regno"', *La Voce*, II, 51.

—— (1912), 'Le sorprese della storia', *La Voce*, IV, 45.

—— (1914), 'La pagina di Prezzolini I', *La Voce*, VI, 1.

—— (1925), *Benito Mussolini*, Rome, Formiggini.

Procacci, Gv. (ed.) (1989), *Stato e Classe Operaia in Italia Durante la Prima Guerra Mondiale*, Milan, Angeli.

—— (1990/91), 'State Coercion and Worker Solidarity in Italy (1915–1918): The Moral and Political Content of Social Unrest', *Estratto da "Annali" della Fondazione Giangiacomo Feltrinelli*: 145–77.

—— (1993), *Soldati e prigionieri italiani nella Grande Guerra*, Rome, Editori Riuniti.

—— (1997), 'L'Italia nella grande guerra', in Sabbatucci, G. and Vidotto, V. (eds), *Storia d'Italia*, Vol. IV, Rome-Bari, Laterza: 3–99.

—— (1999), *Dalla rassegnazione alla rivolta*, Rome, Bulzoni.

Procacci, Giu. (1966), 'Appunti in tema di crisi dello Stato liberale e di origini del fascismo', *Studi Storici*, 2: 221–37.

Rafaelli, S. (1996), 'I nomi delle vie', in Isnenghi, M. (ed.), *I luoghi della memoria: Simboli e miti dell'Italia unita*, Rome-Bari, Laterza: 217–42.

Ratnam, K. J. (1964), 'Charisma and Political Leadership', *Political Studies*, October: 341–54.

Rocca, G. (1985), *Cadorna*, Milan, Mondadori.

Rocco, A. (15 December 1918), 'Manifesto di "Politica"', *Politica*, I, 1: 1–17.

Rochat, G. (1961), 'La preparazione dell'esercito italiano nell'inverno 1914–1915 in relazione alle informazioni disponibili sulla guerra di posizione', *Risorgimento*, 13: 10–32.

—— (1976), *L'Italia nella prima guerra mondiale: Problemi di interpretazione e prospettive di ricerca*, Milan, Feltrinelli.

—— (1981), *Gli arditi della Grande Guerra: origini, battaglie e miti*, Milan, Feltrinelli.

—— (1991), *L'esercito italiano in pace e in guerra: Studi in storia militare*, Milan, RARA.

Rossini, D. (1991), 'Wilson e il Patto di Londra nel 1917–18', *Storia Contemporanea*, 3, June: 473–512.

Rostan, P. (1974), *L'Europa in pericolo: Caporetto, 1917*, Milan, Club degli editori.

Ruffo, M. (1998), *L'Italia nella Triplice Alleanza*, Rome, USSME.

Rumi, G. (1963), 'Mussolini e il "programma" di San Sepolcro', *Il movimento di liberazione in Italia*, April–June: 3–26.

Sabbatucci, G. (1974), *I combattenti nel primo dopoguerra*, Rome-Bari, Laterza.

Salandra, A. (1928), *La neutralità italiana (1914): Ricordi e pensieri*, Milan, Mondadori.

Salinari, C. and Ricci, C. (1975) [first published 1962], *Storia della Letteratura Italiana*, III, i, Rome-Bari, Laterza.

Salvetti, P. (1987), 'Il movimento migratorio italiano durante la Prima Guerra Mondiale', *Studi emigrazione*, 87: 282–94.

Sarfatti, M. (1926), *Dux*, Milan, Mondadori.

Schindler, J. R. (2001), *Isonzo: The Forgotten Sacrifice of the Great War*, London, Praeger.

Schweitzer, A. (1974), 'Theory and Political Charisma', *Comparative Studies in Society and History*, 2: 150–81.

Sema, A. (1997), *Fiume Nord Est: I Bersaglieri sul fronte dell'Isonzo 1915–1917*, Gorizia, Libreria Editrice Goriziana.

Serpieri, A. (1930), *La guerra e le classi rurali italiane*, Rome-Bari, Laterza.

Serra, E. (1950), *Camille Barrère e l'intesa italo-francese*, Milan, Mondadori.

Settimelli, E. (1922), *Benito Mussolini*, Piacenza, Societa tipografice editoriale.

Snyder, J. (1984), *The Ideology of the Offensive: Military Decision Making and the Disasters of 1914*, Ithaca, NY, Cornell University Press.

Sorel, G. (1999) [first published 1905], *Reflections on Violence*, Cambridge, Cambridge University Press.

Spriano, P. (1960), *Torino operaia nella grande guerra (1914–1918)*, Turin, Einaudi.

Stouffer S. A. (1949), *The American Soldier*, 2 Vols, Princeton, NJ, Princeton University Press.

Tamborra, A. (1963), 'L'idea di nazionalità e la guerra 1914–1918', *Istituto per la Storia del Risorgimento Italiano*, Atti del XLI Congresso: 177–291.

Tancredi, L. (7 October 1914), 'Un uomo di paglia: Lettera aperta a Benito Mussolini', *Il Resto del Carlino*.

Tranfaglia, N. (1995), *La prima guerra mondiale e il fascismo*, Turin, UTET.

Treves, C. (1983), *Scritti e discorsi 1897–1933*, Milan, Guanda.

Trotsky, L. (1967) [first published 1932–33], *History of the Russian Revolution*, 3 Vols, London, Sphere Books.

—— (1971), *The Struggle Against Fascism in Germany*, New York, Pathfinder.

Turati, F. and Kuliscioff, A. (1977), *Carteggio*, 6 Vols, Turin, Einaudi.

USSME, (1929), *L'esercito italiano nella grande guerra 1915–1918*, Vol. II-*bis*, Rome, Istituto Poligrafico dello Stato.

Valiani, L. (1966a), *La dissoluzione dell'Austria-Ungheria*, Milan, Il Saggiatore.
—— (1966b), 'Italian–Austro-Hungarian Negotiations 1914–1915', *The Journal of Contemporary History*, 1: 113–36.
—— (1977), *Il Partito Socialista nel periodo della neutralità 1914–1915*, Milan, Feltrinelli.
Van Gennep, A. (1981) [first published 1909], *I Riti di Passaggio*, Turin, Bollati Boringhieri.
Vigezzi, B. (1959), 'Le "Radiose giornate" del maggio 1915 nei rapporti dei prefetti', *Nuova Rivista Storica*, September–December: 313–44.
—— (1960), 'Le "Radiose giornate" del maggio 1915 nei rapporti dei prefetti', *Nuova Rivista Storica*, January–April: 54–111.
—— (1961), 'I problemi della neutralità e della guerra nel carteggio Salandra–Sonnino (1914–1917)', *Nuova Rivista Storica*, XLV, September–December: 397–466.
—— (1969), *Da Giolitti a Salandra,* Florence, Vallecchi.
Violante, L. (1976), 'La repressione del dissenso politico nell'Italia liberale: stati d'assedio e giustizia militare', *Rivista di Storia Contemporanea*, V, October: 481–524.
Vivarelli, R. (1981), *Il fallimento del liberalismo: Studi sulle origini del fascismo,* Bologna, Il Mulino.
—— (1991) [first published 1967], *Storia delle origini del fascismo: l'Italia dalla grande guerra alla marcia su Roma*, 2 Vols, Bologna, Il Mulino.
Voce, La (1911a), 'L'illusione tripolina', *La Voce*, III, 20.
—— (1911b), 'Perché non si deve andare a Tripoli', *La Voce*, III, 33.
—— (1911c), 'I socialisti', *La Voce*, III, 39.
—— (1911d), 'A Tripoli', *La Voce*, III, 40.
Weber, M. (1968) [first published 1922 & 1925], *Economy and Society: An Outline of Interpretive Sociology*, 3 Vols, Gerth, H. and Wright Mills, C. (eds), New York, Bedminster.
Webster, R. A. (1975), *Industrial Imperialism in Italy, 1908–1915*, Berkeley, CA, University of California Press.
Whittam, J. (1977), *The Politics of the Italian Army*, London, Croom Helm.
Wilson, W. (1969), *Woodrow Wilson 1856–1924: Chronology-Documents-Bibliographical Aids*, Vexler, R. I. (ed.), Dobbs Ferry, NY, Oceana Publications.
Zingarelli, N. (ed.) (2000), *Vocabolario della lingua italiana*, Milan, Zanichelli.
Zunino, P. G. (1985), *L'ideologia del fascismo: Miti, credenze e valori nella stabilizzazione del regime*, Bologna, Il Mulino.

Index